You and Your Baby

THE FIRST WONDROUS YEAR

You and Your Baby

THE FIRST WONDROUS YEAR

Edited by

Richard A. Chase, M.D.

and

Richard R. Rubin, Ph.D.

Johnson & Johnson

Child Development Publications

First published as the ''Guide to the Infant Development Program''

MACMILLAN PUBLISHING CO., INC.
New York

COLLIER MACMILLAN PUBLISHERS
London

Library of Congress Cataloging in Publication Data
Main entry under title:

The First Wondrous Year
    ''First published as the 'Guide to the infant develop-
ment program' ''
    Includes index.
    1. Infants—Care and hygiene. 2. Infants—
Growth. I. Chase, Richard A. II. Rubin, Richard R.
III. Johnson and Johnson, inc.
RJ61.G965   1979   649'.122   79-21997
ISBN 0-02-559530-X

Macmillan Publishing Co., Inc.
866 Third Avenue, New York, N.Y. 10022
Collier Macmillan Canada, Ltd.

First Macmillan Edition 1979

Printed in the United States of America

CONTENTS

A Message to Parents

No experience holds more wonder, hope and opportunity for self-growth than becoming a parent.

Quite naturally, it is also a time of some puzzlement and many questions — a time when parents feel a deep need to know everything that will help their new infant flourish.

This need embraces three major concerns:
1. Mastering the basic routines for the physical care of your baby,
2. Enjoying your relationship with your baby to the fullest, and
3. Doing everything possible to help your baby develop to his or her fullest potential.

Ample material exists to advise parents on the physical care of the baby. It is less easy to obtain advice and information you can trust on your other two major concerns.

Although there has been a substantial amount of scientific research on infant development in recent years, most of this new information has been confined to technical papers and professional publications. And where books for parents have been written, many have tended to promote pet theories. In some cases they have made it sound as if babies developed identically. But no two babies are alike, and no "pet theory" is going to satisfy the new parent's need for reliable information.

A Message to Parents

Aware that the information parents needed was not available, Johnson and Johnson Baby Products Company set out to develop a single, easy-to-understand source. To create it a team of professional child-care specialists, distinguished researchers, and many parents reviewed all the best information on development in the first year of life. We chose the first year because it is a period during which the way parents relate to their baby profoundly affects the child's future development. A warm day-to-day physical and emotional relationship between the infant and those who care for him is the foundation for healthy growth.

The project involved years of sifting and analyzing thousands of scientific reports, books, and articles in addition to our own extensive research studies.

Only after we had gleaned from this effort the very best and latest information did we attempt to write about the most important aspects of infant development and play. And only after the material had been scrutinized by a distinguished Editorial Advisory Board would we permit it to be published.

The result is this book. Even parents with more than one child will find that the book helps them to recognize and enjoy aspects of infant behavior that may not have been evident to them with their first child.

In fact, as you look through *The First Wondrous Year,* you will see that it has been designed and written so that even other children in the family can better understand the new arrival and their own relationship to him.

The short introduction gives you the main points of how your baby will develop in the first year of life. Babies come in both sexes, so throughout the text we have used he and she interchangeably.

Parts One and Two tell about the baby's own feelings and responses to parental behavior. The information gathered here will explain how early experiences influence your child. It will help you to communicate with him from the earliest days of life and to predict his future develop-

ment. Most important, it will help you provide your baby with experiences that will develop his mind, his emotions, and his ability to get along with other people and live a productive life.

The third and fourth parts address themselves to specifics of infant development and provide guidance for play and learning techniques. Here you will discover how babies learn to move, to think, to talk. You will learn how to choose toys that are safe and that will help your baby to learn new skills.

Finally in "Further Information" we mention other sources of information that you may find useful. These include books that we have examined and can recommend, and other sources of good current information about topics of interest to parents.

You will notice that this book contains many photographs. There are two reasons for all these illustrations. One is to show the many actual changes in a baby's behavior during the important and exciting first year of life. The other reason is to show that babies at the same stage can differ in the style of their development. Pictures can often tell more than words.

The First Wondrous Year by Johnson & Johnson gives you real insight into your baby's first twelve months. It helps you to understand your role as parents, your baby's needs, and how you can best meet them. It provides practical guidelines on how and when you can do things to aid all phases of your baby's development.

We created this guide to help you encourage and enhance your baby's growth and development as you enjoy your first year together. We believe you will find it a never-to-be-forgotten adventure in learning, communication, and love.

Richard A. Chase, M.D.
Richard R. Rubin, Ph.D.
Editors

Introduction:
The Meaning of
"Infant Development"

When we speak of the development of an infant, we are referring to his physical growth, plus all the changes in personality and skills that occur as the baby matures.

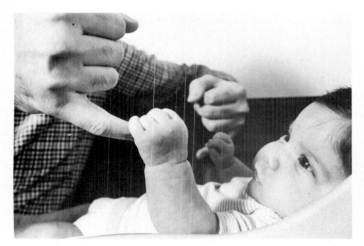

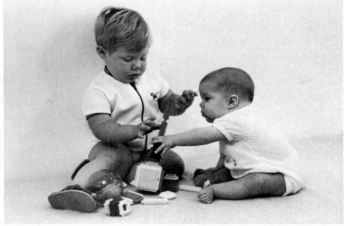

Many of these changes occur naturally in almost all children. The ability to stand upright, the ability to grasp and manipulate objects, to reason, plan, imagine, dream, to communicate and to feel concern for others, develop according to a general plan of nature.

However, nature is not the only force at work on the
flowering of these skills. Society also makes certain demands and plans for the raising of children, and so does
each set of parents, all trying to influence children's
growth in order to affect their behavior as adults. The
skills that infants begin to gain will have a bearing on their
own welfare as adults as well as on the survival of society
as a whole.

It is not surprising then to find that as society's needs
change, plans for the raising of children are modified.

For example, in the Middle Ages, Europe was intent on
the struggle for survival. As a result, many families put

their children to work as soon as they could. Childhood was simply a short waiting period before the beginning of a life of work. In later periods, the concept of discipline, the hardening of body and spirit, became the most important concern for meeting society's needs.

The first ideas of what we now regard as important requirements for the development of personality appeared in the 19th century. It was then that authors began to write books especially for children. Some of the books were still occupied with the concept of "improvement," but others winked at the sober attitudes of the day and opened doors to fantasy and fun. *Alice's Adventures in Wonderland* was published in 1866 and it was a great success.

Attitudes toward childhood have continued to change throughout the 20th century.

In the early decades of this century, great emphasis was placed on hygiene, on the cleanliness of the baby, his room, and his clothing. By the 1930's and 1940's, the psychological and educational needs of the child came to the fore. Children's attitudes and feelings, and their early educational experiences, became the important concerns. The fields of child psychology and early childhood education blossomed, and soon the ideas of professional workers in these new fields began to influence parents' attitudes about their own children.

The concepts of psychology, however, were still very new. Faced with these revolutionary and threatening ideas, parents and professionals alike began to focus on the supposed "dangers" to a child's personality. Mainly they worried about "spoiling" the child. Would a baby be spoiled if he were fed on demand instead of on a fixed schedule? Would he be spoiled if he were picked up when he cried? You may have heard your parents or grandparents discussing child care in these terms.

The question of "spoiling" seems a good one with which to launch a summarized account of what we now believe is important to the development of a child.

Obviously, we have assumed a much more relaxed attitude. We regard feeding a baby when he is hungry and

comforting him when he cries as good things to do. They add to a baby's comfort and we have no evidence that he is spoiled by comfortable feelings. On the other hand, babies, like adults, need some order to their lives and it seems only sensible to develop schedules for eating and sleeping that bring him both comfort and predictability.

In short, we now think less about whether we are *spoiling* the baby and more about what we are doing to increase his sense of *well-being*.

The Meaning of "Infant Development"

We have learned how important it is for a baby that at least one adult understands the baby's needs and meets them effectively. We have learned that strong feelings of love and trust between a baby and the persons who care for him are essential. We also understand that even the youngest babies are eager to explore the world around them, but that the comfort, love, and trust must come first. Without them, babies find it difficult to express their inborn curiosity and reap the rewards of learning and the satisfaction of accomplishment and skill.

Understanding this sequence has changed our views about infancy. We now realize that it is not just a time to protect babies. It is also a time of active learning, during which the foundations of all future development are laid.

We have also discovered something further about this active learning period. Babies, we have found, develop distinct and different emotional strengths at various stages of growth.

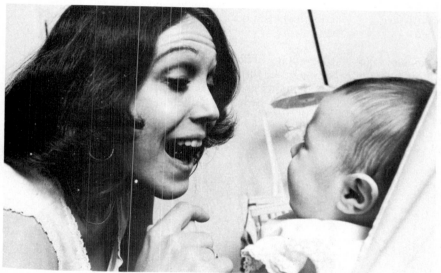

The first 6 months of life, for instance, are a critical period for building strong attachments to adults. Very young babies are extremely responsive to human faces, voices, and physical contact. During that time, the few adults who are closest to the baby and who are most sensitive and responsive to the baby's needs develop a strong sense of attachment to her. She, in turn, treats them in a special way, being happiest when they arrive and most responsive to them. Her well-being depends heavily on these strong relationships.

During the second half of the first year, the baby begins to model speech patterns after the speech of those around him. He may have been listening carefully during the first 6 months, but he begins imitating during the second 6 months.

The baby's sense of trust develops throughout the entire first year. Sensitivity to his needs during this period, and consistency in meeting them, make him feel that the world he lives in can be trusted.

A baby's motivation to explore and to tolerate risks and frustrations is also activated during this same period, as is his sense of self-esteem and self-confidence. The foundation of these lifelong attitudes is developed as he learns to move about and to explore the properties of objects.

The Meaning of "Infant Development"

There will be changes in your baby's behavior which will look like setbacks. They are part of the normal course of a baby's growth. There are times when a baby learns less quickly, when he is less responsive to people and objects, when the pattern of his sleeping and eating is upset. The setbacks seldom last long, but understanding and patience are required to avoid feeling discouraged.

Setbacks, we have found, occur for several reasons. One is a change in the special conditions under which the baby has first learned a new skill. A baby who has recently learned to roll over may seem to have lost her new ability if she is placed on a surface that is too soft or if her clothing gets in her way. Later, after more practice, she will be able to roll over under many different conditions.

Setbacks also appear when a baby is giving most of her attention to mastering a new skill. A baby just learning to crawl might omit close visual inspection of nearby objects because her interest is now focused on moving. A baby just learning to walk might neglect eating, sleeping, or even speech because it distracts her from the task at hand.

A new stage of development may also precipitate a setback. On the threshold of a new increase in independence, an infant may become insecure or irritable and forget a skill he has already mastered.

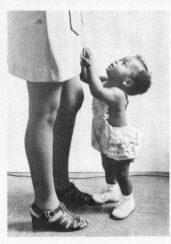

A baby's "state," we have learned, also affects his speed of development. Some of these states change with age. For instance, babies are awake much more after they are about 6 weeks old, and requirements for sleep continue to decrease into adult life. An infant's state, however, also varies throughout the day and a perfectly healthy baby will move in and out of several stages of sleep and wakefulness.

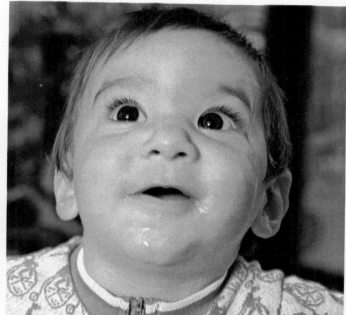

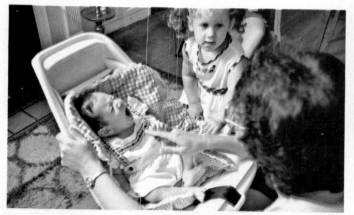

The Meaning of "Infant Development"

At the same time that we have been learning these facts that hold true for *all* babies, we have also learned that each baby develops at its own rate and in its own style. No two babies are the same, and they differ in many ways:

some babies are more active than others;

some show greater regularity and predictability;

some react with eagerness to new situations, while others are initially upset by changes of any kind;

some react to small changes in the environment, such as a whisper, while others don't respond to anything much less than a drum roll;

some are friendly and happy most of the time, while others are more reserved;

some stay involved in activities for long periods of time, while others do things for much shorter periods;

some like to be cuddled, while others (usually the more active babies) chafe at being restrained;

some babies move through the stages of development with little assistance, while others need much help with each new ability they practice;

some cry much more than others;

and some are more easily comforted than others.

This list covers only some of the ways in which babies differ from each other. The list could go on and on, with much more detail. For example, babies who are more regular and predictable in some aspects of their behavior won't be regular and predictable in everything that they do. They may be very regular in their patterns of sleeping and waking, but quite irregular in their patterns of feeding.

There is really no limit to the ways in which babies differ. Later, this marvelous, almost limitless variety in babies provides society with its abundance of differing talents and skills.

In infancy, however, this great diversity means that no one can say what is best for a *particular* baby on the basis of what is known about *most* babies. Thus, parents must learn to understand their individual infant. It then becomes the parents' special privilege and responsibility to decide what will best suit their baby.

But parents have differing needs and desires, too. Father may want to hold the baby more than the baby wants to be held. Mother may like to play more actively than the baby wishes. How a baby fits in with other members of the family is an important subject that you will read about in the first two parts of this guide.

Clearly, in the past 30 or 40 years we have learned a great deal about what is called "infant development." As you read on, you will find many more interesting discoveries and many suggestions for helping your baby develop well during his first year. Before you begin reading, however, it might help to review the following goals of infant development and the requirements for achieving them:

A. Goals of a Baby's Development

1. Learning to trust and to enjoy being with people.

2. Learning to influence the environment.

3. Achieving a sense of self-confidence and self-esteem.

4. Learning to enjoy new experiences, and to enjoy the process of learning itself.

5. Attaining skill in touching, holding, and moving.

6. Understanding the qualities of objects, how things work, how to use objects as tools, how to plan, and how to make a plan work.

7. Learning to communicate with people through gestures and words.

B. Basic Requirements for Achieving These Goals

1. Loving and responsive people who devote time and attention to understanding the baby's needs and who meet the baby's needs in reliable and effective ways.

2. Opportunities to have an effect on the environment, in-cluding objects that change as a result of being manipulated by the baby.

3. Exposure to varied, stimulating, and challenging experiences.

4. Encouragement of curiosity, exploration, and play.

5. Examples of skills the baby is trying to learn, such as fitting objects together, and making speech sounds.

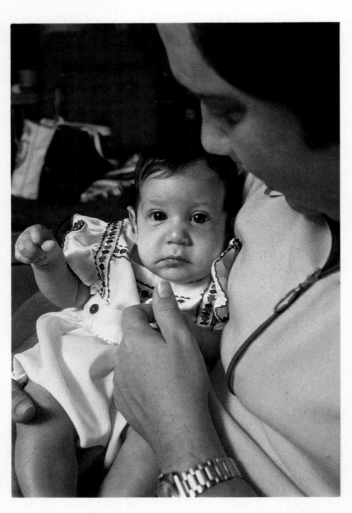

PART ONE: PARENTING

1. Relating to Your Baby— An Emerging Partnership

Parents want to have a good relationship with their baby. And babies *need* to have good relationships with their parents. Because this is so necessary for your baby's healthy growth and development, nature has seen to it that right from birth he is equipped to tell you what you can do to help him. You're not alone in your parenting job; your baby's involved in the process.

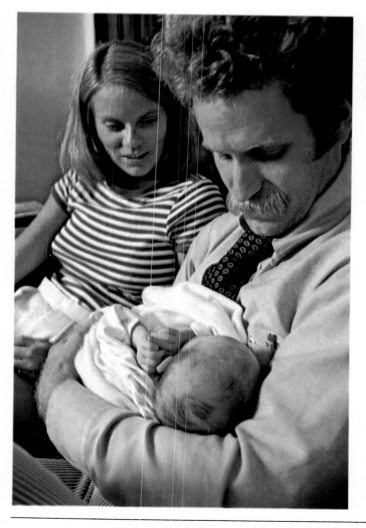

Relating to Your Baby —
An Emerging Partnership

Babies' Ways of Interacting

Although newborns don't yet have the thoughts and feelings they will later have, they are nevertheless social people, with many ways of being in communication with other human beings. For example, they are born with the capacity to *perceive*. They can see your face, particularly your eyes and your smiles, and hear your voice. And from birth on, babies can *respond* to you. When they hear voices or see faces, they turn their heads to listen and watch, and they quiet their activities in order to pay attention. They react to your voice differently when you are happy or sad.

A baby not only can perceive and respond to you, he can also *initiate* interactions. Babies are active participants in what goes on around them; they start approximately 50% of the interactions they're involved in. From birth on, babies use crying, facial expressions, and body movements to compel us to pay attention to them and to tell us their needs. Later they learn how to smile, gurgle, and coo to charm us.

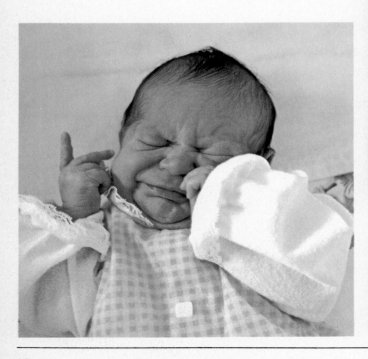

In time, you will learn to ''read'' the meaning of these expressive behaviors, but during these first few weeks, the going may be rough, because you will still be figuring out your baby's messages. Gradually you will come to understand what he is saying, and then the job will be much easier. Here is some general advice for building the partnership between you and your baby:

A. Respond to your baby's needs. Among your baby's most important psychological needs are those for physical contact with you, for verbal communication, and for your smiles. One of the best things you can do for your baby is to smile at her. Tender words, songs, and other sounds also communicate your love. And being touched stimulates her physically and emotionally. Just as you gather information about a person from the way he shakes your hand, your baby feels your love for her from the way you hold her. Your tender loving care makes all the difference to your baby. To prosper, she needs to be caressed, cuddled, rocked, patted, and carried around.

B. Respond when your baby initiates interaction. Your baby needs to know he can trust you to pay attention when he communicates with you. That's how he develops the desirable image of himself as a person who has ways of making things happen. He is also learning that making efforts pays off. So when he calls to you by his cries or his coos, respond promptly whenever possible.

C. Respect your baby's limited ability to interact. After the baby's birth, people often become so excited about having their baby respond to them, they forget to think about the baby's limits. Parents or relatives trying to get their baby to look at them should remember not to put their heads so close to the infant's that he can't withdraw his attention from them. He is able to tell you when he needs to withdraw by turning his head away, yawning, or going into a dull or sleepy state, by turning his body away, or by crying or fussing. If babies are able to withdraw when they need to, they can return with enthusiasm.

**Relating to Your Baby —
An Emerging Partnership**

D. Protect your baby from unnecessary disruptions.
Another way to be sensitive to your baby is to smooth out
transitions for her, especially when she is very young.
Babies can't rapidly shift their attention from one thing to
another. They require a slower pace than adults are used
to. For instance, if you are playing with your baby in your
lap and it's time to change her diapers, it's easier for her if
you indicate something new is about to happen. Get her
attention and tell her she's going to change activities.

E. Be patient. Babies develop slowly. You can't expect a
6-month-old baby to do what a 9-month-old can. Each
baby also grows at her own speed, so you can't expect
your 6-month-old to be exactly the same as other babies
her age. Your baby might learn to sit up earlier than your
neighbor's baby, but the other baby might crawl before
yours. It's important to accept your baby as she is.

Every baby has a built-in drive to learn new skills. In a
supportive environment, she will initiate many activities.
This means you should not feel you must teach your baby
everything. Sometimes parents try to involve a baby in
games they believe are educational without paying attention to what the baby is indicating she wants to do.

Babies need practice. That's the way they learn; they repeat new skills over and over until they've perfected them. On the way to mastery, your baby will make lots of mistakes. Difficult as it may be to be patient, you need to overcome the impulse to jump in and help out. Wait until your baby lets you know he's ready for some help, except, of course, when he is in danger. Older babies often refuse help and get upset when parents intercede, even when the babies' attempts are unsuccessful.

When you can control your urges to help your baby out, it's exciting to watch him explore his world. One baby recently learned about the wonders of a clothespin. He discovered on his own that it could be fitted into holes all around the house and dropped into various containers. It became his favorite game — to poke the clothespin into whatever he could find, to see if it fit. While his first attempts at getting the clothespin in a hole were wobbly, practice enabled him to insert it with ease.

F. Respond to your baby's need for consistency. Be consistent in your responses to your baby and in your care of her. Babies try hard to make sense of the enormous amount of information that surrounds them. The best way to help them understand how their world works is to provide some order in their lives. If you regularly play with your baby when she wakes from her morning nap, or if you sing songs as she falls asleep at night, she begins to develop a sense of the predictability of her life. Just as you derive some feelings of comfort from your morning routine of reading the newspaper over your first cup of coffee, or from whatever other patterns you have in your life, babies also feel secure when there are things they can count on.

Consistency is especially important when someone else is taking care of your baby while you're away. If you explain the routine you and your baby have worked out, you'll be helping your baby adjust as easily as possible to this new person and to your baby's time without you.

Some babies have a greater need for consistency than others. You will soon learn whether your baby is one of them from the amount of frustration he experiences when his routine is interrupted for any reason. For instance, some babies fall asleep wherever they are when their nap time arrives; others happily wait for their nap until they get home. Still other babies, who have a strong need to stick to established patterns, cry inconsolably until safely at home in a familiar setting. However your baby responds, respecting her needs makes things easier for everyone.

At the same time you are trying to be generally consistent with your baby, you also need to remain flexible, for she will be changing rapidly. By paying attention to what she says, you will notice when your baby's signals tell you something that worked well yesterday no longer suits her.

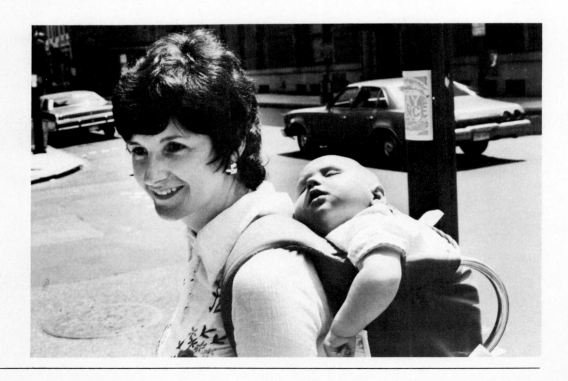

G. Respect your baby's temperament. The match between your needs and those of your baby influences the ease of your relationship. One father may be overjoyed that his baby is a cuddler, while another may feel uncomfortable about what he sees as his baby's clinginess. If a tense mother is matched with an easy-going baby, the relationship may be smooth; if the baby happens also to be tense, the relationship will probably be more difficult. A mother who loves to roughhouse and be physical with her baby has an easy time if her baby happens to enjoy roughhousing. It is more difficult for that mother if her baby prefers quiet play.

In most cases, people whose temperaments are similar have a fairly smooth time in a relationship. But when a person accepts another's differences, it can be interesting, and each person will learn a lot. When a man who is sociable and enjoys spending time talking with people is married to a woman who prefers being alone and reading, it may be difficult at first; but if they respect each other's differences, they can share what each has to offer. The same is true for you and your baby. The main thing is to respect your baby's individuality, just as you respect that of any person you love.

**Relating to Your Baby —
An Emerging Partnership**

H. Accept the "bad days." Because your baby is an active participant from the start in your relationship with him, keep in mind that his moods and temperament influence you just as yours influence him. You'll each have some "bad days." Babies are often more sensitive than adults are to the moods of people around them. When you're nervous or upset, your baby is also likely to be somewhat on edge. He might cry more or get off his schedule. But it won't hurt him as long as there are more good days than bad days.

As in any love relationship, making up is great fun. If your baby, or you, or both, have been cross, kiss and make up as soon as you can.

I. Enjoy being a parent. It's important that parents not feel as if they are constantly *working* at being parents. If you have fun playing with your baby and watching her develop, you will help her grow up with a sense that life is joyful and exciting.

2. New Baby, New Parents— The First Few Weeks

Becoming a parent is like starting a new job—you feel happy and excited about the possibilities, yet nervous, too. You wonder whether you will really be able to handle this great new responsibility. Fortunately, you can. It just takes time to learn your new role and to adjust to it. Many parents say that the adjustments they made to parenthood were even greater than those they made to marriage. Your life is different after you have a baby. As new parents you go from a freer, more independent life to one focusing more on your family and home. For some months, your sleep will be interrupted at least once a night by your baby's crying for food. Your pace will probably slow down as you spend time getting acquainted with your baby.

2

New Baby, New Parents —
The First Few Weeks

**Meeting Your New Baby's Needs
and Your Own, Too**

In the first weeks after the birth of their baby, a new father and new mother quickly find they must continually put the baby's needs ahead of their own. When he needs to be fed, everything else must wait! And taking care of a new baby demands so much of your time that you just can't do some things that used to be important to you. This change in priorities can be even more difficult for new mothers than for new fathers, since women have often been brought up to think they should take care of everything. A new mother may feel that she ought to work extra hard to make sure her husband doesn't feel left out, to see that her mother who has come to help with the new baby isn't overworked, to entertain visitors hospitably, and to keep her house clean as well. But if the new mother actually tries to do all that, she'll be physically worn out and emotionally drained. Her husband shouldn't want her to overextend herself, for if she does, she'll have little emotional energy left for the baby, for herself, or for the couple relationship. If at first you limit your concerns to meeting your baby's needs and your own needs, you will get back in shape faster to do other things. Don't worry if you don't get around to keeping your house in its previous tip-top shape. And though your friends will be anxious to see you and the new baby, keep their visits short, or even wait until you and your baby are feeling rested and relaxed before seeing any but your closest friends. If you are a new father and your boss wants you to work overtime, find out if it's absolutely necessary, explaining you're needed at home. Remember, this is a special time in your lives. You and your baby are making big adjustments.

It is also a time for cooperation between husband and wife. During these first few weeks, a husband may have to cook more dinners or do more housework than he is accustomed to doing. He may have to handle all the well-wishers who telephone. When one parent is exhausted from walking the baby to get him to sleep, the other can take over. Both partners have to work together, balancing the burdens so they can also share the joys of this new stage in their lives.

Besides taking care of yourself physically, take care of yourself emotionally. Make extra efforts to be gentle on yourself—take a long bath, sit under a tree, read a book, call a friend, compliment yourself on a job well done—whatever you can do to feel *good about yourself*. It's hard to nurture your baby when you don't feel nurtured yourself.

Caring for a Baby Is a Learning Experience

Unfortunately, few new parents have much experience caring for a baby before they have their own. A few generations ago, people usually lived close to parents, grandparents, aunts, uncles, sisters, and brothers. There were always babies around, so people had lots of experience before having their own baby. Things are different today. Since many couples don't live near their families, caring for an infant is often a new endeavor. Frequently parents or other relatives live so far away that getting day-to-day advice is impractical. As a result, new parents often feel very much alone. Besides, ideas about raising children have changed, and new parents are sometimes reluctant to turn to their own parents for guidance.

Producing a child brings joy, awe, and a sense of creativity that is wonderful to feel. But some difficult feelings are also common to most new parents, and people who haven't had much experience with babies aren't always prepared for them.

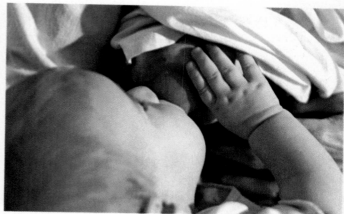

**New Baby, New Parents —
The First Few Weeks**

Baby Blues

Once the elation over the baby's birth has passed, many mothers feel moody and sad. After 9 months of being so close to her baby, a mother can feel strangely empty. These feelings may be especially strong if her baby is cared for in tne hospital nursery, instead of next to her in a rooming-in arrangement.

Mothers seem to feel most upset the first few days they have complete charge of their baby. That's not surprising. Being a parent *is* a big responsibility. And you're not at your best when you're exhausted! You may be giving your daughter her first bath at home, all the time longing to settle into a hot tub yourself.

When the blues hit, mothers typically feel that *everything* is going wrong. They may cry over every little thing. A mother feels particularly strange when she finds herself crying for what seems to be no reason at all. Sometimes you may just look down at your baby and, with a confusing mixture of emotions, start sobbing. These strange feelings may come in waves through a period that may last as long as a few months.

But as a mother learns that she *can* manage all of her new responsibilities, and as she sees that baby, father, and mother are all doing well, these emotional days will be far less common.

For a few women, the adjustments to motherhood are too difficult to manage on their own. If you're too uncomfortable with your reactions, talk to your pediatrician. He's well acquainted with feelings mothers have. He may say you just need to wait a few weeks longer to "outgrow" your difficulties, or he may suggest a counselor to help you with your feelings. In any case, it will be helpful to get his support and understanding.

Feelings About the Baby

Many parents have been led to believe they will love their baby at first sight. This does happen to some parents, just as there are some people who fall in love with their spouses at first sight. But people differ. For many parents, getting to love their baby is a slower, more gradual process that happens as they get to know the baby. In the beginning, baby and parents are strangers to each other. Every day you spend together you learn something new about your baby—what she enjoys, what her sighs mean, and when she is most ready for play. You're not only learning your baby's ways; she's learning and adapting to yours also. So every day that passes helps make the next day better, easier, and happier.

People frequently have a romantic image of parenthood. They envision a happy, smiling face beaming up at them, a soft, tender body snuggling in their arms, and a few tears that are quickly dried with a gentle kiss. They feel sadly disappointed when life with their baby isn't smooth and free of problems. Parents sometimes feel there's something wrong with *them* when their baby isn't as contented and smiling as they had imagined he would be. It's hard to remember that the baby's cries are not criticisms, but merely signals of his needs.

Some parents experience anxiety about their tiny baby. They fear they might hurt him, or that he will suddenly die. New parents worry if their baby cries a lot, and they worry if he doesn't seem to cry enough. Often parents go to check their sleeping baby to make sure he's still breathing.

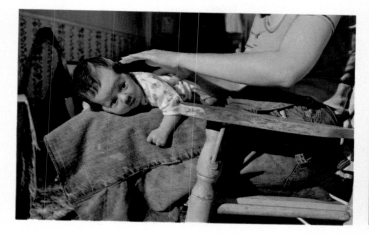

**New Baby, New Parents —
The First Few Weeks**

One common emotion that parents are often shocked to feel is resentment towards the baby. There are a number of good reasons why you might feel this way. You may find yourself angry that your life seems so much more complicated, that you can no longer go out whenever you like. And even when you're at home, you can't devote long periods of time to any projects without being interrupted. Learning to take care of a baby can make you feel helpless and incompetent when you are used to feeling pretty good at what you do. One time new parents are most likely to feel resentful is when they try hard to get their baby to stop crying and nothing works. Sometimes, when their baby just cries and cries they themselves feel frustrated almost to the point of tears.

And then the worst moment of all, when you wonder, "Why did we ever have this baby?" That's when you feel you must be the worst parent in the world for having such a thought!

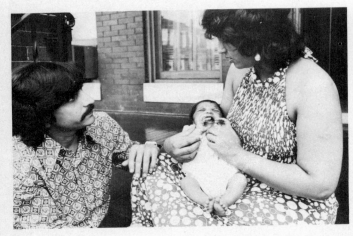

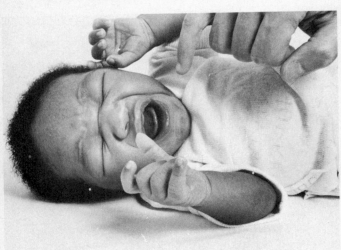

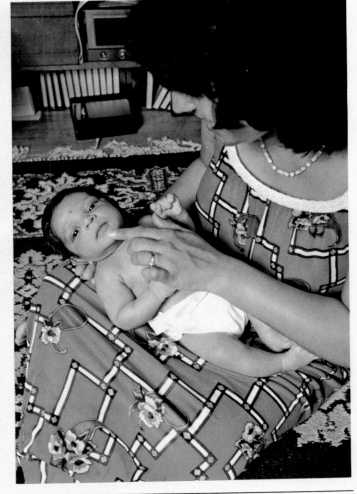

Your Feelings Are Natural

At times like these it's good to remember that every new parent has such desperate moments, that your concerns are completely understandable, and that most parents experience them to some degree. It's also important to remember that the intensity of your negative feelings won't last very long. When you're feeling overwhelmed, it seems as if there is no end in sight to the massive effect your newborn child has on your lives. But in a relatively short time, things will return to a more normal state. When you can keep this in mind, you can cope with the temporary stresses more easily.

Humor

A sense of humor helps. Being able to laugh about the toils and troubles of raising a baby eases your life during these difficult days. You can develop family jokes about traumatic incidents you've survived. For example, there was the first time you were so carefully putting the diaper pin in, making sure it didn't hit the baby. Instead you stuck it halfway through your thumb!

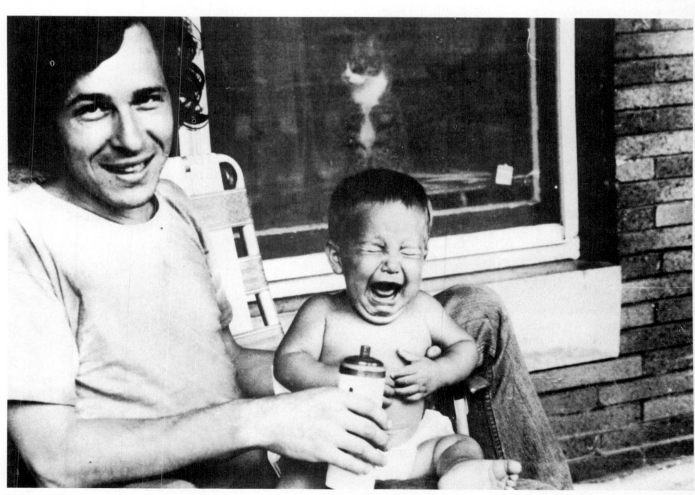

**New Baby, New Parents —
The First Few Weeks**

Sleep Can Help a Lot

Besides trying to keep a cheerful perspective, try to avoid exhaustion. Do all you can to get enough sleep!

Everything about taking care of a baby is more difficult when you are exhausted. Anyone who has stayed up all night working can remember being unfit for human company the next day. It's much worse for new parents who are kept awake for hours night after night!

Getting extra sleep may seem impossible, but there *are* ways. When your baby takes her nap, you too can head for bed. Many parents learn to catnap for the first time. Take the nap even though it may be getting close to dinner time. You'll enjoy your dinner and your baby a lot more later on. And get to bed early whenever you can.

A husband can help in a number of different ways, especially on the weekend when he may be better able to lose some sleep during the night. When the mother isn't breast-feeding and the father is able to get up, dividing the night is a good idea, with each person taking responsibility for different hours, to let the other sleep. If a mother is breast-feeding, her husband might open his eyes just long enough to give his wife a supportive hug while she nurses. That doesn't help her get any extra sleep, but it can make her feel less alone during the wee hours. Sometimes a mother is too exhausted to do the final

details of a feeding. The father might burp the baby and put her back in her cradle, especially if she needs to be rocked back to sleep.

As a mother, sometimes you'll find that even if your husband is around to take care of the baby, you have developed such a "mother's ear" that you have difficulty sleeping when you can hear the baby crying. Ask your husband to take the baby out for a walk or ride during your nap time. If your husband isn't home, ask a friend or neighbor to take your baby for a few hours so you can nap. Keep in mind that the most difficult period of adjustment lasts only a month or two.

Other Helpful Things to Do

It's helpful to be able to talk to others who have had similar experiences. Seek out other parents for help and support. Even neighbors who don't know you well might be happy to talk to you at times of special stress.

Parenting

If This Isn't Your First Child
Some parents worry they aren't doing as much for their second child as they did for the first. It's not unusual for the second child to have a half-empty baby book, if she has one at all. Instead she has parents who are more relaxed and practiced, who've learned a lot from having been through it all before. And she has an older sibling who will entertain her for hours and teach her about life from his own inimitable child's point of view.

Your Older Child's Feelings
Older children always have mixed feelings about their younger brothers and sisters; this is a normal part of living together. When you first bring the baby home, don't go overboard in your involvement with your baby and forget about your older child. It's helpful to arrange that visitors pay attention to him as well as to the baby. You can discreetly ask grandparents and others who are special to your older child to take extra care with him.

37

New Baby, New Parents — The First Few Weeks

The negative feelings your child may show are a reaction to his mother having been gone for a few days. It will be helpful to him if you respond by reassuring him that you are home to stay now and by acknowledging his right to be upset, rather than by dwelling on his reaction to the baby. Since you won't have as much time to spend with your older child as he has been accustomed to, take advantage of whatever special opportunities you do have. Your baby's feeding time often works well as a time to read or talk to your first child.

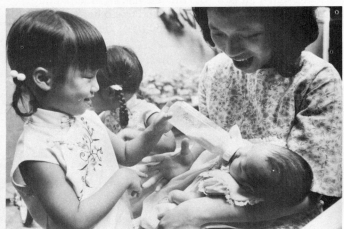

The new baby can be integrated in the family in ways that help the older child feel included. It's important not to develop the habit of saying, "Don't touch." Help him "hold" the baby, with your assistance. After a feeding, sit the baby on your lap, and let her older brother burp her. She can take it, even if he burps her less gently than you do. Think of ways your older child can help in baby care that will enable him to feel useful and important. If your child enjoys carrying things for the baby when you go places, let him do it.

**New Baby, New Parents —
The First Few Weeks**

Parenthood Is a Process
Just as your baby will grow and develop, you will grow and develop as parents. After all, being a parent is a new experience for you—you've never done it before, at least with this child.

The process of parenthood goes through 3 stages. When you've just had a baby, you look at your tiny newborn and feel many different emotions: pride in the wondrous being you have produced, excitement about the challenge of growing together, and uncertainty or even fear about your ability to be a good father or mother. The tears replace fears as you experience temporary frustration and fatigue. It takes practice and patience to be a parent, but if you give yourself time to adjust to the new person in your life, your final feeling will be one of satisfaction and pleasure.

3. Two Become Three— How Your Marriage Changes

Sharing the experience of having a baby brings new depths to the feelings a new mother and a new father have for each other. However, because a baby directs the attention of his parents away from each other, there is bound to be a time of adjustment before a couple can relate as smoothly as they did before the baby was born. Your relationship is never going to return to what it was before the baby. You wouldn't really want it to, though there certainly will be times when you long to be free of all the responsibilities just for a while. The adjustment to parenthood is part of maturing, and rich rewards accompany that change. You need to find ways to alter your relationship that will support being close and loving with each other during your child-rearing years. In this chapter, we'll discuss some of the difficulties you may encounter and offer some practical suggestions for minimizing those difficulties.

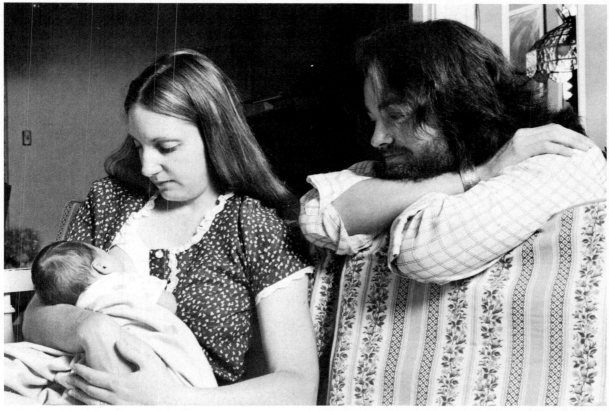

header

— n

Two Become Three — How Your Marriage Changes

Not Enough Time

Going to the movies, to ballgames, to concerts, or on long walks are common ways couples enjoy themselves and feel close to each other. You won't be able to do those things so easily now. When your baby is born, you suddenly assume responsibility for responding totally to another person's physical and emotional needs. All the extra work keeps you hopping. Even when caring for your baby doesn't keep you busy every minute, you may feel "tied down" by her. Going out seems so complicated.

Not only is it more difficult to arrange, but you often feel too tired. And, on evenings when you are at home together, you can't really count on the peaceful, quiet times you used to enjoy. Babies' schedules aren't very regular, especially when they're young. They often need food or attention at the most awkward moments. You'll just settle down for some relaxing time together, and . . . WAAAHHHH!

Jealousy and Envy

When a third person enters their lives, parents are apt to feel jealous. A husband may envy the large amounts of time and attention his wife gives their baby, particularly when it appears to be at the expense of time he and his wife used to spend together. She may have similar feelings if her husband returns from work and dashes in to see the baby instead of spending a few moments with her. If a woman was working before the baby came, she may be envious of her husband's freedom to leave the house while she stays home all day, especially if she is out of touch with other adults.

Irritability

New parents are made more irritable than they were before the baby was born by the pressures of their new situation, the lack of sleep, and the lack of time to talk things out. The husband may come home to find that dinner isn't ready or the house still hasn't been cleaned. The wife may badly want to tell her husband some wonderful new things the baby has done that day, but he doesn't listen when she tries to tell him the exciting news, because he has come home still thinking about some problem from work.

Your Sexual Relationship

The disruption of the couple's sexual relationship presents an added pressure. New parents may worry that sex will never again be full of passion and abandon. Some women fear a permanent loss of attractiveness. For breast-feeding mothers there is the awkward problem of the initially overflowing milk supply, which can be messy. Also, some women start to feel that their breasts are the baby's property. In addition to all these factors, it's hard to relax and enjoy each other when your baby may wake up and need attention at any time.

Now we will describe some of the ways parents have found to deal with these problems, to successfully make the transition from being a couple to being a family.

Time Away from Your Baby

During the first few weeks with their baby, parents may not feel like going out in the evenings. Often they're both tired, and being near their baby is far more fun than going to the movies. But most couples do eventually need time away from their baby, time when they don't have to think about changing diapers or the next feeding. Once you find someone you trust to care for him, you're on your way.

Parents often wonder if it's all right to leave the baby with another person, particularly the first time they do it. If you find the right babysitter, your baby actually benefits from being around other people. When he is sensitively cared for by another person, he begins to learn that he can trust other people besides his parents.

Babies *do* need consistency in their care. When you ask someone to care for your baby, make sure she (or he) understands how you relate to him, so she will do things in similar ways. Spend time helping her get to know your baby. Tell her about his schedule and his likes and dislikes, particularly in relation to eating and sleeping. Have her take care of the baby at least once while you are around, so that you can give her suggestions and see how well she and your baby get along.

Who are you going to get to babysit? Among the most likely candidates are relatives, if you're lucky enough to have them close by. Grandparents can be very special people for your baby. They are usually delighted with their new grandchild, especially since they don't have constant responsibility for her. They are free to love the baby in a unique way, and of course they retain the knowledge they gained from raising you.

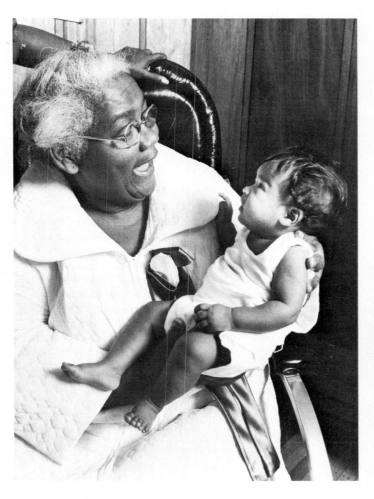

Two Become Three — How Your Marriage Changes

The next place to look for babysitters is among your friends. Those who have children past the baby stage might love the chance to re-experience a tiny one. Those who don't have children might be interested in finding out more about them. Some parents have found it convenient to form "sitter swaps" with other parents of small children. These swaps can save money while providing your baby with experienced and dependable babysitters.

When relatives or friends aren't available, it's a good idea to have one regular babysitter who will be familiar to your baby. You will want to find someone who loves babies, is reliable, and can handle any difficulties that might arise. It's always nice to find someone who has had experience with babies, but don't rule out teenagers, except perhaps when your infant is very young.

You can get names of babysitters from other parents. In addition, local high schools, colleges, and nursing schools often have referral services. You may be able to find older people who would like to babysit through a nearby church, synagogue, or senior citizen's organization.

Now—where are you off to? Wherever you used to go before your baby was born! Going out to dinner can be a huge relief from your usual household chores. There's something extra pleasant about being waited on for a change. An idea that is attractive to some parents, when the baby's feeding schedule allows it, is to take a whole night off. Go to a nearby hotel or motel for a very special time alone with each other. What a joy to have a night's sleep with no interruptions! You will probably return the next morning refreshed and eager to see your baby again.

Sharing Responsibilities

Since there's so much more work when there's a baby in the house, it's important that both parents feel comfortable with arrangements for sharing the new responsibilities. Sit down together as needs change to discuss who does what.

A nice way to handle the extra housework is to do it together, evenings or weekends. Although it's hard for husbands to imagine doing housework in the evening after a long day at work, remember that what your wife has been doing all day has been equally taxing. It's always more fun doing those kinds of chores if someone else is around doing them, too. Put on a relaxing record and enjoy yourselves. If your baby wakes up, he'll probably want to join the fun.

valid and high-priority complaint — a signal that the harried parent needs to leave the baby with the spouse and take a break.

A word of caution: when one spouse comes home from work, he or she needs a little time to unwind. Don't expect your wife to start cooking the minute she walks in the door. Don't hand your husband the crying child as soon as he gets home. Try to have a quiet relaxing time first, and then move on to the evening's projects.

Baby chores can also be more enjoyable if your partner is around. While one of you is making dinner, the other can play with the baby in the kitchen. At bath time, one can wash and the other watch.

It can be beneficial to sometimes share the baby in "shifts." It's also important to have an understanding between you that "I can't take it another minute" is a

**Two Become Three —
How Your Marriage
Changes**

Being Together with the Baby
Taking the baby with you when you go places is one of
the pleasures of being a family. It can also help relieve
those feelings of being "tied down." Of course, this depends on your baby's temperament, and on yours, but
babies are often remarkably adaptable. They usually enjoy being in different settings. In fact, sometimes babies
do better when taken out. Being driven in the car and being carried around often relax them. If the baby has been
fretful, going to visit friends may reduce the tensions all
around so that everyone can have an enjoyable evening.
With a sling, stroller, or back pack you can take a baby
almost anywhere. And most babies get used to sleeping in
different places, if you start them early.

Although it's practical for parents to take turns with the baby, arrange some times when all of you are together. It is important for the baby to experience the family together, and it is vital to the couple's relationship. There is a special kind of intimacy between a husband and wife alone with their child. The intimacy is reinforced by watching each other being tender and loving with the child or by seeing each other as competent and able to handle the responsibilities of caring for a baby.

Playing with the baby is a special time. Parents can coo, clown, and make faces to amuse the baby in ways that would ordinarily make them feel foolish. In this case, the baby enjoys it, they enjoy it, and it helps endear each parent to the other. Adulthood doesn't often allow us to be silly, so take advantage of your opportunity to be playful with your baby.

Two Become Three — How Your Marriage Changes

Improving Communication

Parents usually experience many new and conflicting emotions during the first weeks after the baby's arrival. Often it's hard to talk about feelings when they are new, especially when you aren't yet certain just what they are. You know you are feeling uncomfortable, but sometimes that's all you know for sure. If you just say that much, probably your mate will sigh with relief that you've brought the subject up. Chances are he or she has been waiting to talk also.

You might try to set aside a time each night to talk about the things you are experiencing as new parents. You probably never had to schedule a "talk time" before — you could talk anytime you felt like it. Other times that some parents have found to be important for maintaining the high quality of their relationship are the first few minutes after waking in the morning and the first few minutes when you greet each other after work, just before you take some time to unwind. In the morning, even though you are jolted awake by the baby's cry, if you just take a moment to smile at each other, it often makes the pressures of the day more manageable.

There are so many things to talk about. It's a good idea to start right from the beginning discussing with each other any questions or problems you might have about the baby.

You might like telling each other ways you've enjoyed the baby that day. You will probably remember wonderful moments you had almost forgotten. Some parents enjoy taking notes together on their child's development. That serves as a way of sharing information with each other and also preserves a record they can enjoy and return to later. You might like to read sections of this Guide aloud to each other and discuss them. There is magic in having created this combination of the two of you. By talking about your hopes and dreams for the life of your new little daughter or son, you can learn a lot about each other you never knew before. Sharing those feelings brings a new closeness.

Money is frequently an issue which needs to be discussed after a new baby arrives. Your budget may be stretched as expenses rise, especially if only one of you is working when two of you previously worked. Fathers often feel more pressure about being a good enough provider, now that they have a child to support. Mothers may forget about that side of things because they feel the pressures of mothering so strongly. It's important to share these feelings and plan how you want to spend money.

Coming to decisions together is not only helpful to your relationship, it's also helpful for your baby. A baby is incredibly sensitive to the feelings that flow around him. When there are happy, loving feelings, he will probably feel and act contented. When there are angry, harsh feelings, he will probably feel and act tense and upset, too.

When misunderstandings occur, as they undoubtedly will, it's important to handle them as gently as possible. For instance, a tired, worn-out mother had finally gotten her baby to rest fairly peacefully in his crib. He was still fussing and fretting a little, but she knew he was close to falling asleep. When her husband came home from work, he heard the fussings and, eager to help, went to the baby's cradle and picked him up. This is one of those times when the mother might feel like yelling at her husband's mistake, but life will be smoother if she stays calm and explains the situation.

4. Fathers and Babies— A Mutually Rewarding Relationship

One father was alone with his 6-week-old baby for the first time. His wife had gone out for the afternoon. It happened to be the day of the "Super Bowl," and a good friend was over to watch the game with him on TV. The baby was sound asleep and everything was fine until the middle of the third quarter, when, suddenly, the baby started to cry. The father went to her and started to change her soggy diaper. She looked up at him, kicked her legs, and flashed him a loving smile. Ten minutes later his friend called out, "Hey, what's taking you so long?" Only then did he realize that he'd become so involved in playing with his baby that he had completely forgotten about the game.

Couples share in the care of their babies in different ways. In some families, mothers do most of the work and fathers help by supporting their wives. But scenes like this are becoming more common. More fathers are involved with their babies, and they are showing their wives and themselves that, with a little experience, they are equally capable of caring for their infants. At the same time, research is showing that fathers are important to their babies.

Fathers and Babies —
A Mutually Rewarding
Relationship

Fathers Are Involved with Their Babies

It used to be that most men didn't have much to do with their children until they were toddlers. Fathers often had the attitude, "Bring him to me when he can talk!" Many people mistakenly believe mothers are more *naturally* responsive to their babies than fathers are. That this is not the case is clear from a study of the way parents relate to their infants in the first few days after birth. Dr. Martin Greenberg of the Langley Porter Neuropsychiatric Institute in San Francisco and Dr. Norman Morris of the Charing Cross Hospital in London found that fathers who had the opportunity to spend time with their babies in the hospital were intensely involved with their newborns. When they were able to hold their infants, they loved looking at them and touching them. They often commented on how soft the babies' skin was, and how "beautiful" and "perfect" they were.

Fathers Are Good Caregivers

Who hasn't seen a cartoon of a frazzled father unable to cope with his baby? Not a flattering image, and quite often, not an accurate one either. A study directed by Dr. Ross Parke of the University of Illinois found that fathers were just as competent as their wives in bottle-feeding their babies. They were also as sensitive as their wives to the babies' signals of distress while feeding, such as sneezing, coughing, or spitting up, and the fathers responded to these cues as effectively as the mothers in the usual ways — by stopping feeding temporarily, looking closely at their babies, burping them, or talking to them.

A father who chooses to be actively involved in taking care of his baby can do just as good a job as a mother in feeding, bathing, or playing with her. He can calm a baby with his voice or a gentle touch just as well as she can. Still, in most families, fathers' participation in child care drops off after the first month or so, for a number of reasons. Recognizing these reasons may help fathers to maintain their involvement, build their competence with their babies, and enjoy the full benefits of fatherhood.

What Keeps Fathers from Participating in Caregiving?

Many men still think it's unmanly to dress a baby or push a stroller. Many women still feel that taking care of babies is ''women's work,'' and they don't encourage their husbands to take part. Some women would like their husbands to take an active role with the baby, but they assume men aren't capable. Some wives are afraid to ask for assistance. They feel guilty for asking ''too much'' of someone who has ''worked all day''; or they feel nervous about further straining their relationship during these difficult times. Even if both husband and wife believe in sharing baby care, many men don't have as much time to

Changing the Pattern

Happily, attitudes are changing, and people are recognizing the advantages for the whole family of the father's active participation in child-rearing. Child care books are now being addressed to both parents. A greater percentage of husbands are present and active at the birth of their children. Even TV ads show fathers with babies. More and more men are realizing that they can be gentle as well as strong. Most mothers are already aware that coping with the demands of caring for an infant takes as much strength as it does gentleness.

spend with their babies as their wives have. As a result, mothers become more skilled than their husbands at caregiving. A woman then finds it easier to slip into the habit of doing all of the baby care, even when her husband is present, because she is more familiar with it. Wives sometimes find themselves jumping in to rescue both husband and baby at the slightest cry of distress from the child. This can quickly become a self-perpetuating cycle, with the husband becoming less and less competent at child care because he doesn't get the chance to practice. The problem is further complicated by his then feeling isolated from the tight unit of mother and child.

Fathers and Babies —
A Mutually Rewarding
Relationship

Every father reading this Guide should know that even if he spends less time with his baby than does his wife, he can do a number of things to increase his competence in caregiving. When his wife is taking care of the baby, he can watch the way she does things and ask her questions about the whys and wherefores. Then he can allow her to make suggestions while he takes over. We're not talking only of such matters as changing a diaper, which really isn't such a complicated skill, but of the ways the signals of the baby are interpreted. It's important that *both* husband and wife be patient with the father's initial efforts.

In addition to learning when you're with your wife, try taking care of your baby by yourself sometimes. Two parents are bound to have some differences between their rhythms and styles of baby care. When alone with his baby, a father can gain confidence in his own style of parenting without the self-consciousness he might feel in the presence of his wife, who has more experience. Slipping back into the old pattern of the mother taking over is

avoided. At least 2 ways to schedule solo baby care by the father have been found to work. Some parents arrange for the father to practice caregiving alone by setting aside specific times as his responsibility. He gains the most experience if these are times when the baby is awake and doesn't need to be breast-fed. The father can always supply a supplementary bottle. Other parents arrange for *activities,* such as bathing the baby, feeding her dinner, or taking her for a walk.

Fathers Are Important to Babies

Until recently, people thought that the only importance of fathers to babies was as a *substitute* caregiver when the mother wasn't around. But current research is showing that fathers are *uniquely* important to babies, and offer them something quite special.

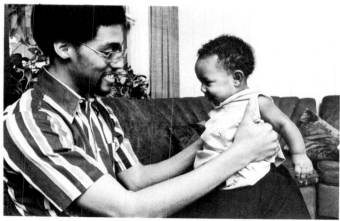

For example, it's been found that a baby as young as 2 weeks can differentiate between his parents, not only by differences in their faces and their voices, but also by differences in the way they relate to him. Two people relating to the baby in different ways makes life more varied for him. Early experience with this kind of variety helps him to learn how to respond to the other new situations he faces every day. You might wonder . . . can variety be provided by any 2 people? It can, and in single-parent families, it often is — by mother and grandmother, for example. But in most two-parent families, the father is the person besides the mother who is closest to the baby.

Fathers and Babies —
A Mutually Rewarding
Relationship

Another special quality fathers have to offer their babies is playfulness. Dr. Michael Lamb of the University of Wisconsin found that the fathers he observed tended to play with their babies differently from mothers. Fathers thought up new ways of playing more often than mothers did, so their play was more varied and unpredictable.

Fathers were also more physical in their play, rough-housing and tossing their babies in the air. A mother may sometimes feel nervous when she sees her husband playing with the baby in a way she fears might hurt the baby. But she needn't worry. Even though it appears Dad's being too rough, babies love the excitement and fun fathers provide. Many babies observed by Dr. Berry Brazelton of Boston Childrens Hospital became excited when they saw their fathers, in anticipation of the kind of play

they had come to expect. With the father-baby relationship being intense and active, the father's behavior has a special impact.

The families most likely to fit the pattern found by Dr. Lamb and Dr. Brazelton are those where the mother does most of the caregiving, and the father's relationship is almost exclusively one of play. Where fathers take on more baby care responsibilities, mothers have more time to relax and play with their babies. What is important for parents to remember is that each has something special to offer the baby, which they can share with each other. Just as fathers can learn about caregiving from mothers, mothers can learn from fathers by watching their special ways of playing with babies.

Time with Your Baby—How Much?
Fathers who don't spend as much time with their babies as they would like are often concerned not only about how well they can take care of their babies, but also about whether their babies will love them. Mothers who work outside the home also share these concerns. However, what matters to a baby is the *quality* of the relationship with a person, not how many hours that person is with him. But what about the father who can give his baby only 20 minutes a day? That may not seem like much, but if you spend 20 minutes completely involved with your baby, it makes a huge difference to him; you convey how deeply you care about him.

Fathers who are able to spend time with their babies can be as loving and nurturing as mothers. However, fathers may need help and encouragement in learning more about their babies and how to care for them. No one is born with the skills needed for taking care of a baby — it's a matter of practice. When a father does actively participate in his baby's life, the baby, the father, and the mother reap the benefits of their close relationship.

5. Babies and Working Mothers

Whether or not a woman works after the birth of her baby is an individual decision based on her own emotional needs and the family's financial situation. Many parents want to know whether their baby will thrive and develop properly if she is left with another person all day while they are working. Research has shown that the *quality* of the baby's relationship with her parents and the *quality* of the care she receives from whomever else takes care of her are the most important influences on her development. A mother who cares for her baby lovingly and attentively when she gets home from work can develop a close relationship with her. What goes on between them when they are together is of great importance. A baby can also benefit from having a close relationship with the person who substitutes for her mother. Just as forming an attachment to her father helps her trust more than 1 person, relating to another person who cares for her can broaden her ability to relate to different people.

Some mothers worry that if their baby spends most of his day with another person he will become more attached to that person than to his mother. Be assured that you are irreplaceable to your baby. Though the person who takes care of your baby will come to love him, her involvement with your child will not have the same intensity as yours. Your strong love for your baby and your special sensitivity to his signals are part of what makes your relationship unique. Your baby will feel this, and he will save both his best and his worst moments for the times when you are together.

Choosing Day Care Situations

When parents are able to leave their baby with someone who is loving and nurturing, in a place where the baby will be happy, they can feel more relaxed about the fact that they are both working away from the home. To help ensure that both parents are comfortable with these arrangements, investigate the possibilities together. If your schedules make this impossible, try to discuss the alternatives fully before making a decision. There are a number of possibilities, which include an individual babysitter, play groups, and day care centers.

Individual Babysitter

When looking for the right person to care for your baby, ask what her experience with children has been. Make certain she enjoys children and is a loving person. When you interview her, let her hold your baby for a few minutes and watch how she responds. You can usually tell when someone is comfortable and is enjoying herself. A warm, sensitive, and practical babysitter will benefit your baby far more than one who is overly concerned with cleanliness and order. Make it clear to her that she's being hired to take care of your baby — not to do your housework.

Your baby may need time to feel at ease with this new person, and the sitter will need time to become familiar enough with your baby's signals to respond appropriately. Because the attachment your baby develops to this new person is an important part of learning to trust people, try to find someone likely to be available for most of the first year. A frequent change of babysitters could be disruptive to your baby.

Finding the right person to fit your specifications may take a good deal of effort on your part. Suggestions for finding a part-time babysitter were offered earlier. If you check the suggested sources and still can't find someone for full-time care of your baby, you can advertise in the newspaper or put up notices on bulletin boards around your neighborhood. Since people who respond to your ad will be strangers, it's extremely important that you check their references, to be certain their past employers can recommend them. How well you like someone, your "gut reaction," will certainly enter into your decision, but also take time to sift through your information on her experience and references.

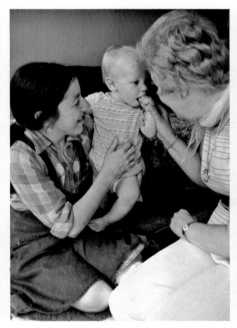

Babies and Working Mothers

Being able to communicate with the babysitter is crucial to maintaining consistency in your baby's care. Find someone you can talk to easily. Ideally her style should complement your own. When interviewing someone, ask how she feels about feeding, crying, naps, discipline, and any other topics that seem important to you. Tell any likely prospect your own views so you can discuss how she feels about them. You might suggest that she also read this Guide. Relatives often work well as babysitters because their ideas about taking care of babies may be similar to yours, and because they may be easier to talk to than people you don't know. On the other hand, if you end up with serious disagreements about baby care, a relative is harder to fire than someone you're not related to.

After you select a babysitter, arrange a trial period — a weekend, a few evenings during the week, or whenever both parents will be free to observe her in action, to make certain both of you like the way she relates to your baby and the way your baby responds to her.

You may feel awkward about hiring someone on a trial basis and observing how she relates to your baby before making a final decision. But a competent, confident person will not mind. She'll understand that you are doing all you can to assure yourself that your baby will be in good hands. In addition, your baby will have time to get used to his new companion gradually, with you still available for comfort.

If your baby is cared for in your home, he will be in a familiar environment, which can be comforting. Some babysitters have their own children and may prefer to care for your baby in their home. This can also benefit your baby because being with other children is usually a stimulating and happy experience for a baby.

Be sure you schedule time every day to talk to the sitter about what your baby has been doing. In the morning, tell the sitter how the night went, what breakfast was like, any new things the baby has just learned, and any changes in his routine.

When you return, ask how the baby's day went, what her moods were like, and about the day's events, such as naps and eating. Both of you will feel more comfortable if each knows as much as possible about the baby so that her care is smooth and consistent.

Play Groups, or Group Care in Homes
Many parents find it convenient to hire 1 or more babysitters to be responsible for a small group of babies, usually no more than 4, either in their own homes or in the sitter's home. This arrangement has at least 3 beneficial features. One, it is less expensive than individualized day care and may be more personal than a day care center. Two, the babies who play together on a regular basis can become friends. Such friendship is special, because they rarely have a chance to be with somebody just as little in a world where everyone else is large. Three, as their babies get to know each other, parents become friends who help each other out in other situations.

The advice given in the previous section about finding an appropriate babysitter applies here as well. However, the entire set of parents will want to get together to discuss the qualifications they are jointly seeking in a sitter. Though such a discussion may be complicated, you will probably be considering this type of day care alternative with parents who generally have the same beliefs that you have about childrearing. This similarity will ease considerably the task of choosing a babysitter acceptable to all.

Babies and Working Mothers

Day Care Center

Day care centers for infants are a fairly new phenomenon and still are not very widespread. In the past, people suspected that babies in an all day group care situation couldn't receive the highly individualized attention they need. In those days, the suspicion may sometimes have been well-founded. Nowadays, however, day care centers for infants are being more carefully developed, and new information is available. Psychologists and child-development researchers are studying infants in day care situations and are discovering that the situation can be a positive one for the baby's development, given the right conditions of infant care, including a stable relationship with a competent caregiver.

When choosing a day care center, make sure the ratio of adults to infants is low—at least 1 adult for every 2 or 3 babies. There should be one individual who will be primarily responsible for your baby, even if others will share in his care at times. This person will get to know your baby's habits and unique characteristics, and your baby will become familiar with her. In order to share information about your baby's development and changes in his behavior or routines, a good center will maintain close communication with you.

One of the most helpful things parents can do when considering a day care center is to talk to parents of other babies in the center. An excellent pamphlet that discusses requirements parents can look for in a good quality infant center is *"The Good Life" for Infants and Toddlers,* by Dr. Mary Elizabeth Keister. It's available from the National Association for the Education of Young Children, 1834 Connecticut Ave., N.W., Washington, D.C. 20009.

Practical Tips: Ways to Make Your Life Easier
No matter how good a day care system you arrange there will be days when emergencies arise. If your baby is sick, one parent will probably want to stay home. On the other hand, if your babysitter is sick, you may want to have a close friend or relative available to care for your baby.

Organizing Time
If both parents have jobs, some sort of schedule can help to get things done. Be clear about your priorities, so you don't waste time on nonessentials. It's more important to spend loving time with your family than to do more work around your house, especially after a long day at the job. For instance, it works well to establish an arrangement that allows you both to relax and be close to your baby

for the first half hour after you arrive home, before either of you cooks dinner. It's nice to remind yourselves how much your baby needs you. If your baby has this special time with you, he won't need as much attention during dinner preparations, and you'll feel less harried. In the same spirit, reserve weekends for leisure time together as a family. Taking a trip to the zoo on a sunny Saturday can be more rewarding than polishing furniture. Going on a picnic with friends rather than preparing an elaborate sit-down dinner will be more relaxing for everyone.

If you regret these sorts of changes, remember that having to make adjustments to simplify your life won't last forever — just the first months while you establish your new routine.

Babies and Working Mothers

Timing Your Return to Work

If the choice of when you go back to work after your baby is born is up to you, your decision should be based partly on your needs and partly on your baby's needs. A mother who plans to continue breast-feeding after she returns to work may want to delay that return until her milk supply and the baby's schedule are regular. This usually happens when the baby is 2 to 3 months old. In this way both can easily adapt to breast-feedings before she leaves for work and when she returns home, with supplementary bottles in between.

How confident a mother feels about taking care of her baby is another consideration. New parents often doubt their own competence. It might work best for a new mother to wait until she feels comfortable about her new role — when she understands the signals her baby gives and when their lives have settled into some kind of pattern — before she returns to work. Being tired from work at the job and also nervous about how well you are managing as a mother could create difficulties.

Departures

A mother frequently wonders whether she is doing the right thing in returning to work, and she regrets being separated from her baby. These feelings are often heightened in the morning when she is leaving for work. It can be particularly difficult for a mother if her baby cries when she departs. If this happens to you, check your behavior. Are you leaving firmly and calmly, or are you unsure and apologetic, so that the baby is reflecting your lack of confidence? Try leaving before your husband leaves, to see if doing that makes things easier for you and your baby. A phone call home after you get to work can reassure you that your baby stopped crying soon after your departure and is back into his routine. Babies differ in how upset they become when their mothers return to work. Your understanding of your own baby's needs is an important guide to your plans for returning to work.

It's important to both parents that you be confident about your decision to return to work. Remember that you are not abandoning your baby; you have carefully selected someone to look after her. You have done everything possible to ensure her well-being and happiness.

PART TWO: SOCIAL AND EMOTIONAL DEVELOPMENT

1. Babies Respond to Other People from Birth

Infants may *look* completely helpless at birth (and until recently even experts described them this way), but new techniques for measuring their abilities reveal how much they have been underestimated. Today a growing number of scientists are ignoring old theories and watching how newborn babies actually behave. As a result, an exciting view of the newborn is emerging. Far from being helpless, all her senses are working at birth. She can hear, see, taste, and smell — and she's especially attracted to the sounds, sights, tastes, and smells of other people!

Voices Are Your Newborn's Favorite Sound

Did you know infants just a few minutes old will become alert and turn their heads to the sound of someone speaking much more often than to any other sound? Drs. Peter Eimas, Einar Siqueland, and Lewis Lipsitt of Brown University have also discovered other signs of the newborn's special adaptation to voices. She comes equipped for the most basic feature of communication — pausing in her own activity to pay attention to what another person has to say. When an infant who is sucking hears a sound other than a voice, she is interrupted only momentarily before resuming a steady sucking pattern. But if she hears a voice, she resumes her sucking with a different pattern, one of bursts and pauses, as if she wanted to hear more and was pausing occasionally to pay attention. Many parents recognize this pattern and naturally adapt to the built-in opportunities it provides for "conversations" at nursing time. They are relatively quiet while the baby is sucking, concentrating their smiling and talking in the pauses between bursts of sucking.

Newborns Love Faces

From the moment of birth, babies are especially attracted to human *sights* as well as to human *sounds*. Research shows that right in the delivery room an infant will pay attention to a person's face or a picture of a face, and will follow its movement with his eyes. If he is shown a picture of a face with its features rearranged, he will stare at it wide-eyed for a long time, but is much less likely to follow it. Even though he's had no contact with other people, his responses seem to say "this is fascinating, but it's not quite right."

Even the youngest baby will follow a person's face with his eyes.

Even the Senses of Taste and Smell Are Specially Adapted to People

Dr. Aidan MacFarlane of Oxford University in England found that babies sucked differently on a bottle containing human milk than on one containing cow's milk formulated to resemble as closely as possible the contents of breast milk. The formula didn't taste or smell the same to the babies although it contained the same ingredients.

Experiments have been conducted recently by Michael Russel at the University of California Medical Center in San Francisco to test the great biologist Charles Darwin's century-old suggestion that infants use odors to identify their mothers. He found most sleeping 2-week-old babies were roused by the odor of a cotton sponge their nursing mothers had worn for 3 hours inside their brassieres — but the odor of another mother was equally effective. At 6 weeks, the babies' sense of smell was more sophisticated. Seven of 10 babies responded to the mother's pad (as they had 4 weeks earlier). However, only 1 of the 7 responded to another mother's pad and his response was "negative" — a head jerk and cry.

Understanding Your Newborn's Built-in Strengths

You may wonder *why* the sights, sounds, and other sensations that most appeal to your baby are all available in the form of adult caregiving humans — namely you. One theory is especially interesting. It suggests that in the early ages of the human race, babies who recognized and adapted to their parents quickly and easily were most likely to survive and to pass these abilities on to their own children. Of course, a baby's preadaptation to people is no longer essential for his physical survival, but it continues to be important for his development. Parents are by far the richest source of help and stimulation in the baby's environment. He adapts most quickly to the world by paying special attention to them.

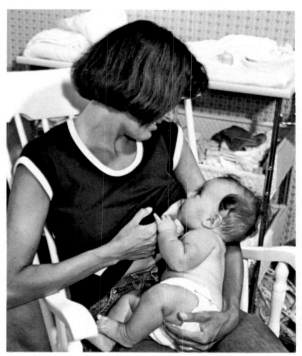

When an infant who is nursing hears her mother's voice, she may pause for a "conversation."

Parents, the source of life, are also the best source of help and stimulation.

**Babies Respond to
Other People from Birth**

Newborns Are Attracted to People,
and the Feeling Is Mutual

Infants are born especially attracted to people, and this attraction is a 2-way street. Many parents are fascinated by their new babies and spend long periods of time watching, touching, and speaking to them. Drs. Marshall Klaus and John Kennell of Case Western Reserve Medical School in Cleveland tape-recorded mothers' "conversations" with their infants the first time they were alone together after delivery. They found that 80% of what was said related to the babies' eyes! The mother

and that he knew it was me . . . I was afraid it was just wishful thinking. But if *you* tell me it's true, I can believe in it and enjoy it.'' This enjoyment seems to generate wider benefits. A group of new parents watched a film showing that newborns are capable and tuned in to people. A month later these parents and a group of parents who hadn't seen the films were observed relating to their babies and were asked a few questions. The results were interesting: the parents who had seen the film seemed to be more comfortable with their babies. They also said they felt closer to their babies and had greater confidence

*New parents often find
their baby irresistible.*

was looking for a sign the baby was "paying attention" or responding to her own excitement and enthusiasm. Of course, your baby's earliest responses *are* especially thrilling. The first stage of your relationship begins at birth and grows out of this mutual attraction and attention.

Can Awareness of a Baby's Abilities
Really Make a Difference?

Dr. Berry Brazelton of Boston Children's Hospital describes the benefits parents derive when he shows them what capable little individuals their newborns really are. Parents tell him "I *knew* he could see and hear me,

in themselves as parents. Apparently (and not surprisingly), when you are aware your baby is a real person from birth, you feel closer to her and relate to her better.

Most of what we know about the abilities of newborns comes from a careful "reading" of their behavior. Now that you know how capable your new baby is, and how helpful an awareness of her abilities can be to you as parents, you may be interested in some hints on understanding behavior throughout the whole first year

2. Communicating with Your Baby in the First Months of Life

We are beginning to recognize that babies have powerful inborn abilities to communicate to us what they need and to shut out what they don't want. Your baby's behavior provides you with some helpful guidelines which you can rely on in caring for him. He's not yet capable of thinking as adults do, but he does *feel* strongly. And these feelings, expressed by the way he behaves, can be trusted as your best single guide to his needs and to his pleasures and displeasures.

Your baby is good at expressing his needs, but they'll only be met if you can figure out what he's telling you when he behaves in a particular way. That's why it's so important to learn how to interpret your baby's behavior, right from the start. Your ability to understand his behavior will still be a big help when he begins to use words. Even as adults we often express feelings most clearly through actions rather than words, though we may not always be aware of it. From the day he's born, your baby uses sounds, facial expressions, and the way he holds and moves his body to signal what he likes and dislikes. At the same time, he is sensitive to the messages *you* send by the way you hold, look at, and speak to him.

What *Is* She Saying?
No baby's needs and feelings are exactly like any other's, but most babies share common ways of expressing themselves. Some of your newborn baby's behavior is fairly subtle. A gradual quieting and alerting when you are holding her gently is a sign of comfort and pleasure.

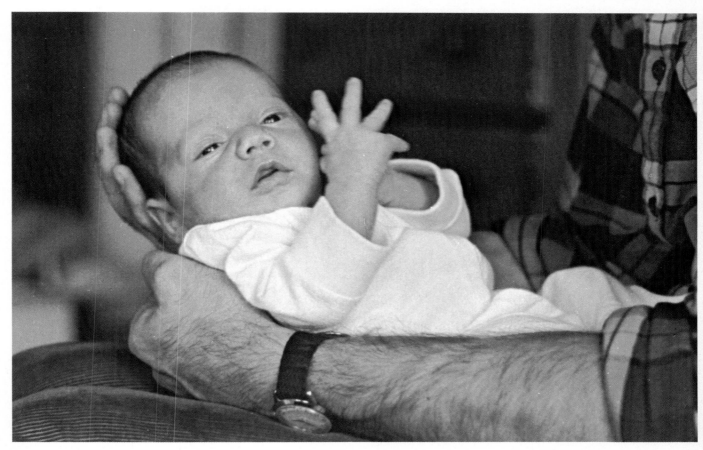

Communicating with Your Baby in the First Months of Life

From the start, your baby has ways of both seeking and avoiding or cutting off contact with other people. Smiling, babbling, and cooing are all gentle come-hither signals, which she uses when she wants company and you are nearby.

Within the first few weeks of life, babies move their eyes and head to look *at* people when they want to relate to them, and *away* when they want to avoid contact — sometimes only momentarily. *Recognizing and respecting your baby's need to look away for a moment every once in a while, even when she's having a good time with you, can keep you from feeling "rejected" and increase her comfort and pleasure.*

Of course fussing or crying are signals that she really needs you.

Your baby may also shut her eyes or even fall asleep when she needs a break from the excitement of play.

After the middle of the first year, your baby develops new ways of using her body to seek, avoid, or cut off contact. When she holds out a toy to you or touches or pets you, she may be saying, ''I like to be near you,'' or ''Let's

play.'' When she pushes your hand away, or tries to wriggle out of your arms, or tries to crawl away, or shakes her head ''no,'' she may be saying ''Leave me alone for a bit, please.'' A serious expression and trembling lip after be-

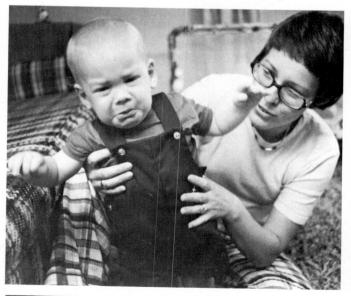

ing approached by an unfamiliar person say ''You aren't someone I know. I'm not sure I feel comfortable with you, and if you don't give me a little room, I'm going to scream.''

**Sometimes His Behavior Alone
Doesn't Tell You What He Needs**
Sometimes you have to rely partly on the *context* in which you see a particular behavior for help in interpreting its meaning. For example — you hear your newborn crying in the middle of the night, several hours after he's last eaten. As soon as you have him in your arms he starts ''rooting'' or groping for the nipple. You put 2 and 2 together and guess he's probably hungry. His active nursing tells you you're right. After he seems full and comfortable you put him back to bed, but a few minutes later he cries again. You know he's probably not hungry, and this time when you turn on the light you see him frantically pulling his legs up against his stomach and stretching them out again. His cries and his actions say, ''My stomach hurts.'' The fact that he's recently eaten tells you burping may help. And it does. Of course most parents respond naturally to this situation because the baby's signals are fairly clear. But there are times when figuring out the problem may be more difficult. What would you do if your baby didn't need burping — and wouldn't nurse either — when you went in the second time? Maybe his need was for company and not food. And what might he need if he did start ''rooting'' again just a few minutes after his meal? Perhaps he's one of those babies who needs his feedings in ''courses.'' In the chapter on crying we'll have much more to say about figuring out and dealing with such situations.

Communicating with Your Baby in the First Months of Life

Communicating with Babies Is a 2-Way Street
Until your baby learns the meaning of the words you use, she relies on the same signals for understanding *you* that you use in "reading" *her* — feelings expressed in behavior. As we mentioned, adults express their feelings through body language continuously, though not always consciously. Communicating feelings to your baby also happens naturally in the day-to-day routine of shared activities. What are some of the ways you can communicate with her?

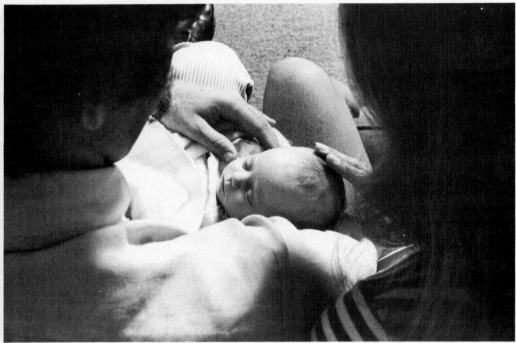

Your baby first experiences the world largely through her skin and her sense of touch. When you hold her securely and caress or stroke her gently, you are expressing your love in a way even the youngest baby can appreciate.

Even a newborn is aware of your feelings when you hold her close and smile at her.

A soothing gentle voice communicates love and pleasure.

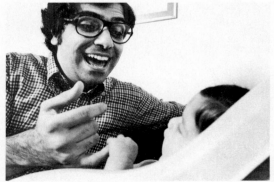

Your voice also expresses your feelings. A sharp, high-pitched tone expresses playful excitement.

"Conversations" in the First Month of Life

Recent research by Dr. Berry Brazelton at Boston Children's Hospital suggests that the communication between newborns and their parents is far more sophisticated than was previously thought. Dr. Brazelton and his colleagues have been observing the "conversations" of mothers and fathers with babies as young as 2 weeks. By the time a baby is 2 or 3 weeks old he is recognizing and responding to his parents' individual styles of relating to him. He has learned quickly to respond with "personalized" messages. Some parents tend to be low-keyed. They gently contain the baby with their hands and with soft words. If his mother's style is low-keyed, a baby also tends to be low-keyed when he is relating to her. He stares at her with fascinated attention, cooing softly and moving his arms and legs in smooth cycling rhythms.

Other parents tend to be much more playful. Their touching is less containing, and often takes the form of little taps and tickles. If his mother's style is more active, a baby's whole manner when relating to her seems to reflect a kind of playful anticipation. He's more bright-faced and wide-eyed, his movements are more active, and instead of love coos, he gives little grunts of excitement.

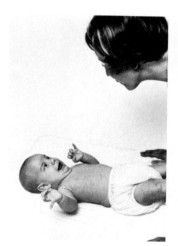

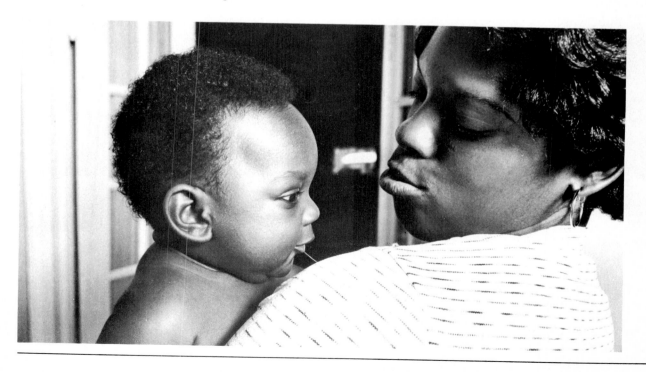

**Communicating with
Your Baby in the First
Months of Life**

Before the end of his first month, your baby is already expressing his love and acknowledging his unique relationship to you. He's letting you know how important you are to him by responding to you in ways *you* find particularly comfortable and enjoyable.

3. Babies Have Personalities, Too

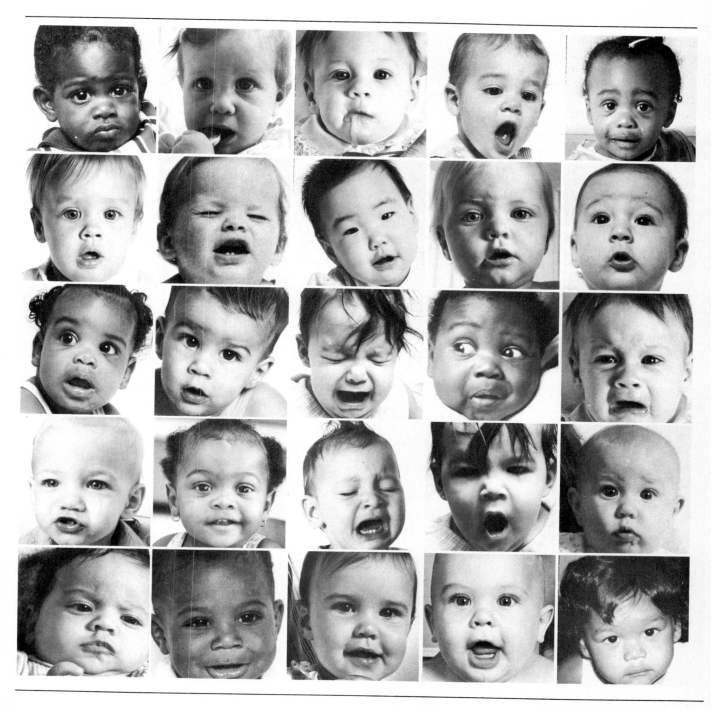

Babies Have Personalities, Too

Your baby is an individual from the moment of birth. This can be important news, especially if your baby came home from the hospital wailing and hasn't let up since. Instead of blaming yourself and trying to figure out what you've done wrong, you might be better off trying to recognize and adjust to your baby's individual style.

No one really knows why one newborn baby's style differs from another's. Part of the difference is almost certainly inherited, part is probably due to experiences in the womb, and at least some of the difference may be attributable to how the baby was born, including the drugs his mother may have received during labor and delivery.

Whatever the *causes* of differences in babies' basic style of reacting to the world around them, the *consequences* of these differences are profound. A baby's activity level, adaptability, sensitivity, and regularity all affect his early experiences and his individual needs. Most parents are capable of meeting their baby's needs, but they must know what these needs are. This chapter is designed to make your early relationship with your baby as enjoyable as possible by helping you recognize and adjust to his individual style or temperament.

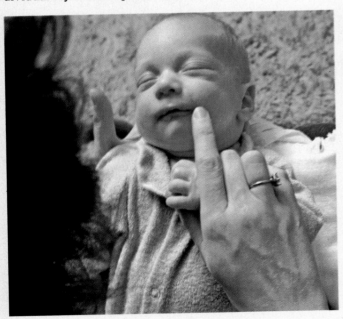

Twenty years ago, a psychiatrist, Dr. Stella Chess, and 2 of her colleagues, interviewed the parents of more than 200 babies to learn about their infants' reactions to routine activities, such as sleeping, eating, dressing, eliminating, and moving about. They found that these babies differed very much in their typical reactions. From the first, there were substantial differences between babies in their general *mood*, in their *activity level*, and in their *adaptability* to changes in routine. Large differences also existed between babies in the *intensity* of their responses; in their tendency to *approach* or *withdraw from* new experiences; in *persistence* (even though it sounds strange to talk about persistence in a young infant, it's certainly there in some babies); and in their *distractibility*. The infants also varied in the *regularity* of their natural sleeping and eating cycles, and in their *sensitivity*. (As their parents know only too well, some babies will wake to the slightest sound). A baby's typical way of reacting in all these 9 categories is what Dr. Chess and her colleagues call *temperament* or the *basic style* of behavior. We might think of it as "personality."

Getting to Know Your Baby as an Individual

During the first few months of your baby's life, much of your time together is spent feeding her. These are excellent opportunities for picking up some of the earliest and best hints to her personality, just by noticing how she reacts when she's hungry, how she nurses, and the way she takes to her first few tastes of food other than milk. For example, the way she reacts to her first mouthfuls of cereal may tell you a great deal about how easily she'll adapt to other changes in her daily life.

No matter what her basic style, every baby can develop beautifully, *if* her parents recognize her personality and respect her special needs.

To help you profile your baby's temperament, we have put together a few easy-to-answer questions, much like those Dr. Chess asked the parents of the babies she studied.

Activity Level and Intensity of Response
One baby lets his parents know he's hungry with a loud,
piercing cry. Another baby cries softly. Still other hungry
babies signal *very* mildly. They may wake and stir a bit,
or move about restlessly. They don't start crying unless
these signals go unnoticed or are ignored.

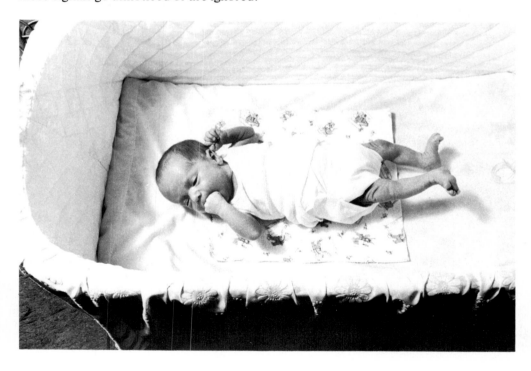

1. How does your baby usually let you know when he's
hungry?

_____

_____

_____

_____

**Babies Have
Personalities, Too**

Active, intense babies who wake up screaming and kicking with hunger tend to gulp down their milk or formula. Less active, milder infants are slower, steadier nursers. They may take an hour or more to drink the same amount.

2. How long do your baby's meals usually last?

Lusty, intense infants who scream for food and drain their bottles quickly will usually make it just as clear when they're full. Some of these babies will clamp their lips tightly when they've finished. And some will kick and scream. But quiet, mild babies may just doze off, letting the nipple slip from their lips.

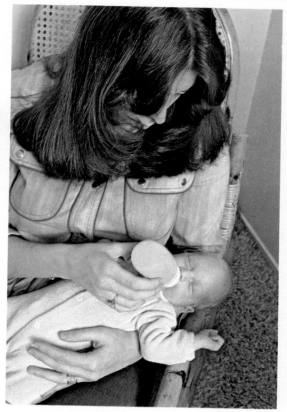

3. How does your baby let you know when he's full?

_____

_____

_____

_____

_____

Babies Have
Personalities, Too

Distractibility
Some hungry infants can be distracted with a plaything or by being picked up or talked to. Other babies keep crying until they taste milk—no amount of jiggling, cooing, or cuddling can distract them, even momentarily.

4. When your baby is hungry, what happens if you try to distract him for a few minutes with a toy while you prepare to feed him?

_____

5. What happens if you hold him and talk to him in the same situation?

_____

_____

_____

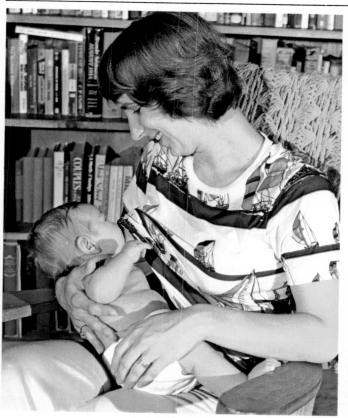

Nondistractible babies usually nurse without interruption until they are full, no matter what is going on around them. A ringing telephone causes only the briefest pause in sucking, and they usually ignore anyone who tries to attract their attention. Other babies will stop nursing to check out every noise or movement.

Nondistractible babies are unusually calm; even ringing telephones don't interrupt their nursing.

6. What does your baby do while he's nursing if the phone rings, or if there is some activity going on around him?

_____

_____

_____

_____

_____

**Babies Have
Personalities, Too**

Regularity

Some babies seem to be born with built-in alarm clocks. By the second or third week, they are hungry at regular times. Their parents can plan the day's activities around predictable nap and meal times. Other babies are different. There is no telling when they will be hungry, how hungry they will be, or when they will be hungry next.

7. Try keeping track of your baby's meals for a few days to get an idea of how regular he is. Remember, babies take from several weeks to several months to settle into a schedule so you may want to try recording mealtimes for a couple of days now, and then for a couple of days in a few weeks or a month, to see whether he's settling into a routine.

Mealtimes A.M.

Day 1 Date	Day 2 Date	Day 3 Date	Day 4 Date	Day 5 Date	Day 6 Date	Day 7 Date	Day 8 Date

Mealtimes P.M.

Reactions to New Experiences
Parents get a chance to see how their baby reacts to new
experiences when they start introducing her to foods
such as fruits, vegetables, juices, and cereals. Some
babies love their first taste of orange juice or other new
foods — they may smile and smack their lips, or even
strain toward a second taste. The parents of other babies
learn to offer new foods only at arm's length — out of
spitting range. Their babies may also twist away from the
food or gag on it. Still other babies fall in between and
have mildly negative reactions to new tastes. They
sometimes turn away from the food and often let it drib-
ble between their lips.

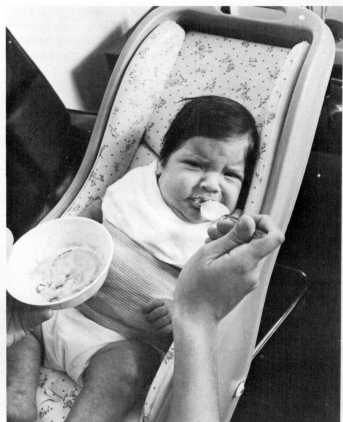

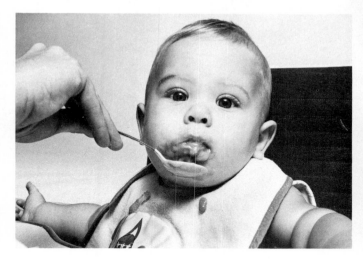

8. How did your baby react the first time you offered her
a taste of a new food?

**Babies Have
Personalities, Too**

Adaptability
Babies who tend to reject new foods will usually learn to
accept the same food eventually *if little tastes are offered
regularly*. Still, there are great differences among babies
in how long this takes. And most babies, like most adults,
have a few foods they will *never* learn to enjoy.

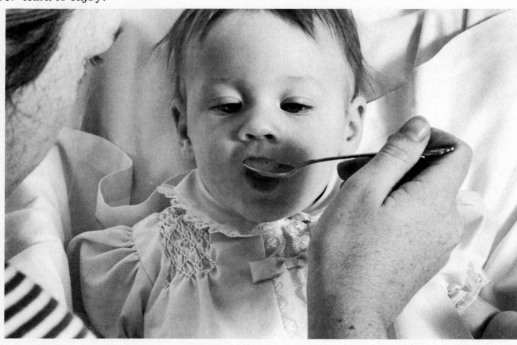

9. If your baby didn't like his first taste of a new food, did
he finally get to the point where he took it willingly?

_____

_____

_____

10. If he did, on about how many occasions did you offer
him a taste before he got used to it?

_____

_____

**An Awareness of Your Baby's Personality
Can Help You Right Now**
Dr. Chess found that a surprisingly large number of babies showed a clear and consistent *pattern* in their reactions to nursing and to new foods. If you think about other regular experiences, such as meeting new people, baths (especially the first one), and sleeping, you will probably notice a pattern similar to your baby's style in feeding. This overall pattern is what we mean when we talk about a baby's personality.

Dr. Chess discovered that most babies seemed to have 1 of 3 basic styles. "Easy" babies take things pretty much as they come and seem comfortable almost all of the time. "Slow-to-warm-up" babies usually need a little time before they feel at ease in new situations. "Difficult" babies tend to have a harder time getting comfortable and staying comfortable. Life with any baby seems to go most smoothly when his parents recognize his basic style and work out a mutually satisfactory compromise between their own needs and their perception of the baby's needs. Let's look now at the overall pattern of behavior and special needs of easy, slow-to-warm-up, and difficult babies.

**Babies Whose Temperaments Differ
React Differently to Daily Events**

Easy Babies:	React mildly when they are hungry
	Nurse steadily
	Signal mildly when they are full
	Can be distracted for a few minutes while their meal is being prepared
	Are not easily distracted by noises in the room while nursing
	Eat, sleep, and move their bowels on a fairly regular schedule
	React with interest and enjoyment to new foods, new people, and other new experiences
Slow-To-Warm-Up Babies:	Have generally mild reactions, like easy babies, BUT
	Tend to withdraw from *new* experiences
	Reject new foods, new people, first baths, and changes in routine
	If treated patiently, tend to adjust and become comfortable with these experiences
Difficult Babies:	Scream when they are hungry
	Nurse very actively
	Signal when they are full by rejecting food
	Cannot be distracted when they are hungry
	Are easily distracted by noises in the room while nursing
	Do not eat, sleep, or move their bowels on a regular schedule
	Reject new foods, new people, and changes in routine; adjust slowly to these experiences

Babies Have
Personalities, Too

"Easy" Babies

For most babies this overall pattern is one of regularity, easy acceptance of new experiences, mild reactions to hunger and other discomfort, and smooth adjustment to changes in day-to-day routine.

Sometimes the parents of an easy baby will say, "He's so good, we hardly know he's around." Actually, this can be a mixed blessing — for them and for him. While they may thank their lucky stars when they compare their lot with that of a couple with a difficult infant, their baby's quiet, calm approach to life may occasionally make them feel he doesn't need them at all. And since an easy baby is so undemanding, his parents may spend less time relating to him than they should, especially if their own activities keep them busy most of the day. These problems can be

avoided. If you have an easy baby you can be grateful, but don't let his politeness allow you to ignore his real need for attention, love, and stimulation.

For most babies, easy acceptance of new experiences such as meeting a new person or taking a bath, denote a smooth adjustment to life.

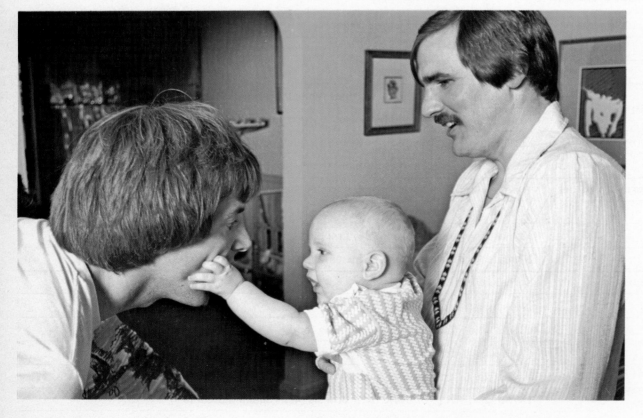

Babies Who Are "Slow-to-Warm-Up"
Other babies share some of the style of easy babies, but
tend to withdraw from new experiences. Because they
gradually adapt to new situations if they are handled
sensitively, they may be thought of as slow-to-warm-up,
or shy. If your baby is shy, what she needs most is the
time to warm up which you can provide by a slow,
calm, tolerant introduction to new experiences.

For example, if your baby is slow-to-warm-up, it's best
not to be too concerned about how long it takes her to
begin eating solid food or to change from 4 to 3 feedings a
day. She'll let you know when she is ready. She shouldn't
be pressured to play at the edge of the surf on her first trip
to the beach. She will gradually work her way closer and
closer to the water, at her own speed, until she finally

puts her toe in. Sometimes parents are very patient with a
shy baby except when she is slow-to-warm-up in social
situations, such as the neighborhood playground. But this
is typical of her reactions to all new situations. Pressuring
will only make her cling more. Holding her on your lap or
giving her a familiar toy to play with near you gives her a
chance to warm up before she gets really involved.

*Slow-to-warm-up babies
tend to withdraw from new
experiences.*

Babies Have Personalities, Too

"Difficult" Babies

For some babies, life seems much more difficult. Just about everything distresses them. These babies express their likes (and much more often dislikes) in no uncertain terms; they generally react forcefully and negatively to new experiences and to even minor changes in routine, and they seem to be hungry and sleepy at completely different times each day. One important point of this chapter is to offer some help if *your* baby is difficult. To start with, you should realize you're not alone — many parents are faced with the problem of adjusting to life with a baby whose basic style is difficult. And since it's *most* unlikely you're to blame for his difficulties, try not to feel guilty. These bad feelings can make matters worse, for you and for him.

If your baby has a difficult temperament, you may worry there is something physically wrong with him. It's unlikely, although you may want to have him checked by your doctor just to reassure yourself. *A difficult baby is unusually vulnerable.* He needs special protection from even the minor stresses of daily life if he's to develop to his fullest. This means you must scale down your expectations — both for the kinds of experiences he'll be able to handle in his early months and for his ability to respond positively day-to-day. You may have to restrict visitors

to a few and introduce them one at a time. Forget about new foods for at least a few months. Be prepared for totally unpredictable meals and naps, and be prepared to give up a good bit of your own sleep and social life. Above all, you might have to endure hours of inconsolable crying, even if you try keeping pressures to the low levels your baby can manage.

Difficult babies can often drive the sturdiest parents to distraction. Frequently parents say the worst part is the fear nothing will help — certainly the baby isn't giving much sign of responding to their sacrifices. *All* parents have a tendency to feel they have failed when they can't soothe their baby. But it's important to keep this in mind — *once you've done all you can to make your baby comfortable, it's not your fault if it doesn't work.* This is especially important if you have a difficult baby.

The fact is, parents *do* help just by maintaining their patience with a difficult baby, by being flexible in their responses to his needs, and by keeping the stress he feels to the lowest levels possible. They are helping him adjust to life at a pace not overwhelming to him, though he will often be uncomfortable. As he reaches the end of his first year, he is likely to begin responding more consistently and easily, except at times of unusual stress. And his basic style may even change over time.

Even the comfort of her mother's arms may not end a difficult baby's distress.

Sometimes difficult babies are thought to be "colicky" and vice versa. There is disagreement among experts on the nature of colic. Some see it as a label that is used for any baby who cries a lot in his first few months. Others think there is evidence that colicky babies suffer occasional intense digestive distress. For more information on colic, see the next chapter.

Your Baby's Personality in the Months to Come
Almost every baby passes the same developmental milestones, but each baby's individuality makes the whole process of development distinctively his own—he moves through the stages of development at his own pace and with his own style. So there is no such thing as a "typical baby" or an "average" 3-, 6-, or 9-month-old. For this reason, our discussions in the following chapters take into account individual differences and the needs of parents for effective ways of relating to babies with different personalities.

4. Crying Is a Call for Help

Crying is nature's way of ensuring that, right from the start, your baby can get help when help is needed. And crying is effective. It makes you feel concerned, and you usually hurry to see what can be done to help.

A young infant's cries are a *reflex reaction* to discomfort. For at least the first few months, your baby has no control whatsoever over his crying. This means he will cry only when in real need, and he won't be able to stop crying until his needs are met or until he is too exhausted to go on.

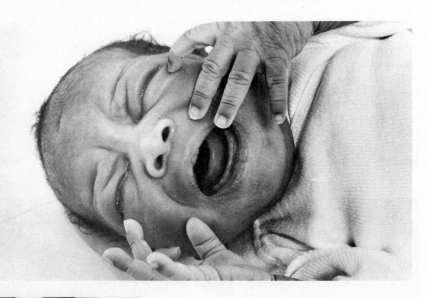

Crying is the only way a baby has to get help, and he will cry whenever he's in need.

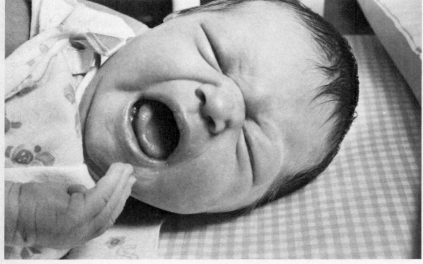

His Cries Form a "Language"

Within a few weeks, your baby's cries begin to form a kind of "language." Each type of cry has its own special sound and meaning. So even while his cries are automatic, they can tell you a lot about what's bothering him and what you can do to help. The most common is the *hunger cry,* building fairly quickly to a loud, demanding rhythm. Babies cry this way when they need to be fed, but it can also indicate another kind of hunger. Your baby's need for warmth, cuddling, and attention are as strong as his need for food, and these cries often express loneliness.

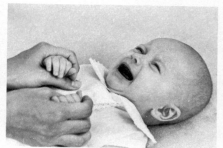

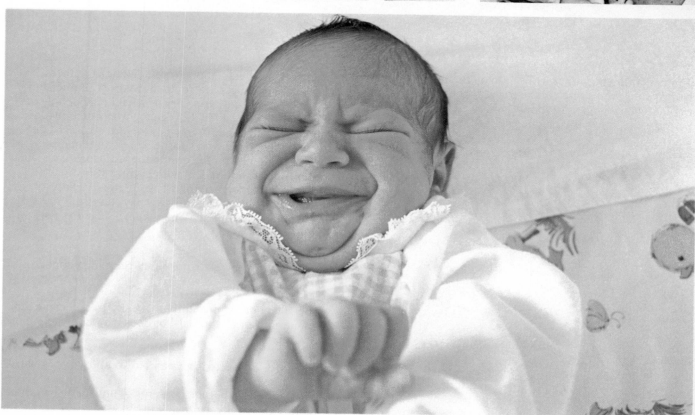

Crying Is a
Call for Help

There's another cry that will send you rushing to your baby's side every time you hear it. It's the shrill *scream of pain,* which begins suddenly, followed by a silent period (while the baby catches her breath) and a series of short gasps.

Many babies cry in a mildly fussy way when they need sleep, company, or a change of scene. If they are not responded to, their *fussiness* usually becomes louder and sounds similar to the basic cry, but a bit more "forced."

Certain cries reflect a more urgent need than others, but every cry is produced by some discomfort. Babies *never* cry "only to annoy," contrary to what many people may tell you. Still, you can be left feeling frustrated, inadequate, and even angry if you can't figure out *why* your baby is crying, or how to soothe him. Your uncertainty may be heightened by the conflicting advice you will hear about how you should deal with crying. Many new parents today recognize their baby's cries as calls for help and respond as promptly as they can. But others don't respond, fearing they may make the baby "demanding" or "spoiled."

In this chapter we will discuss some common concerns about crying:

Does responding promptly to a baby's cries make him demanding and "spoiled" or does it actually help him develop?

What are some effective ways to soothe a crying baby?

What advice is there for parents of unusually irritable babies, or colicky babies?

Responding to Crying and Your Baby's Development
Since crying is the earliest reliable guide to your baby's needs, responding promptly when she cries helps make her comfortable and happy. However, many people feel that consistently responding in this way encourages crying and "spoils" the baby because they think it makes her more demanding. This is not the case. Recently Drs. Silvia Bell and Mary Ainsworth of The Johns Hopkins University found that mothers who responded promptly to their babies' cries and to their other signals had babies who cried *less often,* and for *shorter periods,* at 12 months. They discovered this by spending over 60 hours in the home of each baby, watching how his mother responded to him. The researchers also noticed that toward the end of the first year, the babies who cried least were also advanced in their ability to get their mothers' attention in other ways. Their facial expressions, gestures, and vocalizations were easier to understand than those of most other babies because they were clearer and more varied. Not only that, at 12 months they were actually more independent than babies whose mothers often let them "cry it out."

Studies such as these have led researchers to conclude that a baby whose crying is responded to promptly, cries less after the first few months because she learns she's not alone and helpless. When her parents also respond promptly to her *noncrying* signals — her gestures, facial expressions, and vocalizations — she learns she can communicate her needs without having to cry, unless pain, exhaustion, fear, or frustration force her to signal more urgently.

Crying Is a
Call for Help

Regardless of how conscientious you are in responding to your baby's cries, you will sometimes be delayed by day-to-day realities, such as a ringing doorbell, food on the stove, or the need to warm her bottle. We do not suggest you constantly be on the run to prevent her from crying. The important thing is the *confidence* she develops in your responsiveness, and *that* doesn't require that she never utter a single cry. As she gets to be nearly a year old, your baby will be even better able to handle the little bit of insecurity involved in waiting for you a few minutes. In fact, as long as the doses are small, they are an important lesson. She begins to see a delay doesn't mean she won't be satisfied.

There will also be times when your baby is fussy and in-consolable no matter what you do. You're then likely to put her to bed, and she'll probably whimper or even yell for a while. It's best to relax yourself for 10 to 15 minutes while you see whether she settles down. Put on some music or do the dishes. If her crying hasn't subsided, go back and try again to soothe her. Sometimes just being away from her for a few minutes gives you a chance to calm down and figure out what's going on.

Effective Ways to Soothe a Crying Baby
While babies differ a good deal in how much they cry, and how easy it is to soothe them, a few soothing methods seem to work well for most babies.

Feeding Is the First Thing to Think of
Whenever your baby is not screaming from pain, the first thing to think of is hunger, especially during the first few months. Most young babies don't get hungry on a predictable schedule, and some need to eat more often than you might imagine. Even when he's not ready for an entire meal, a snack might work wonders, since being nursed provides him with much more than food. The sucking, the comfort of being held, and the stimulation of being moved are also effective soothers.

When He's Not Hungry, He May Be Lonely
Even the youngest baby will often cry for lack of company. He misses the pleasure of physical contact with his parents. If they feel he has a "right" to cry only when there is something *physically* wrong, they are overlooking a very basic *psychological* need. For crying caused by loneliness or boredom, try this highly effective soothing method: put him to your shoulder and walk around slowly, cuddling him in that position. The body contact is comforting, and several experimental studies by Dr. Anneliese Korner at the Stanford University School of Medicine show that holding a baby in an upright position and moving him about stimulates him to alertness. Though visual experiences are one of the few ways young

babies can get acquainted with the world, the average baby is quietly alert only about 30 minutes every 4 hours during his first weeks. Picking up your baby when he's crying can increase the opportunities he has for learning about the things around him. It puts him in the right "state" and provides a marvelous view — especially compared with being on his stomach or on his back.

Slings for carrying your baby when he's young, and backpacks for use later, provide some of the same benefits, and they leave your hands free, too. Dr. Benjamin Spock, in a recent article, recommends using a sling or back carrier instead of a plastic infant seat to carry a baby from place to place. Two American pediatricians in Guatemala were amazed to find that the Guatemalan children, who were carried everywhere in slings on their mothers' backs, showed no signs at all of the fretfulness and unexplained crying so common among babies in our country.

Some other methods for soothing that you may find effective in relieving your baby's loneliness or boredom include: cradling him while you sit; singing or talking while you hold him; and cuddling him while you rock in a rocking chair.

**Crying Is a
Call for Help**

Cuddling Doesn't Comfort Some Babies
There are babies who stiffen and twist away when someone tries to cuddle them. Their parents often feel rejected, which only adds to the problem of finding ways to soothe the babies' crying. A study by Drs. H. R. Schaffer and Peggy Emerson at the University of Strathclyde in Scotland found that a "noncuddler's" resistance to close physical contact is a characteristic of her unusually active nature, *not* a rejection of her parents. She is uncomfortable when restrained, no matter how tender the cuddling, and she's trying to let her parents know she needs to be

soothed in other ways. For the noncuddler (and for other babies, too, when your hands are full), try a commercial infant swinging device, or talking to her, or touching her without picking her up.

At least occasionally, any baby will continue to cry when picked up. Any time your baby isn't comforted by cuddling you should try some of these other methods. And even if you feel you have a genuine noncuddler, you should be aware that she may occasionally signal, "I *could* use a little cuddling now."

Why Is Rocking So Soothing to Young Babies?
Snuggling against you while you rock in a rocking chair, jiggling along in a carriage or in your arms or a sling as you walk, and swaying back and forth in a commercial baby swing can be wonderfully soothing for a young baby. He's just spent 9 months rocking every time his mother moved, and now the rocking you provide seems to remind him of the comfort of the womb and eases his transition to the outside world.

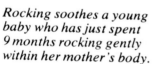

Rocking soothes a young baby who has just spent 9 months rocking gently within her mother's body.

Crying Is a Call for Help

Pacifiers and Thumbs

Many parents discover that a pacifier works well to help stop crying, especially when the baby is tired. Sucking on a pacifier not only relaxes the baby and helps him to sleep, it also seems to protect his sleep. Noises and other disturbances that would otherwise wake a baby and lead to crying just make a baby with a pacifier suck more vigorously. At first, your baby may have some difficulty holding the pacifier in his mouth, and some infants never get any real comfort from it. But it works well for many babies, particularly those who don't use their thumbs for the same purpose. If you like the idea, try providing the pacifier at least a few times.

Many parents resist letting their baby comfort himself with a pacifier (or his thumb) for 2 reasons — they don't like the way it looks, especially when the baby gets older, and they have heard it may damage his teeth. The first issue is largely one of personal choice, though you might consider letting your baby use a pacifier for at least his first 6 to 8 months, when his sucking needs are greatest. If you really object to the idea of continuing past that point, you can stop then. The question of the damage pacifiers do to teeth is *not* a simple one. The *type* of pacifier is important. Those that are "anatomically correct" (the package says so) seem to be all right. Many dentists, *but not all, say some* kind of tooth deformity

will result in about half of those children who make sub-stantial use of other varieties of pacifiers past the first 6 to 12 months of life. If you let your baby use a pacifier that isn't "anatomically correct" (and unfortunately, not all babies enjoy this variety), have your dentist look at her teeth just after she's a year old and follow his advice.

Most dentists take pretty much the same position on thumb sucking as they do on pacifiers. Of course, there's an added complication: it's pretty hard to take a thumb away from your baby. It's not a good idea to cover your baby's hands to keep him from sucking his thumb. They should be free so he can explore the world around him.

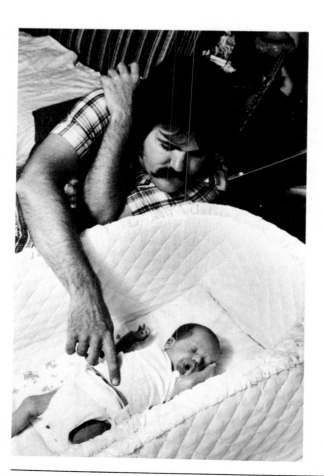

*A pacifier not only soothes
a baby but also seems to
protect her sleep.*

Mistiming Stimulation Can Cause Crying
Babies love to be played with, and the stimulation is es-sential for their social and emotional development and for their growing understanding of the world around them. But anybody, including your baby, needs an occasional break from even the most enjoyable play. Your baby lets you know when he needs to "tune out" for a moment—he looks away. If he's prevented from looking away because you miss the message and continue trying to get his attention, he will begin to fuss or cry.

Many kinds of stimulation that your baby may enjoy when he's alert and happy can have the opposite effect if he's tired or fussy. Talking to him, rocking him, swinging him, or tickling him can all cause distress if they're done to "cheer him up" when he really needs food, sleep, or to be by himself for a while.

Many parents have a few tried and true soothing tech-niques that seem to work well for their baby. But every once in a while these old standbys just don't do the trick. When this happens, be ready to try new ones. Your baby will tell you when you hit on one that works.

One thing to keep in mind above all else—it's much easier to soothe your baby when you are calm yourself. If you are tense or angry, your baby will sense it by the way you look, the sound of your voice, and the way you hold her. When she feels your tension, there's almost no way for her to relax. It's time then to hand her over to someone else for comforting, if that's possible. If it isn't, put her in a carriage and rock her gently, or take her for a long walk.

Crying Is a
Call for Help

"Colicky" Babies and Unusually Irritable Babies

Babies differ a great deal in how much they cry and how hard it is to soothe them. As many as 1 baby in 5 has a condition often called colic. Babies thought to be colicky sometimes cry for hours at a time, usually at about the same time each day, often in the early evening. Their parents *feel* as if the crying is almost non-stop. There's no certainty about what colic is, though it has long been thought to involve digestive discomfort. At about 3 months, when a baby's digestive system matures a bit, the distress of many colicky babies seems to subside. Since there's no clear evidence of an abnormality in these babies, some experts feel colic is simply a *label* given to any baby who cries a lot and is difficult to soothe. The frequent crying of a baby, for whatever reason, is hard on her and her parents. They're all frazzled and frustrated, and a happy relationship often seems out of reach. However, with time and patience, a positive relationship does develop.

If your baby seems to be colicky, or if she cries a great deal for *any* reason, you may want to try some of the following suggestions, each of which has helped some babies:

One of the most useful responses is more frequent smaller feedings.

You can offer her a pacifier. Extra sucking may relax the digestive system.

Burp her with special care, particularly after a crying spell when she may have swallowed air.

Laying her on a lukewarm hot water bottle or heating pad may help her relax.

Extra cuddling, walking, singing, and rocking are also worth a try.

Motion often helps, especially if it's fairly active. Put your baby on her stomach over your knees and thump your heels on the floor as you rub or pat her back. Or take her for a ride in her carriage or in your family car.

You can try changing the formula, if you are using one, although the formula is usually not to blame.

Breast milk is the most easily digestible food you can give your baby. However, the physical demands of nursing can be a real strain on the mother of a colicky or difficult baby. In this case, an understanding pediatrician can help her decide what feeding method is best for her and her baby.

None of these suggestions is guaranteed to work. You'll often provide only temporary relief; just as you get your hopes up, she'll start to scream again.

If you have a colicky baby, the most important things to
do are relax as much as you are able, stop blaming yourself or the baby, and arrange for some time away from
her. It's important to get help from relatives, friends,
and neighbors because you need a break from the constant stress. A colicky baby makes her parents nervous,
so that they find it even harder to help. You can also look
forward to the ending of her colic. Three or 4 months can
seem like an eternity, but it isn't. Don't be surprised if,
when she outgrows her acute distress, she blossoms into
an unusually alert, active, and responsive baby. No one
knows how to explain this sequence, but maybe the extra
holding, soothing, and stimulation most colicky babies
receive give many of them a developmental boost.

A "difficult baby", who is unusually vulnerable to the
normal stresses of day-to-day life, also cries a great deal.
His greatest need is for protection from the stresses that
make him uncomfortable and cause his crying. In the last
chapter, we offered some suggestions for reducing the
stress. The burden on his parents can be monumental,
but if they keep trying, he often learns to function more
easily and consistently, except under the pressure of
major changes and unusual demands.

Quite naturally, crying is the first and most common concern of many new parents. But the early weeks of a
baby's life also bring some happy, exciting developments, which we'll talk about in our next chapter.

5. Really Relating to You at Last!

As we've said, a baby has an inborn attraction to people's faces and voices and soon shows a special interest in those of her parents. Right from the start, you naturally provide stimulation perfectly suited to encouraging your baby's responsiveness to you. When you hold her in your arms for feeding, lean over to change her, or cuddle and talk to her as you rock in a rocking chair, your face is in just the right position for her to focus on it clearly.

A newborn's vision is like a fixed-focus camera. She can only focus clearly on things at a certain distance — approximately 8 to 12 inches from her eyes. By the time she's 4 months old, she can focus clearly at various distances, just like an adult.

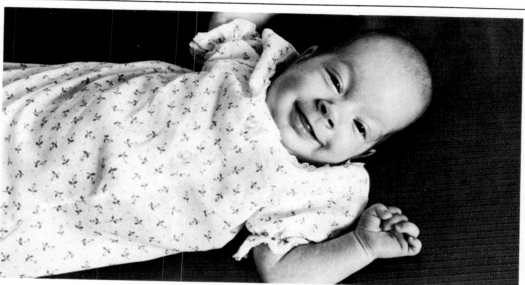

Eye contact and smiling are part of any meaningful relationship, and the first time your baby's eyes light up when seeing you may be among your happiest times as a parent.

Sometime between your baby's third and sixth week, you may notice a subtle but important change in her response to you. For the first time she focuses on your eyes when she looks at you, as if she were making real eye contact. Because this change is often hard to detect, many parents don't notice it. Within a few weeks, however, eye contact sets the stage for a new development in responsiveness — one you're sure to notice. During one of these moments of eye contact, your baby breaks into a *big,* beautiful, toothless grin. No bells toll, and no guns salute, but you don't need them to tell you something very special just happened. She's never smiled this way before. Her earlier smiles were often no more than little twitches at the corners of her mouth. You probably noticed them mostly when she was drowsy or sleeping fitfully. These first smiles were spontaneous reactions of her young nervous system and not the result of "gas," as many people believe. Her new smiles are something else altogether — they are broader, they come when she is awake and alert, and they are clearly directed to you. In fact, they seem to light up her face the moment your eyes meet.

Now It Feels Like a Real Relationship
Eye contact and smiling are a part of any meaningful rela-

tionship between people. There's a beautiful old song with a title that captures this perfectly — "Drink to Me Only with Thine Eyes, and I Will Pledge with Mine." Many parents feel a real 2-way relationship with their baby begins when he is able to respond in these ways, since it's an unmistakable sign he enjoys being near them. They sometimes make comments like, "Now he's so much fun to play with," and "He can really see me now," when their baby begins to make eye contact. When a group of first time mothers with 2-month-old babies were asked what they enjoyed most about the baby, 75% answered, "the fact that he smiles at me." Some parents don't really feel much love for their baby until the very first time he makes eye contact and smiles. Contrary to the popular cliché, many parents don't love their baby at birth—and this is perfectly normal. In a recent study of 54 women having their first babies, only half had positive feelings about the baby right away, and only 7 of the women described their feelings as love. Many had some initial feelings of "distance" and unfamiliarity, which lasted a month or 2. Interestingly, it was the baby's ability to "see" his mother and respond by smiling that most often triggered her feelings of love — feelings that seemed to have something to do with being recognized and appreciated in a highly personal and intimate way.

**Really Relating to You
at Last!**

Your Baby's Smiles "Hook" You into Playing with Him
Your baby uses eye contact and his winning smile to
reach out to you. When he looks you in the eyes and
smiles and coos, it's irresistible — you have to smile and
coo in return. Your responses increase his excitement
and pleasure, and a beautiful cycle begins, not only increasing your pleasure, and his, but drawing you closer
and strengthening your ties to each other as well.

According to the descriptions of Dr. Berry Brazelton and
his colleagues at Boston Children's Hospital, as a parent
plays with a baby as young as 3 weeks old, the
infant's excitement builds quickly. He smiles, makes
noises, and waves his arms and legs.

Then his excitement peaks. He may bring his hand to his
mouth, suck on his tongue, clasp his hands, or yawn, apparently in an effort to control his excitement. You may
notice he's smiling less and making fewer sounds. He
may look serious or grimace as well.

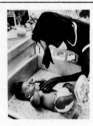

Then he looks down or turns away from you slightly, all
the while keeping you in sight out of the corner of his eye.
If *you* turn away at this point, he may turn back quickly
to re-establish contact. Often he fingers your hand absent-
mindedly or smiles into the distance while he's looking
away. He uses the period of looking away to recover
from his excitement and to absorb what he's learned.

Then he turns to you again. And the whole cycle begins
once more. Dr. Brazelton has found that during play, this
cycle is repeated an average of 4.4 times a minute.

Here's a detailed view of the entire play sequence.

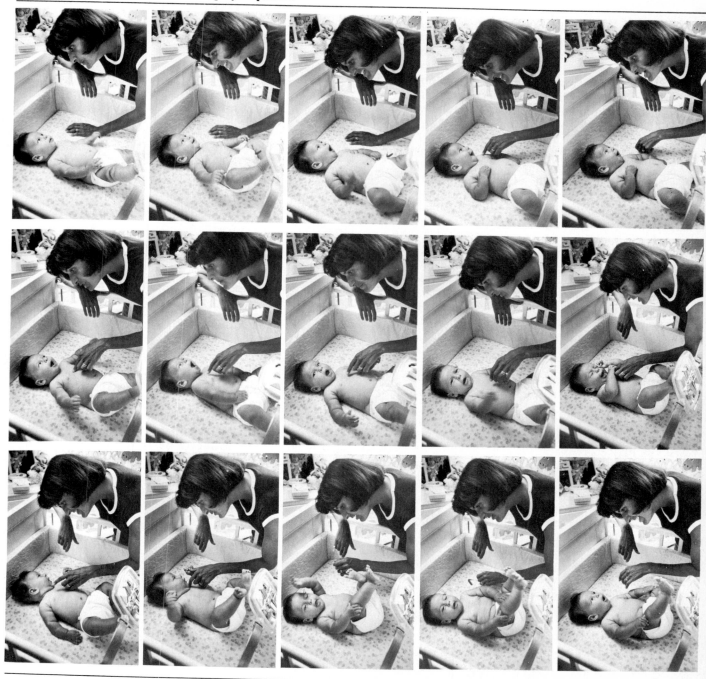

Really Relating to You at Last!

By allowing for his temporary turning away without feeling frustrated, you'll be helping with a necessary "recovery phase" of your baby's play. He'll be more comfortable and relaxed, and you'll be rewarded by longer and more enjoyable periods of play. Dr. Brazelton provides a beautiful description of a mother, similar to the one in these photographs, who showed outstanding sensitivity to her baby's signals during play:

> One of our mothers was particularly striking in her capacity to subside as he decreased his attention to her. She relaxed back in her chair smiling softly, reducing other activity such as vocalizing and moving, waiting for him to return. When he did look back, she began slowly to add behavior on behavior, as if she were feeling out how much he could master. She also sensed his need to reciprocate. She vocalized, then waited for his response. When she smiled, she waited until he smiled before she began to build up her own smiling again. Her moving in close to him was paced sensitively to coincide with his body cycling, and if he became excited or jerky in his movements she subsided back into her chair.

Often babies respond slowly to stimulation; they like to become oriented before they become involved. Sometimes an adult will begin smiling and speaking to a baby and become distracted or lose the patience to wait for her response. By the time the baby has begun to smile back, the adult may no longer be paying attention. Relating to a baby is stimulating for her only if she has a chance to relate back and to have her response acknowledged.

Her sensitivity led her to alter her behavior smoothly and almost constantly, using as cues the changes in her baby's behavior.

Other Things to Keep in Mind When You Play Together

Your baby's interest and pleasure are your best guides to the way you should play with her. Here are several things you might want to keep in mind:

There's no use trying to play with your baby when she's exhausted and needs to be asleep, or when she's hungry and needs to be fed. Her relaxed alertness should be the cue for playtime, and her looks, smiles, and gestures will tell you when she's in that state. A newborn is alert only about 30 minutes every 4 hours. This period triples by the time she's 2 to 3 months old.

Infants who differ in sensitivity may experience identical stimulation quite differently. Rough-and-tumble games and other forms of active play may delight one baby and overwhelm another; gentle lullabies might not catch the attention of the first baby, but might provide great pleasure to the second. Your baby will let you know the intensity of stimulation that is strong enough to be noticeable but still is not too strong. If it's not strong enough, it won't hold her attention. If it's too strong, she'll startle, turn away, or even fuss or cry.

The Importance of Early Face-to-Face
Play for Babies

Watching parents relate to their babies is fascinating. The more the parent clowns — cocking and wagging his head, exaggerating his facial expressions, his gestures, and the sounds he makes — the more his baby enjoys it. Next time you are playing with your baby near a mirror, try catching a glimpse of yourself. You'll see that the funnier you look, the greater your baby's delight.

The clowning most people naturally fall into when playing with a baby not only increases her enjoyment, but also helps her learn how people relate to each other.

When you clown with your baby, your behavior is in many ways a simplified, exaggerated, slowed down version of normal communication. The form and pace of your words, gestures, and facial expressions make them as easy as possible for your baby to recognize and understand.

Parents often mimic their baby's behavior without being aware of it.

When he's playing with you, your baby also constantly experiences his impact on the world around him. When he makes a face or a sound, you often respond by imitating him. You may not always be completely aware how closely your behavior mimics his, but haven't you often caught yourself with your mouth open while trying to get him to "open up" for a spoonful of food? When he's joyous or in pain, your facial expressions, your gestures, and the tone of your voice are immediately and visibly responsive to what he is experiencing. You mirror and

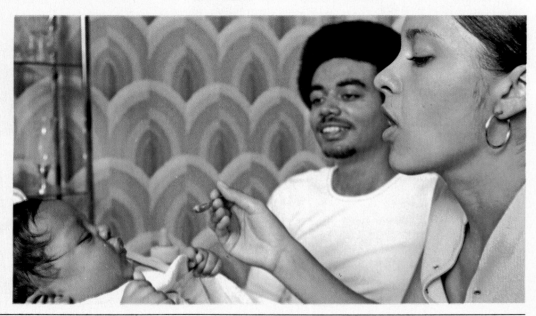

Parents are just doing what comes naturally when they play with their baby. At the same time, they are encouraging his ability to understand the world around him.

respond to what he does and how he feels. The opportunity to see the results of our own actions is the key to learning at any age. During the first months of life, the rich and immediate responsiveness of face-to-face interaction is crucial for your baby's confidence in his ability to figure things out on his own. He learns that when he does something, he gets results, and he is encouraged to go on to try something else — he is "learning to learn."

Of course, most parents rarely think about the fact that they are encouraging their baby's ability to relate to other people or his ability to figure things out when they play with him. They are just doing what comes naturally — and that's the real beauty of it! When you're involved in play, you stimulate your baby in the ways he enjoys most and needs most for his emotional development, and for his growing understanding of the world around him.

The Benefits of Early Interaction for Parents
Early feelings of closeness which grow out of play are just as important for parents as they are for babies. They provide needed fuel for the continuing effort that good parenting requires.

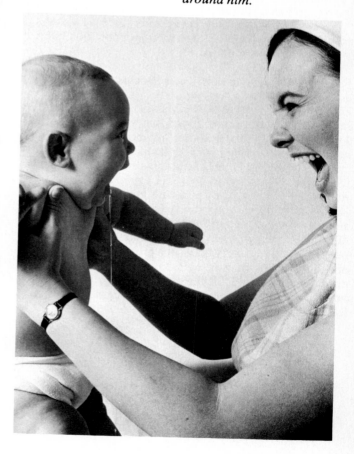

6. The Growth of Love

When adults fall in love they want to be together as much as possible. Separations can be painful, and reunions are a joy. Often the couple's intimacy is so intensely felt that they may even treat other people as intruders. As your baby develops, you'll see that these are the very same ways she expresses her love for you. For example, from her first few weeks she responds differently to you than she does to other people. And when she's 6 to 8 months old she may give the clear impression that you are the only ones in the world for her. Many babies this age become more upset than before over separations from their parents. At the same time, less familiar faces may produce tears instead of smiles.

It's exciting to be able to recognize when your baby says "I love you" in a new way, especially since we know now that mothers don't have a monopoly on their babies' love, as was once believed.

**Newborns Respond to Both Their Parents
in Special Ways**
In a study described in the Play and Learning section, Dr. Genevieve Carpenter found that babies as young as 2 weeks clearly signal that they are more comfortable with their mothers than with unfamiliar people. In similar studies, Dr. Berry Brazelton and his colleagues found that babies 2 weeks and older feel a special closeness to *both* their parents. They pick up signals from differences in the ways their parents and strangers relate to them, and they respond accordingly with a whole different set of facial expressions, body movements, and sounds. A person new to the baby stays at a greater distance when playing with him than parents do, and the baby signals his need to maintain this distance. He is less actively involved with the stranger, looking at her less, and often leaning his body away from her.

Expressions of Love Grow as He Develops
You will probably notice new signs of your baby's growing attachment to you during his second or third month. If he's crying and someone else tries to comfort him, he may keep on crying. But when you pick him up, he nearly always stops crying.

At 3 months, babies will smile at most friendly people, but they smile faster, more broadly, more often, and longer at one of their parents than at an unfamiliar person.

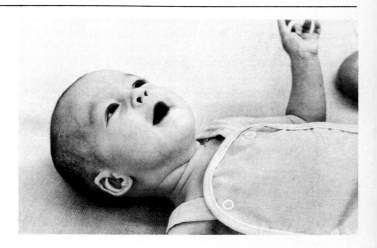

By the time he's 4 months old, a baby will babble and coo to his parents more readily than to someone he's never seen before.

At this age a baby may also show his love for his parents in another way: by his comfort in their presence. In studying a baby's attachment to his mother, Drs. Donelda Stayton, Mary Ainsworth, and Mary Main of The Johns Hopkins University noticed that a 4-month-old was free and confident when he was sitting on his mother's lap. He actively explored her face, her clothes, and her hair. On the lap of an unfamiliar woman, the baby was much more restrained, often barely touching her.

The Growth of Love

New Expressions of Love at 6 Months

When your baby is 6 months or a bit older, you may notice *new* gestures of closeness she reserves for you alone. Many babies of this age greet their parents by clapping their hands or lifting their arms to show that they want to be picked up, and by clinging or snuggling close when they are.

When she is able, your baby may even go to meet you — creeping or walking in your direction as soon as she sees you.

Sometimes a baby's attachment is expressed by the way she seeks out her parents for security. Dr. Ainsworth and her colleagues found that when a 6-month-old was upset, she often buried her face in her mother's lap, but never sought this kind of comfort from an unfamiliar person.

These signs of your baby's love and attachment are wonderfully heartwarming and give you a growing confidence in yourself as a parent.

His Attachment to Each Parent Grows
Even the youngest baby tends to have a different relationship with his mother and his father. As he develops, his experiences with each of them and his new physical and social skills make these differences clearer.

Dr. Michael Lamb of the University of Wisconsin spent many hours in homes of infants 6 to 12 months old, observing how parents and babies spent their time together. One thing that interested Dr. Lamb was the kind of physical contact each parent had with the baby. As you might expect, when a mother held her baby, it was most often for feeding, changing, or other physical care. Fathers held their babies far less often, and for shorter

Studies such as these show that babies form strong attachments to both parents, but their attachment to each parent tends to differ in important ways. This doesn't mean there's anything predetermined or unchangeable about these patterns — they are based on the way *mothers and fathers* typically relate to *babies*. Babies tend to look to their mothers as primary sources of security because, in most families, mothers have the major responsibility for their care and comfort. The playful relationship most fathers have with their babies makes them an important source of excitement and pleasure. And the strength of babies' attachments to their fathers reflects the importance to infants of this kind of intense, highly stimulating relationship.

periods, but almost all of this father-baby contact involved active, highly stimulating play.

Dr. Lamb was also interested in differences in the way babies related to each parent. When he observed a baby with both parents, he found the baby stayed closer to *his mother* and spent more time touching her and trying to get her to pick him up. When the baby was under stress — when he was tired or an unfamiliar person entered the room — he almost always went to his mother. At other times, however, the baby tended to relate more closely to *his father,* especially when he wasn't in physical contact with either parent. Most of the baby's looking, smiling, laughing, and "talking" were directed toward his father.

Shifting patterns of responsibility for family income and
for child care are more and more common in families
today, making it increasingly difficult to draw general
conclusions about which parent is the baby's source of
security and which his source of playful excitement. Of
course, either parent can provide both qualities of comfort and excitement. The fact that babies need both comfort and excitement means they will continue to love both
parents, no matter how the parents share the responsibility for satisfying each of these important needs.

Brothers, Sisters, and Friends
Babies are fascinated by older children. If your baby is not your first child, you'll soon discover that she is often as interested in her brother or sister as she is in you. Once she's old enough for them to play together, this will be one of her favorite pastimes. If you provide the opportunity and encouragement for this kind of play, you benefit your whole family. You get a brief relief from baby care. More important, you help your children form the foundation of a strong and lasting relationship. If you let your older child play with the baby when he wants to, he gains a sense of pride in his ability to entertain her and to show her how the world works. She's sure to appreciate his help with her stacking cups, with the hat she can't get to stay on her head, and with the toy on the shelf she can't reach.

Most parents recognize the importance of a baby's relationship with his older brother or sister. Fewer parents realize how early a baby can begin to form friendships

with children his own age, or how strong and meaningful these relationships can be. Dr. Michael Lewis of the Educational Testing Service in Princeton, New Jersey, has observed 1-year-olds playing in a room with their mothers and with other babies their own age. Once the babies had spent a few hours together, they began to relate to each other as friends. They played very close to each other, imitated each other, shared toys, and smiled and laughed together.

Playing with children her own age helps your baby's development. It not only provides her with early experience in getting along with her peers, but also increases her feelings of self-confidence. Most people that a baby relates to are much bigger and more capable then she is, so to a substantial degree they guide, direct, and control what goes on. Babies, on the other hand, are more or less equal in their abilities. They can influence one another in ways they can't influence adults.

Many babies form strong relationships with their older brothers or sisters.

The Growth of Love

Separation Sorrows

At about 6 months many babies become more upset than before when separated from their parents, even briefly. When your baby is about this age, he may suddenly act as if he can't let you out of his sight. He will do everything he can to keep close to you, clinging desperately when you attempt to put him down, crying when you leave the room, and trying to follow you, if he's able to crawl.

These reactions reflect the anxiety and fear your baby may feel when he temporarily loses the people he loves. These emotions are striking in many babies, but they aren't universal. Some babies seem to reach the end of their first year without ever experiencing much distress over separation.

Whenever a separation *does* upset your baby, it's upsetting to you, too, especially because often you're just not sure what to do. It certainly seems he needs you, but sometimes you have to leave him. So what to do can be a real problem.

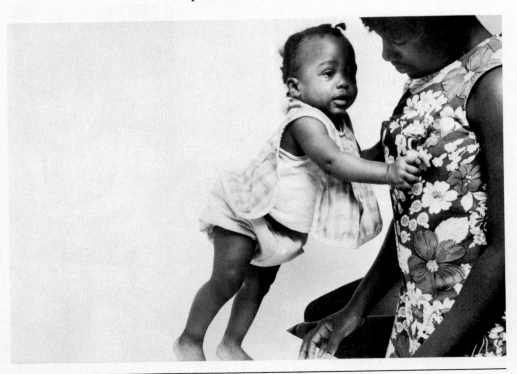

Making Separations More Bearable

Separations come in 2 sizes — short and long. Short separations occur when you leave your baby alone for a few minutes while you move about the house taking care of business. Longer separations occur when you leave your baby at home and go shopping, or to work, or just out for some time on your own.

When you have to leave your baby for a moment, try using some standard phrase such as "Back in a minute," and keep talking while you are gone, as long as you're within earshot. Hearing you, she knows you haven't vanished completely. She may cry when you leave the room, but every time you reappear, her confidence that you *will* return after each separation grows a little stronger.

If even these short separations are really upsetting to her, you might try carrying her with you when you'd otherwise leave her for a minute or 2. Sometimes this is difficult because your arms are full. Putting her in a backpack can give you the freedom you need to get your work done *and* keep her comfortable at the same time.

But what about longer separations? Every parent is tempted to try to avoid a scene, either by putting the baby to sleep before leaving the house or by trying to sneak out unnoticed once the sitter has arrived. Unfortunately, this can make matters worse. Unless the sitter is someone your baby knows well, you will be violating the baby's basic sense of trust when she realizes you're gone. She may become more clingy and really scared each time you leave the room, fearing you're sneaking away any time you're out of sight. Whenever you leave your baby with a sitter it's best to introduce them, and stay until they've become comfortable. Then let your baby know you're going out for a while. Better yet, have the sitter come over to spend time on a day you're *not* going out so you can see how she handles your baby and instruct her directly on your baby's needs, what she finds comforting, what she enjoys doing, and anything else that might help her help your baby adjust to being without you. This way your baby will also get to know her in the most secure possible setting.

Of course, none of this guarantees that your baby won't cry when you leave her. She'll probably cry for a short while. But it's much more likely she'll be crying to express her momentary regret on seeing you depart, and not because she is intensely fearful. If, when you return home, you find she never got over her initial unhappiness, maybe your sitter isn't doing as good a job substituting for you as she might be doing. Try another sitter if the first one just doesn't seem to be working out. Fortunately, it's almost always possible to find some sensitive, loving person with whom your baby will feel comfortable after a period of adjustment.

The Growth of Love

**Babies Develop Their Own Ways to
Deal with Separation**
You may notice that your baby is developing her own
means of reassurance in periods of separation from you
and at times when she's tired, bored, or frustrated. Her
use of a bottle, pacifier, favorite teddy bear, blanket, or
her thumb for security may indicate she is beginning to
develop her own resources for coping with stress, even
while she is still dependent and needful of care. It's also
interesting that many babies become fascinated with
playing ''peek-a-boo'' at the same time that they are
struggling with the feelings they have when their parents
disappear. Perhaps repeating the events of disappearance
and reappearance, under conditions they can *control,*
helps babies overcome their anxiety. They can see where
things go when they disappear and bring them back as
quickly as they want. The game allows babies to turn a
situation which is painful in reality into a manageable and
pleasant experience. Children even as young as 6 months
often seem to get pleasure from situations which have a
hint of manageable fear involved.

Reactions to Unfamiliar People
As we've said, many 6-to 8-month-old babies express
their growing sense of belonging to their parents by getting upset when they're separated. Many also show
they've singled out their parents by shunning *new* faces.
For a time, scientists thought almost all infants this age
were distressed by unfamiliar people. It's now clear that
babies react to new people in a wide variety of ways.

Intensely negative reactions such as crying, twisting
away, and trying to escape are less common than clearly
positive reactions such as smiling, showing or offering a
toy, or a friendly approach.

Neutral reactions, particularly a serious, watchful stare,
are also common.

Some babies seem to flirt with an unfamiliar person —
looking at him until he looks back, then looking away,
and back, and away and back again. After a few moments, the baby usually smiles and warms up, though she
may still be more comfortable if the new person keeps his
distance.

A baby may also fear someone she sees infrequently, not
for what she doesn't know about him, but for what she
does. For example, she may have been hurt by an injection the pediatrician gave her on her last visit. This time,
as soon as her mother carries her into the doctor's office,
the baby takes one look at the pediatrician, screams, and
clutches her mother in fear. Fortunately, most pediatricians have developed ways of easing a baby's discomfort
in this situation.

Helping Your Baby Make New Friends

It's often difficult for grandparents and family friends to understand why an infant gets upset on seeing them or being picked up by them, especially if he was all smiles last visit. You may have noticed that your baby's reactions to unfamiliar people depend to a great extent on the *circumstances:* the *way* in which the "introductions" are made, the setting, and his mood.

Patience is the key to helping your baby feel comfortable with unfamiliar people. Think about how you might feel in his place. Of course, some of us are more shy than others, but practically anyone would be taken aback if a total stranger came up to him on the street and started to hug or tickle him. Yet parents often hand their babies over to this kind of treatment. Unfortunately, this is almost bound to increase the baby's tendency to shy away.

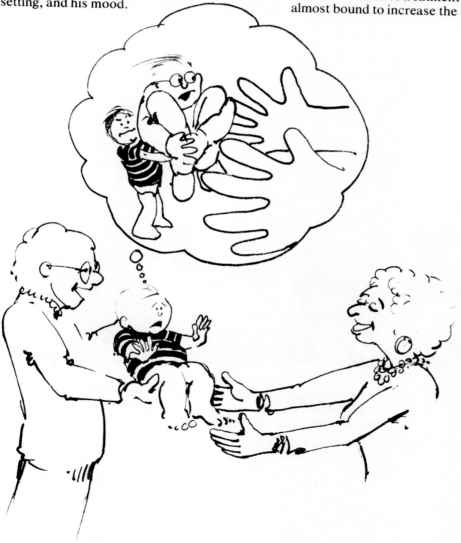

The Growth of Love

The first step toward getting your baby comfortable is to help her realize that the strange person is really all right. Hold your baby in your arms and smile while you speak to the person in a somewhat exaggerated, friendly way. And try to help the person understand what you're doing, so she'll give your baby a little room.

Then have the person make some friendly gesture toward *you,* such as offering a toy your baby might like. Keys or a piece of paper also work well. This can be an ice-breaker. If you accept the object and play with it, you are letting your baby know that this person is someone who can be trusted. And since babies 6 months and older like to imitate their parents, you have that inclination going for you as well.

When your baby meets someone for the first time, you should hold the baby in your arms as you smile and talk to the stranger.

The next step is to have the stranger offer you something the baby might like.

When you accept the object and play with it, . . .

Now you can see if your baby is beginning to warm up to the stranger. If she seems to be getting comfortable, the person can try to relate to her directly. This should begin with a smile and a few words. If she responds, the other person can offer the baby something to play with. Gifts are a key to anyone's affections. From this point, they can continue to make friends at whatever pace seems comfortable for your baby. In most cases, unless the baby is feeling tired or ill, or the surroundings are strange and uncomfortable, your patient guidance and her natural curiosity will likely win out. Remember: even after your baby has warmed up, she may feel more comfortable staying in your arms while she relates to her new friend.

Sometimes no amount of patience will make your baby comfortable with an unfamiliar person. The best thing to do then is to wait until another day. Forcing your baby will only upset her more. Try to patch up everyone's hurt feelings, including your own. Then wait a week or so and arrange another meeting.

. . . the baby gets the idea that this is someone who can be trusted.

If the baby starts to warm up, her new friend can approach her directly . . .

. . . but gently at first.

The Growth of Love

Why Are Some Babies More Upset Than Others by Separations or by Strangers?
You may wonder what makes one baby more clingy or more fearful of separations and new people than another. No really conclusive answers to this question are known. Several things seem to be involved. Babies who have spent a good deal of time with both parents, with relatives, and with other adults may not be quite so dependent on the presence of any *one* person for security as those who spend all or almost all of their time with their mothers.

There's also some evidence that babies whose parents give them a chance to experience a wide variety of objects and settings are less distressed by the novelty of unfamiliar people when they are 8 and 9 months old.

Of course, babies who tend to be difficult or who are slow-to-warm-up need their parents to be very patient and sensitive, to help make separations and new people as manageable as possible.

Even when you and your baby are working through difficulties with separations and reactions to unfamiliar people, he is starting to *initiate* separations from you. His secure dependency on you gives him a base for beginning to discover his individuality, to strike out on his own.

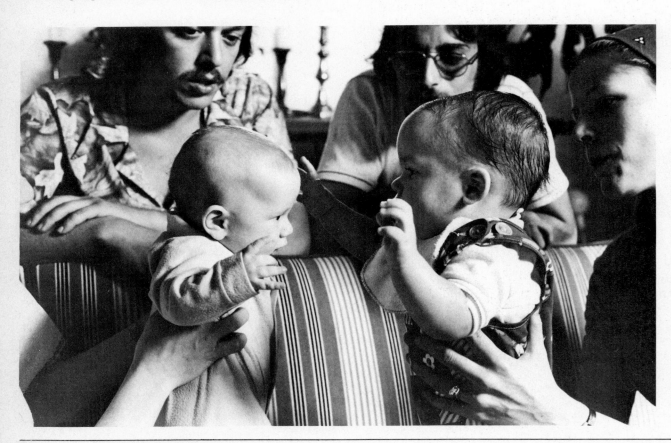

7. Striking Out on Their Own

Most babies become active explorers in the last few months of their first year. They begin to crawl or to stand up and toddle around a room, hanging onto one piece of furniture and then another. Some babies even take a few steps on their own before their first birthday. However they do it, they do get around! Once a baby can crawl, he'll get intensely involved in exploration if given half a chance. After all, he's spent many months *looking* at a world of fascinating things that were out of reach.

Striking Out
on Their Own

There's a whole new air of independence about her, from her explorations to the way she asserts herself at mealtimes. Many 9-month-old babies *insist* on trying to feed themselves. They often let you know how strongly they feel about it by forcefully rejecting your efforts to help them. Babies of this age also assert themselves by shouting for attention and screaming in anger and frustration if their other efforts to get people involved with them don't succeed. The anger babies seem to feel at these times is actually a sign they are growing up. Anger and frustration are a natural part of learning to cope with new and challenging situations.

Curiosity, exploration, and independence — these are some of the most exciting and important developments in your baby's life, but they can also create problems. The same curiosity that leads him to pick up a little ball of dust missed by the vacuum cleaner will also draw him to your glasses, to every exposed electrical outlet in the house, and to that cherished china figure standing on the

end table beside the couch. That's what makes their baby's "striking out on his own" such a trial for many parents. You want your baby to be able to explore and learn about the world. But you also need to keep him safe from danger, and to keep your breakable household treasures safe from *him*. Somehow, it often feels as if it's nearly impossible to balance these requirements.

One thing is clear — a baby *needs* "room to grow in." His curiosity demands space and equipment (pots, pans, toys, etc.). Just as important are his parents' attitudes, which tell him they share his pleasure in what he is doing and learning. Your baby needs your support in learning how things work. Don't get carried away in your understandable concern for safety and order. It's been shown that barricading babies behind fences and playpens, subjecting them to a constant barrage of "No's," stunts their natural curiosity and love of learning. It must be pretty difficult for a baby to be in conflict between his need for his parents' approval and his need to explore.

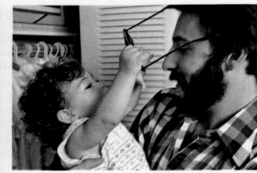

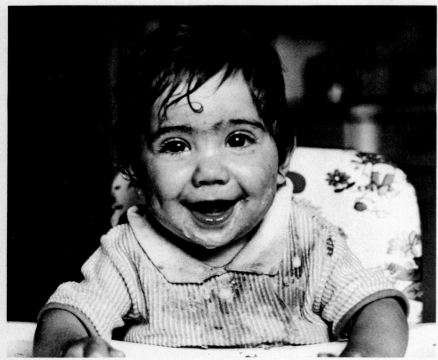

"Baby-Proofing" Can Help

Baby-proofing your home by removing anything that could hurt him, or which he could damage, can dramatically reduce the need for watching him and controlling what he does. When most things that are "out of bounds" are out of reach, nearly everything else can be used by the baby. But for many people, making a home baby-safe can feel like a real sacrifice of their lifestyle. Ornaments, books, and records have to be put out of reach; coffee tables are no longer a safe place to put cups of hot coffee; and television sets must be raised, covered, or put away when not in use — the control knobs are fascinating to most babies.

Fortunately the sacrifice is temporary, and it's an important investment in your baby's happy and healthy development, now and in the future. For suggestions on baby-proofing, see the chapter on "Designing Your Baby's Environment" in the Play and Learning section.

**Striking Out
on Their Own**

But You Still Need to Keep Your Eyes Peeled

Of course baby-proofing your home can't protect your baby from *every* danger or ensure she'll *never* get to an object she shouldn't touch. You still have to stay on your toes, and be ready to act when the need arises. Right now your baby is too young to understand why she shouldn't touch certain things. Your prime goal is to minimize the frustration involved in distracting her and in removing her from the situation. Try to avoid the "No!" syndrome. Give her some *information* — say "Hot" or "Sharp" to help her understand the danger, and then help to take her mind off the forbidden fascination. She may be momentarily upset and angry when she isn't allowed to handle an object she's discovered, but an attractive substitute almost always turns off the tears. By the time your child is old enough to see through the techniques of distraction and substitution, she will also be old enough to understand why certain situations must be avoided.

If you stop a child infrequently and are *consistent* about acting when it's absolutely necessary, she will trust your judgment and her own. She will know you stop her only when a real danger exists, and she can have faith in her own judgment and initiative in other situations.

Even when real dangers are anticipated and avoided, there are always minor annoyances that may keep you on the go — a wastebasket overturned and emptied, cushions pulled off the couch, and the dog's ears yanked.

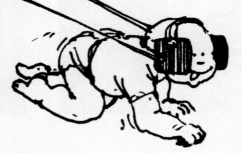

Encouraging Your Baby's Cooperation
Of course you don't want to live in a baby-proofed house
longer than necessary. As soon as possible, you want
your baby to begin cooperating with (or "obeying") certain basic rules for protecting both him and household
breakables. There's a tremendous controversy over the
most effective ways of encouraging babies to cooperate,
but a recent study by Drs. Donelda Stayton, Robert
Hogan and Mary Ainsworth of The Johns Hopkins University shows that a parent's efforts to "train" or "discipline" her baby by physically forcing him to do as she
wishes or by slapping his hand are not effective in the
long run. More effective are efforts to *cooperate with the
baby* and to respond sensitively to *his* signals. It turned
out that babies who responded earliest (at about 9 or 10
months) to commands such as "Come here," and pro-
hibitions such as "No, No," were those whose mothers
always responded promptly and sensitively to *their*
signals — not the babies whose mothers tried to "train"
or to "discipline" them.

Your baby is a person — a little person who loves you
and wants to please you. The more responsive and
cooperative you are with him, the more you will provide
the "fuel" and the experience he needs in order to cooperate with you. His desire to please you will grow, and his
understanding of *how* people go about cooperating with
each other will increase

*Cooperation, not discipline, is the key word with babies. If
you cooperate when she needs you, she'll be more likely
to cooperate when you tell her not to do something.*

**Striking Out
on Their Own**

During the last few months of her first year, your baby's principal needs are the same 2 she has had all along — room to pursue her natural curiosity and prompt help when required. Drs. Mary Ainsworth and Silvia Bell of The Johns Hopkins University found that when mothers gave their babies freedom to explore on their own *and* responded sensitively to their signals, the infants were accelerated in their development at 12 months:

physically, emotionally, and in their ability to figure things out. If you meet your baby's dual needs, you've done everything possible to help her become a happy, independent, and cooperative 1-year-old, ready for the active, fulfilling years of toddlerhood, and beyond. And she'll be sturdy enough to weather the occasional storms that are a part of every child's growing up.

PART THREE: PHYSICAL DEVELOPMENT

1. Summary of Physical Development

The story of how every baby develops through the first year of life is interesting. But the story of how *your* baby develops is *exciting* — because you will see all of the changes that occur — and you will have a chance to help them happen. That experience will be one of your life's great adventures.

We tell the story of physical development from birth to 1 year in small "bite-size" pieces — to let you follow its details easily.

Each of the next 5 chapters is devoted to one area of physical development: Moving, Touching and Holding, Seeing, Hearing, and Making Sounds. Each chapter covers a baby's first year in 3-month periods: birth to 3 months, 3 months to 6 months, 6 months to 9 months, and 9 months to 1 year. We tell you about the major changes that occur within each 3-month period. Each new point is written as a headline at the top of a page. After each headline you get more details about that part of behavior development. The pictures make the story even clearer.

The 3-month time periods are only approximate. Don't worry if your baby doesn't do everything we talk about, and don't worry if she does some things a bit earlier or later than the time periods we note. Every baby develops at her own pace and in her own way. And that's just the way it should be — we are unique individuals right from the beginning! But if your baby is considerably late in doing things, or if you have any other concerns about your baby's development, ask your doctor. Answering questions about infant development is part of a doctor's job.

Remember, in writing this book, we talk about the things that *most* babies do. When you read it, you will be thinking about the things that *your own baby* does and the special way in which he does things. Keep your own baby in mind as you read — and make this a book about *him*. You can pick up your pen and add notes that describe the things *he* does.

Before reading the chapters on behavior development, it might help to read a list of headlines, so that you can get a complete view of what we will be talking about. You can refer back to this list whenever you want a quick summary of the changes that occur during the first year of a baby's life.

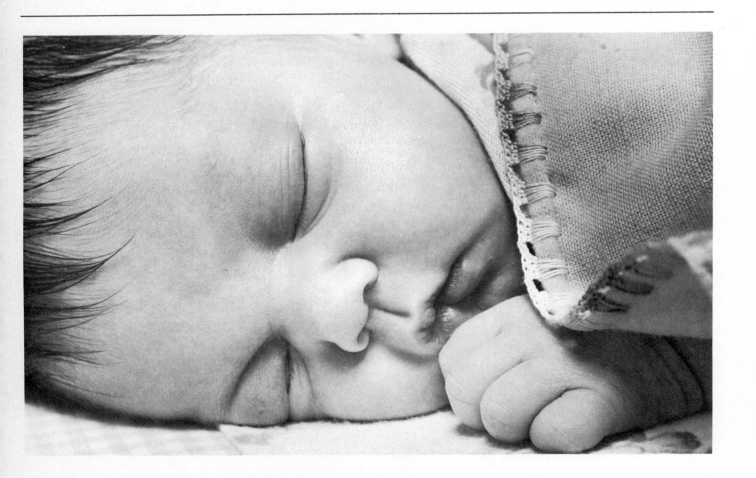

Between the time he takes his first breath of air and the
time you light his first birthday candle, your baby
changes from a sleepy, curled-up newborn to a standing
child with independent interests and skills.

Moving	Movements of the newborn baby
	Gains control over the position of his head
	By 3 months, the body is uncurled, and movements of head, shoulders, arms, and legs are stronger and better coordinated
	Babies enjoy being held, rocked, and carried about
Touching and Holding	Hands are closed or partly closed much of the time
	Grasps objects placed in his open hand
	Between 6 weeks and 3 months, reflex grasping is replaced by voluntary grasping
	Swipes at objects with his arms and hands
	By 3 months your baby's hands are open most of the time, and she is eager to have more objects to touch and hold
Seeing	Visual abilities of the newborn
	Parents can influence the ways their babies look at the world
	Looking at objects produces changes in a baby's body movements
	Enjoys looking at slowly moving objects
	Enjoys looking at faces
	Enjoys looking at patterns
	Babies become excited when they see objects they will soon be able to grasp
	Looks at his hands for long periods of time
	By 2 to 3 months, babies can keep an object in focus from several feet away to 4 to 6 inches in front of their eyes
	By 3 months babies examine objects carefully, and they recognize familiar things
Hearing	Babies can hear before they are born
	Newborn babies react to sounds differently when they are awake, sleeping, feeding, and crying
	Babies look to see where a sound comes from
	Babies respond differently to different sounds
	Babies listen to speech in a special way
Making Sounds	Newborn babies have no control over the sounds they make but they do have an inborn readiness to communicate
	Babies learn that crying brings mother
	A baby's pain cry is different from her hunger cry
	Babies make sounds when they hear sounds and see faces
	Your baby has a big tongue
	She coos and gurgles

**Summary of
Physical Development**

Moving	Learns to roll over
	Learns to sit
	Legs and feet move in new ways
	Physical exercise becomes a great source of enjoyment
Touching and Holding	Plays with hands and feet
	Brings most objects to his mouth
	Looks, reaches, grasps, and mouths objects in a swift and accurate *sequence* of movements
	Explores 1 object at a time
	Reaches in different ways for different kinds of objects
	Increases his use of fingers to touch, hold, and examine objects
	Moves arms up and down and side to side: hitting, waving, patting, and shaking
Seeing	Your baby now watches what is going on in all parts of the room
	Babies like to look at some colors more than others
	Babies enjoy looking into mirrors
	Looks at small objects
	As reaching and grasping improve, babies spend more time looking at objects they want to hold
	Babies enjoy looking at facial expressions
	Babies come to enjoy more complex and realistic pictures
Hearing	Sounds have more meaning for your baby
	He knows the differences between angry, happy, and sad tones of voice
	Babies hear the differences between one speech sound and another
	Your baby is getting better at finding where sounds come from
	He likes to hear himself talk
	Babies like to be talked to in a special way
	Your baby sometimes ignores you when you talk
Making Sounds	He becomes more expressive
	Your baby makes long "speeches" when looking at interesting things
	Your baby chuckles and laughs
	She experiments with making sounds
	Babies make sounds with objects in their mouths

Moving	Moves to a sitting position, and maintains it without help
	Many babies begin to crawl
	Stands holding onto furniture and other stable objects

Touching and Holding	Babies learn to predict how heavy objects are
	Manipulates objects in many new ways
	Objects are now handled in ways that differ according to their size and character
	Uses objects as tools
	Transfers objects from one hand to the other

Seeing	More time is now spent closely examining objects with the eyes and hands
	Fascinated by tiny objects
	Learns to understand depth
	Loses interest in a toy if it is covered up

Hearing	He knows the sounds that go with familiar toys and people
	Babies can hear the differences between different sentence tunes
	Babies enjoy music
	Babies begin to learn games like ''peek-a-boo''

Making Sounds	Your baby's sounds are becoming more like speech
	Babies talk differently to people and things
	Your baby stares at your mouth when you talk
	She imitates her own sounds when you say them back to her
	Babies use their voices to get what they want
	Babies begin to make more difficult sounds

**Summary of
Physical Development**

Moving	Crawling becomes a well-coordinated and speedy way of moving
	Loves to climb stairs
	Pulls up to a standing position
	Walks around holding on to furniture and other sturdy objects
	Takes a few steps while holding on to your hands
	Walks without being supported
Touching and Holding	Uses a cup with less spillage and attempts ''self-feeding'' with a spoon
	Holds small objects between the tips of the thumb and index finger
	Shows objects, but usually doesn't let go of them
	Drops and throws objects
	A baby uses objects to assist the growth of understanding
	Your examples and encouragement strongly influence the way your baby handles objects
Seeing	Enjoys looking at other children playing
	Crawling is often interrupted to look at interesting objects
	Wants to get back toys that have fallen out of sight
	Interested in books that are easy to handle
Hearing	She copies your sounds
	Your baby likes to hear new things
	He knows his own name and the names of familiar people
	Babies try to do what people ask them to do
	She understands more than she can say
Making Sounds	Your baby makes more complicated speeches
	Babies babble to people as well as objects
	Your baby makes different sounds for different wants and needs
	He imitates new sounds
	She talks most when there is plenty of action and everyone attends to her
	Babies make their first word-like sounds

2. Moving

Changes in Positions of Baby's Body and Ability to Move

Many parents mark the stages of their baby's development by 4 important "firsts" — the first time he sits without help, crawls, stands, and walks. Less dramatic than these major milestones in development, but just as important are other signs that your baby's body is slowly becoming responsive to his intentions — like turning around to see where a sound is coming from, or taking objects apart to see how they work. We will also discuss the changes in body positions and postures that allow his movements to become more elaborate and skillful. Altogether, this is the story of the changes that turn a curled-up newborn into a standing 1-year-old.

You will see your baby work to get his body to move as he wants it to, and you will learn how to help him with his efforts. Some parents think that helping a baby means doing things to speed up his development. There is no evidence to suggest that speeding up a baby's development is a good thing to do. Babies who are pushed by their parents may find it harder to be satisfied with themselves as they grow up. It's best to let your baby develop in his own way, and at his own rate. You will get better and better at understanding the signals your baby uses to let you know when he wants your help. If you take your cues from him, you can't go wrong.

Moving

Changes in Positions of Baby's Body and Ability to Move

This introduction outlines the general sequence of changes in a baby's moving, or "motor development," during the first year of his life. It will also point out some of the principles at work in your baby's swiftly growing ability to move where he wants to, when he wants to, and how he wants to.

Motor development follows a general plan for all babies. The ability to sit comes before the ability to crawl, and the ability to crawl comes before standing and walking. But babies differ a great deal in the ages at which they first make new movements, and also in the ways they make these movements. Each baby moves a bit differently from every other one. You may enjoy taking some photographs of your baby when he lifts his head and chest, handles objects, sits, crawls, stands, and takes his first steps. You can place your favorite pictures on the following pages. They are designed to let you make your own photographic record of *the individual way* your baby achieves these major milestones in development.

Moving

Lifts his head and chest off the ground
when lying on his stomach

Baby's age when these photographs were taken

Handles objects

Baby's age when these photographs were taken

Sits alone

Baby's age when these photographs were taken

Moving

Crawls

Baby's age when these photographs were taken

Moving

Stands alone

Baby's age when these photographs were taken

Moving

First steps

Baby's age when these photographs were taken

Moving

Changes in Positions of Baby's Body and Ability to Move

Physical development follows a fixed sequence. It proceeds from the head down to the feet. Your baby will learn to control his head and neck muscles first, then his arms and hands, body, legs, and feet.

When your baby is learning to move in new ways, he needs to concentrate, and this may slow down his movements. With practice, his movements become swift and smooth, and they begin to achieve goals. Like an adult learning to drive a car, your baby's movements become *skillful.*

Your baby concentrates much effort during his first year on acquiring new motor abilities. When he achieves one, he enjoys practicing it over and over again. Success in the growth of motor abilities is one of the earliest and most important forms of success a baby can experience. Motor skills build his confidence and motivation to explore, and exploring is one of the ways he learns.

Through his growing ability to move about on his own, your baby also has opportunities to cope with challenges, and he learns to be resilient in the face of frustration.

Here is a list of ways to help your baby develop:
(1) Psychological
As your baby develops new motor skills, you can encourage his self-confidence. Even a very young baby can be quite sensitive. Don't add to his feeling of embarrassment at a temporary failure. When you feel like laughing as your baby works to develop a new skill, make sure that the laughter can be shared by you *and* the baby. Of course, if your baby laughs first, by all means join in! Babies can also sense your impatience, anxiety, and bad temper. Such feelings on your part can also discourage his experiments with body movement. He wants to please you, so if he feels you are displeased, he can become inhibited.

(2) Physical
You will have to provide conditions that allow your baby to exercise his motor abilities freely. Early practice with reaching and grasping are easier in a sitting position, but you will have to provide that opportunity. For example, you may have to remove any clothing that hampers your baby when he is trying to learn to roll over. He also needs a firm surface to practice his rolling, because soft sur-

faces give way as he presses against them. Strengthening his legs in preparation for walking is easy and fun to achieve by giving your baby chances to jump and dance on your lap. By providing opportunities for positions that encourage a newly emerging motor ability, you are also making a contribution to the growth of your baby's trust in you and confidence in himself. When you manage your baby's development in an atmosphere of play, both of you can share his enjoyment in learning new skills. And when the hard work of practicing a new way of moving makes him tired or frustrated, you can step in and entertain him so that he has a chance to rest. Favorite games, songs, or a massage, can help to relax him and to let him know how much you appreciate his efforts.

Your baby can be given *too much* help, particularly when a new ability is emerging. When he seems slow and clumsy, you may be tempted to step in and take over. Try to be patient. Let the baby do as much as he can do and wants to do on his own. Only then offer help.

Moving

Movements of the Newborn Baby

Some babies prefer lying on their stomachs, while others prefer lying on their backs. Whichever position your baby prefers, you may want to move her once in a while to provide more varied experience. Whether lying on their stomachs or on their backs, newborn babies tend to curl up when they are still.

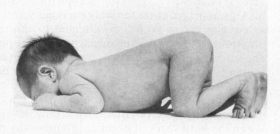
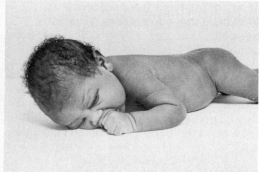

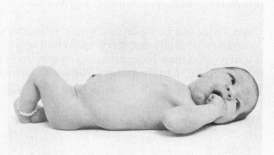
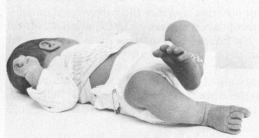

When not lying still, babies wave, kick, and squirm about. Sometimes very young babies are uncomfortable with their own movements, and may fuss and cry. Wrapping them up snugly sometimes helps to quiet them.

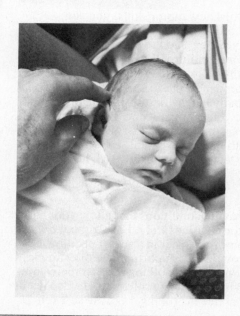

Moving

Movements of the Newborn Baby

Babies are born with a number of reflex movements that help them adjust to life outside the mother's body. Some of these reflexes are directly related to life-supporting activities — such as turning her head to find the nipple, sucking, and swallowing. Other reflexes help protect her — such as blinking, sneezing, coughing, and turning her head when an object presses against her nose or mouth and interferes with breathing. Still other reflexes are forerunners of skills she will develop later.

Rooting and Sucking

When you stroke the corner of your baby's mouth and move your finger slowly toward his ear, you will see that his tongue, mouth, and sometimes even his head move to follow your hand. This reflex helps babies to locate the nipple for feeding.

If your baby catches up with your finger, he will suck it vigorously, as he will suck most objects placed in his mouth. This reflex helps to assure the success of feeding in the newborn period.

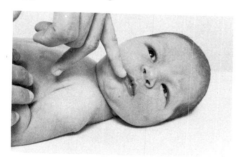 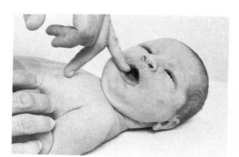 

Startle Response (Moro Reflex)

Newborn babies are startled either when they hear very loud sounds or when their positions are changed too abruptly, so that they feel a loss of support. The startle response involves extending the arms and legs, often accompanied by crying. If the response is vigorous, the baby's back may curve up and his arms may tremble. The startle response is strongest and occurs most frequently during the first 6 to 8 weeks of life.

Babies differ in their sensitivity to sound and handling. The startle response helps your baby tell you about her own sensitivities. In this way she helps you learn how to control the level of sound in her environment, and how to handle her so that she doesn't become uncomfortable.

Moving

Movements of the Newborn Baby

Tonic Neck Reflex

A very young baby holds his head toward a preferred side, usually the right, when lying on his stomach or back. The arm and leg on that side are extended, while the arm and leg on the other side are held closer to the body. By 3 months his body positions vary much more. Meanwhile, during the first 2 months, place objects that you want your baby to see on the side he prefers to look toward, and place objects that you want him to touch in the hand that is freer to move.

Reflex Crawling

When very young babies are placed stomach down on a solid surface, many make reflex crawling movements. When they are placed in water and securely supported, their crawling movements are even more smoothly coordinated, like those shown in this drawing.

Reflex crawling may stimulate the baby's development, both in the fluid environment of the mother and after birth.

Like many reflex movements, crawling tends to disappear, to be built up again later as learned, voluntary behavior if the baby needs it to get along in his environment.

Adapted from: McGraw M.
The neuromuscular maturation of the human infant.
New York: Hafner Press© 1945, 1974

Moving

Movements of the Newborn Baby

Reflex Walking
When newborns are held under their arms, with their feet touching a firm, flat surface, they perform reflex walking movements like those of an adult. This reflex usually disappears around 8 weeks of age.

Research workers have wondered whether giving infants the opportunity to make reflex walking movements will help them learn to walk earlier. In one experiment, infants were given an opportunity to practice reflex stepping during four 3-minute sessions each day from the second through the eighth week of life. At 2 months these infants were stepping more quickly and more skillfully than the infants in the experiment who were not given these opportunities. And they began to walk by themselves at an earlier age. Five of the 6 were walking at 10 months.

Of course, most babies learn to walk by themselves between 9 and 18 months of age. This study shows that early and continuing opportunities to use the stepping reflex speed up the learning of voluntary walking. There is no evidence that babies benefit from early walking. If you want to try it, you can decide about whether to continue it or not, depending on how you and your baby feel about it.

Moving

Gains Control over the Position of His Head

During the early months of life, your baby's head is too heavy for the muscles of his neck and back to support, so it's important that *you* support it when you lift him. Your support prevents *sudden* or *extreme* stretching or twisting of the neck muscles and bones. But you don't have to support your baby's head as if the slightest movement could harm him. He's really pretty tough — even at this early age. He'll need less and less help as he matures.

Obtaining control over the position of the head is a major achievement in the first 3 months of life. It allows your baby to look at things that interest him, and it prepares the way for him to be able to sit up.

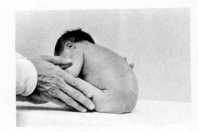

By 3 weeks of age, his ability to hold his head steady improves considerably. When you carry him, he's able to hold his head clear of your shoulder for a few seconds. By 6 weeks of age, he will be able to do this for several minutes at a time. Be careful to avoid sudden movements that might cause him to lose his balance.

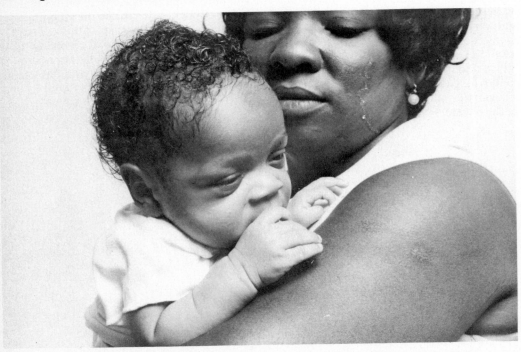

Moving

Birth-3 Months

Gains Control over the Position of His Head

Even after your baby begins to hold his head clear of your shoulder, his head, neck, and back will sag when you pull him to a sitting position. The ability to control the lower neck and back muscles grows more slowly than the ability to hold the head steady.

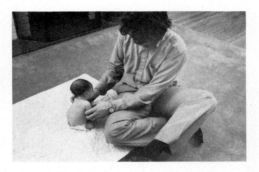

He also holds his head steady when held upright in your arms. This position is one of the best he can be in for getting a good view of the world about him.

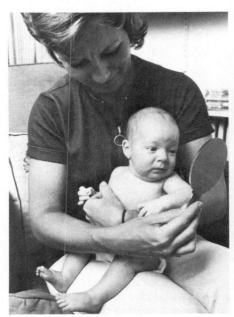

By 3 to 4 months of age, he also shows improvement in the strength of his back muscles. Now when you gently pull him to a sitting position, his head, neck, and back sag far less than they did earlier. He is now ready to spend more time propped in a more upright sitting position.

Moving

Gains Control over the Position of His Head

You can help your baby strengthen his neck and back muscles by placing him on his stomach several times each day. In this position, he will practice lifting his head and neck. At 4 weeks he lifts his head briefly. By 8 weeks he lifts his head and chest, and holds his head up longer.

By 3 months of age, your baby lifts his head quite well when lying on his stomach, supporting his weight on his forearms and, later, on his hands. His head is now much higher off the ground, and he is able to see much more of what is going on around him.

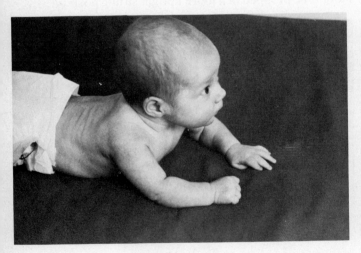

Your baby's eagerness to see the world is a strong incentive to practice moving his head in ways that give him a better view. You can also help by moving him around so that he always has some new things to see.

Moving

By 3 Months the Body Is Uncurled, and Movements of Head, Shoulders, Arms, and Legs Are Stronger and Better Coordinated

Your 3-month-old baby is a much more active person than she used to be. Increased strength and coordination permit smoother movements of her arms and legs, and a marked increase in the *pleasure* she gets from moving.

She even uses her new motor abilities to help communicate her feelings.

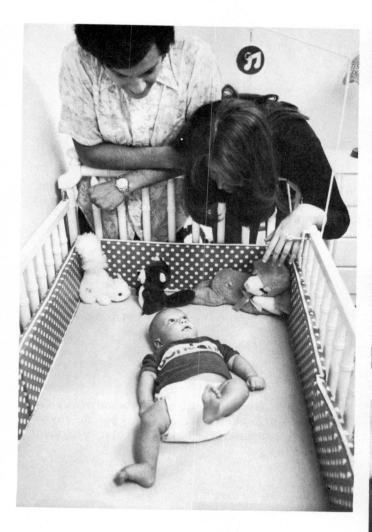

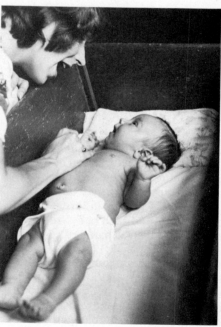

Moving

Babies Enjoy Being Held, Rocked, and Carried About

Rocking a baby in your arms, or by using a cradle or rocking chair, can soothe a fretful baby or add to the enjoyment of a happy one. Rocking, holding, stroking, and carrying have been found to benefit all aspects of an infant's development. But no one has yet been able to discover why. It's possible that movement maintains an alert state that helps the baby to learn.

Many newborn infants who are handled and rocked as a routine part of their care cry less, even when they are left alone. By using this effective way to reduce crying, you become a trusted source of comfort. And your ability to comfort your baby increases your self-confidence and self-esteem.

When you lift your baby to your shoulder and rock him, he will become more alert, and look about more actively and attentively.

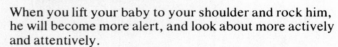

When you lift your crying baby to your shoulder to comfort him, rocking in an up-and-down direction may be even more effective in calming him than rocking in a side-to-side direction, and vigorous rocking may be more calming than gentle rocking. Of course, different babies will respond in different ways, and each baby will have individual preferences as to how he is handled.

Many modern devices allow a baby to be carried close to his mother's or father's body, and many parents enjoy using them so that they can have their babies with them wherever they go.

In some cultures, babies are carried around strapped to their mothers for long periods every day. Doing this provides them with movement that benefits their motor, social, and intellectual development, and it also allows them to see more and hear more. The prolonged close contact can also help the mother and baby get to know each other.

Moving

Learns to Roll Over

Between 3 and 6 months your baby learns to roll over. At first he is barely able to roll up onto his side and roll back down again, whether he is lying on his back or on his stomach. You can help him in these early efforts by making sure his clothing isn't getting in his way, and that he has a firm surface to practice on. You can roll him gently onto his side, so that he gets the feeling of this new movement. To encourage him, you can make sounds or wave a favorite toy. Finally, to help him complete attempts that don't quite succeed, you can give him a gentle pull.

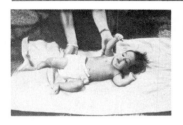 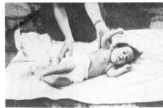 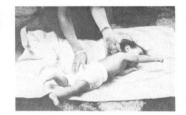 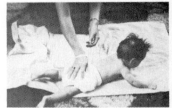

Soon he is able to turn over completely.

As with all newly developing motor abilities, your baby will practice rolling over again and again. And as his rolling improves, he will have this additional way of changing his view of the world by himself.

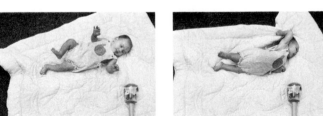 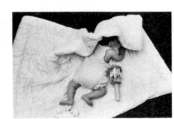

Moving

Learns to Sit

By 3 months, your baby thoroughly enjoys the sitting position, provided she has sufficient support for her back. Hold her in your lap, prop her up with pillows, or sit her in an infant seat, car seat, or swing.

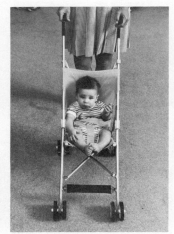

Pulling your baby slowly and gently to a sitting position makes a nice game. It is also good exercise for her back muscles. As the strength increases in the muscles of her head, neck, shoulder, and back, you will see less and less sagging as you pull her up.

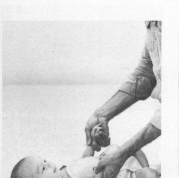

Moving

Learns to Sit

Soon she will take your extended hands and pull *herself* to a sitting position. Now she sits with little support.

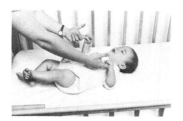 

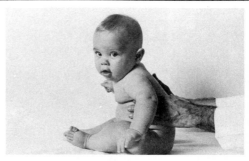

A bit later, she provides most of the power to sit up herself, and holds on to your hands simply to help her balance.

By 6 months her back muscles are strong enough so that she can sit comfortably with only 1 pillow behind her. She may even be able to sit for a brief time with no support at all.

When babies are first learning to sit alone, they often have difficulty getting *out* of the sitting position. Be alert to signs of fatigue — a slumping back, an unhappy face — and help her onto her stomach or back, or pick her up and hold her for a while.

Much of the attention must be given to the act of sitting, so if she sees something that interests her, or if she is otherwise distracted, she may topple over.

During the months your baby is learning to sit, surround her with some cushions, or place her on a quilt or thick mat. In these ways you can reduce the discouragement that falling can cause.

Babies who have just learned to sit alone sometimes lean far forward and support themselves on their arms and hands. Later, as the strength of their back muscles and the ability to maintain good balance improve, they can sit without the support of their arms, which become free for grasping and holding.

Moving

Legs and Feet Move in New Ways

Your baby will now lift his feet and legs off the floor or
mattress while lying on his back.

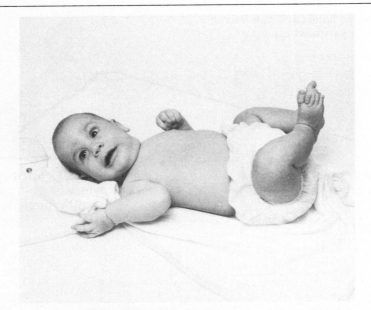

Moving

Legs and Feet Move in New Ways

By 6 months most babies enjoy the standing position when they are supported under their arms. Held this way in your lap, your baby will enjoy bouncing and jumping. And your own pleasure will add to her enjoyment. Using your lap as a trampoline is both a game and an important step toward learning how to walk. Some parents wonder whether these activities can make a baby bowlegged. The answer is ''No.'' When a baby is strong enough to bounce and jump in your lap, it's safe for him to do it as much as he likes. In fact, the exercise helps his legs to get stronger.

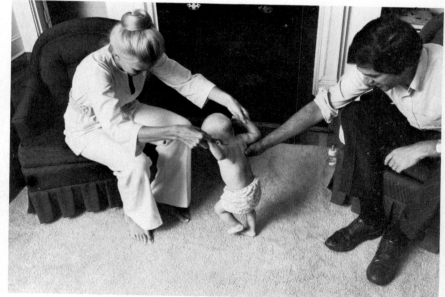

Moving

Legs and Feet Move in New Ways

Kicking and thrusting of the legs occur more frequently now. If you hold your hands firmly against the bottoms of your baby's feet, he will kick and thrust even more. This form of play brings him the special pleasure of practicing a new ability, and it also helps improve his strength and coordination.

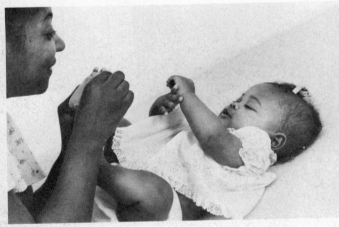

Kicking movements bring the legs and feet into view, and your baby becomes fascinated with them. He looks at them with the same interest he had in looking at his arms and hands some months before. He works hard at getting hold of his moving feet, and once he succeeds, he pulls them to his mouth for further exploration.

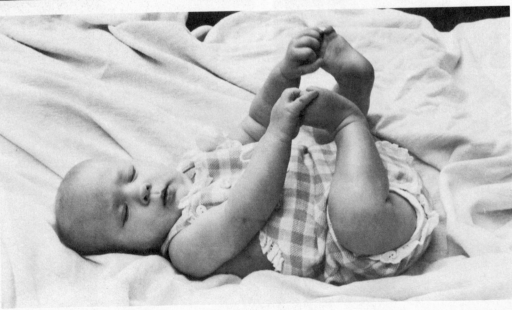

Moving

Physical Exercise Becomes a Great Source of Enjoyment

Exercising the large muscles of her body — by kicking
her feet, waving her arms, and rolling over — provides your baby long periods of enjoyment.

Moving

Moves to a Sitting Position, and Maintains It without Help

From 6 to 9 months babies learn to get into and out of a sitting position whenever they want to, and they become very confident about keeping their balance. They use their arms and hands freely to reach, grasp, and manipulate a wide range of objects, with little concern about toppling over. The whole body can now be turned while sitting.

Moving

Many Babies Begin to Crawl

While staring ahead, a 6- to 7-month-old baby alternately lifts her chest and her bottom from the floor, supporting her weight on her arms and legs. It looks as if she is about to move into a crawling position. But it just doesn't quite work yet. She doesn't lift her chest and her bottom together — and so she is more likely to rock back and forth than go forward. By 7 to 8 months she begins to move. At first she may go backward instead of forward — or she may pull herself forward by moving her arms together, dragging her legs and stomach along the floor. She knows where she wants to go, but it takes her a while to discover the best way to get there.

Later, the arms begin to reach out in alternating movements, like the strokes of a swimmer. The legs start to move more, and the stomach is lifted off the floor.

As her ability to crawl improves, the baby's elbows and knees are used more than her arms and legs.

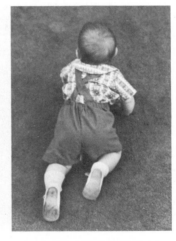

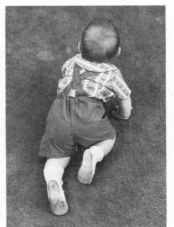

Moving

Many Babies Begin to Crawl

Babies move forward in many different ways. Some don't really crawl. They prefer to roll over, or to push themselves forward while in a sitting position, or to squirm with such strength and determination that they start moving across the room.

Your baby's curiosity encourages her to crawl. You can help her to practice crawling by holding favorite toys in front of her and adding encouragement with smiles and words.

Moving

Stands Holding on to Furniture and Other Stable Objects

As your baby's legs gain strength, she will enjoy having you lift her to a standing position near something she can grasp firmly, like the rail of her crib. Now it's important to be sure that the crib rail is securely locked in the "up" position.

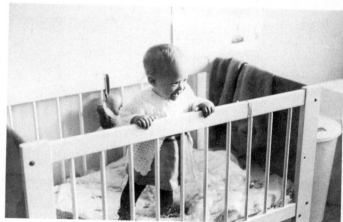

Moving

Crawling Becomes a Well-Coordinated and Speedy Way of Moving

Between 9 and 12 months the crawling movements of earlier months become more rhythmical and much more rapid. Your baby now moves on his hands and knees. His chest and stomach are lifted far off the floor.

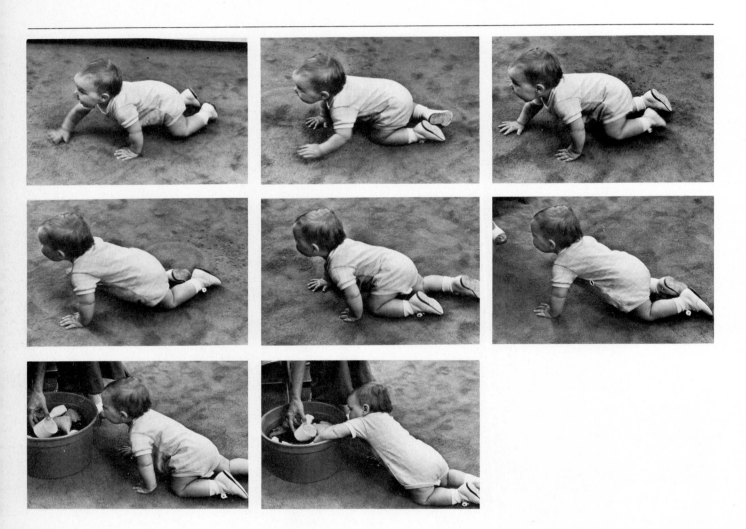

Moving

**Crawling Becomes a Well-Coordinated
and Speedy Way of Moving**

Some babies even manage to move on their hands and
feet instead of their hands and knees.

Some babies are so good at creeping that they put off
learning to walk for many months. A few babies don't
creep much at all, preferring to go right ahead with learning to stand and walk. These differences in the ways
babies learn to move are all normal.

Moving

**Crawling Becomes a Well-Coordinated
and Speedy Way of Moving**

No matter how quickly or in what way your baby decides
to crawl, stand, and walk, the ability to move about the
room brings her an important new freedom. Her curiosity
prompts her to crawl into strange new places even when
she has no idea of what she will find there. You will have
to think ahead about possible dangers to your baby, and
keep her from getting into trouble. But you will also want
to encourage her exploration and her independence.
These 2 points of view can conflict, so you should
think about how much freedom you feel she should have.
This question will be coming up over and over again as
she grows, and you will want to make your decisions
thoughtfully.

Your baby's safety can be better ensured if you clear
some generous portion of floor space for her explorations. But she wants to be near you and other people
more than she wants to be alone in her own play area.
She needs to feel part of the social life of the house. That
is why it is so important to baby-proof your home — to
make *the whole house safe* for a baby who can creep,
and who will soon be climbing, standing, and walking.

Moving

9 - 12 Months

Loves to Climb Stairs

Once your baby becomes reasonably skillful at crawling and creeping, she begins going up the stairs with the enthusiasm of a mountain climber. Stairs hold a special fascination for babies, who are capable of climbing them over and over again on all fours without getting tired or bored. Stair-climbing play always needs to be carefully supervised.

Climbing up stairs is much easier than climbing back down. Some parents teach their babies to move down stairs by sliding, using their hands and feet to control their movement. With your supervision, this can be a safe way to move down stairs. Other parents prefer to carry their babies down so that they can start up again. Whatever you decide to do, you'll probably get tired of your baby's playing on the stairs before she will. A gate will help to keep the stairs "off limits" when you are too tired or too busy for another climbing expedition.

169

Moving

Pulls Up to a Standing Position

Most babies will pull themselves up to a standing position for the first time between 9 and 12 months, by holding on to a steady support — such as furniture, the clothing of adults, or crib rails. Once your baby is successful at pulling himself up to a standing position, he is well on his way to learning how to walk.

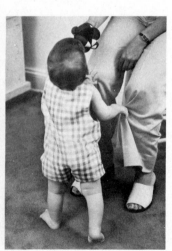

When your baby first starts pulling to a standing position, he may need your help to get up. But he soon learns to manage the getting-up part by himself. Pulling himself to a standing position is easier for your baby than getting back down. His inability to get back down can frighten him, and he may cry for help. But within a few weeks he also learns to get down by himself.

Once he is confident about his ability to pull himself up and get himself down again, your baby will want to spend more and more time standing up. As a baby begins standing on his own feet, we see babyhood coming to an end and childhood beginning.

Moving

Walks Around Holding on to Furniture and Other Sturdy Objects

By 12 months most babies are able to walk while holding on to furniture. At first, most babies move along using a sideways step while holding on with both hands. They often lean against objects for added support.

Moving

**Walks Around Holding on to Furniture
and Other Sturdy Objects**

As your baby becomes more confident about her movements, she will begin to stand farther away from the furniture she is holding. Now she uses it for balance only, and the full weight of her body is being supported on her legs. She may be able to hold on with 1 hand only.

Falls are common when babies first start walking, even when they are holding on to sturdy objects. Since learning how to walk requires real courage, and since too many falls can lead to fear and discouragement, it is wise to place cushions or blankets nearby, so falls will be less painful and frightening. Make sure that the furniture she holds on to is sturdy enough to support her. Your reassurance and help will tide her over discouraging moments. If you laugh and say "Ooops" when she falls, she'll get up a lot faster than if you look frightened and say "Oh, oh!"

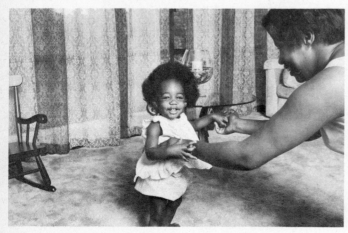

Moving

**Walks Around Holding on to Furniture
and Other Sturdy Objects**

Many ingenious devices have been invented to help babies with their early efforts at walking.

This picture was first printed in the 15th Century. It shows "the ages of man" from infancy to old age. Just to the left of the infant in the cradle there is an older infant walking with the help of a sturdy frame mounted on wheels.

This picture shows infants and toddlers being cared for in the nursery of a French community started around 1860. The people in this community believed in sharing the work of caring for children. They also believed in helping children to become independent. These ideas are expressed in the device they built to help children learn to walk. Infants crawled to the circular railings, pulled themselves to a standing position, and walked by themselves.

This baby is using a modern walking device.

Moving

Takes a Few Steps While Holding on to Your Hands

After he's confident in his ability to walk while holding on to sturdy objects, your baby will be ready to take a few steps while holding on to your hands. Doing this is frightening to him at first, so limit these early walks together to just a few steps, unless your baby clearly wants to keep on going. Many parents become excited and happy during these first walks, and their enthusiasm becomes part of the baby's adventure in learning to walk.

Moving

Walks without Being Supported

The ages at which babies walk differ widely. Some babies will take a few steps on their own by 10 months. Others wait until they are 15 or 16 months old. Most begin between these extremes. All babies will be improving their walking abilities through the second year of life.

Even in the earliest stages of learning how to walk, babies show a great deal of individuality. Some prefer to take a few slow and deliberate steps, lifting their legs high in the air and bringing them cautiously down again with long pauses in between. Others will take a few quick running steps and then topple over.

Your baby does other things to improve her balance and make it easier for her to walk. She holds her feet far apart and she points her toes in or out. This helps her to balance, but it makes walking slower, too. She holds her arms up, both to aid balance and to provide protection in case of a fall. And she sometimes looks down at her feet for added control and reassurance.

Moving

Walks without Being Supported

Both the shape of the baby's body and her tendency to bend at the hip and at the knees, bring her weight low to the ground and make it easier for her to keep her balance while walking (A). Later, her posture becomes more erect, and she walks as older children and adults do.

As her coordination and balance improve, and falls become less frequent, the baby's arms become more relaxed and are held closer to her body (B). Finally they begin to swing right alongside the body in rhythm with the stepping movements of her legs. As her balance improves, she walks with her feet closer together, and she bends less at the hips and knees. Her steps become better coordinated and more rapid. Her feet stop hitting the ground "flat-footed" — with the entire sole touching the ground during each step. Now the heel of the front foot hits the ground as the back foot is raised up on its toes (C).

These changes are shown in the diagrams drawn from motion pictures of babies who are learning how to walk.

A.

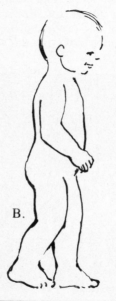

B.

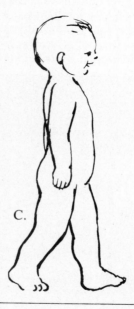

C.

Adapted from: McGraw M. The neuromuscular maturation of the human infant. New York; Hafner Press© 1945, 1974.

3. Touching and Holding

Movements of Arms and Hands during the First Year

A newborn infant has a grasp and a reaching reflex. He will automatically close his fingers tightly around any object placed in the palm of his hand. When he is alert and held so that his arms are free to move, he will sometimes reach toward objects placed in front of him.

Voluntary grasping replaces reflex grasping between 6 weeks and 3 months of age. At first babies don't hold things as firmly or as long as they did when they automatically grasped everything placed in the palms of their hands. Some parents worry about whether their babies are becoming clumsy at this stage of development. Actually, the baby is making a big step forward. He is beginning to replace an automatic response with a voluntary one. By learning to grasp those things he wants to grasp, he is gaining a great deal of independence.

After several months of practice, his voluntary grasp will become skillful.

Babies start voluntary reaching at 4 to 5 months. At first, voluntary reaching is slow and clumsy, and the baby watches his arm and hand movements closely. After a few months of practice, reaching becomes swift and accurate, and the baby no longer needs to watch his movements so closely.

During the first year, a baby's fingers move in increasingly independent ways. Reflex grasping and early voluntary grasping involve all of the fingers working together to press objects into the palm. By 6 months babies can hold objects between their extended fingers, and by 12 months they can pick up and hold small objects between the tip of the thumb and the tip of the index finger.

Touching and Holding

Hands Are Closed or Partly Closed Much of the Time

During the first 6 weeks of life, your baby's hands will usually be curled up in little fists. When he cries, his hands will often move and his fingers will open and close. When he sleeps, his hands will be more relaxed—loosely fisted, partially open, or even fully open.

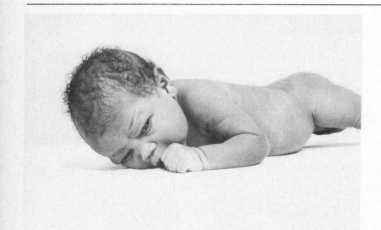

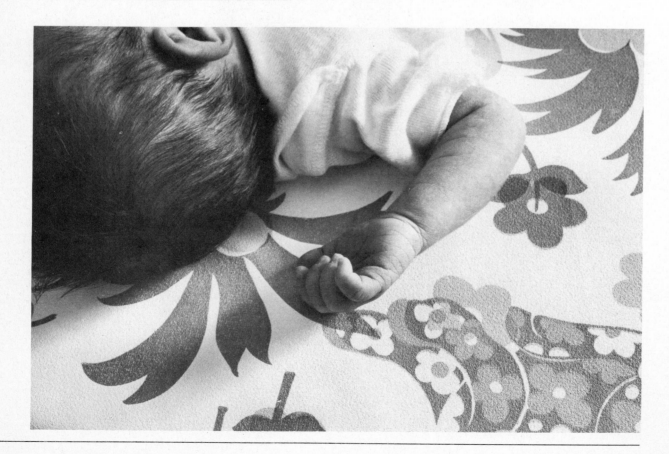

Touching and Holding

Grasps Objects Placed in His Open Hand

During most of the first 2 months of life, your baby firmly grasps any object placed in the palm of his hand. He has no voluntary control over this early form of grasping. It is 1 of the reflexes he is born with. The grasp reflex helps him hold on to you, contributing to his safety and sense of security. It also helps you feel closer to him.

When a large ring is placed in this baby's partially opened hand, his fingers automatically close around it. He moves the ring about as if it were part of his own body — and he hardly bothers to look at it. The eyes and hands are not yet working together to learn about objects by combining everything the hand can feel with everything the eye can see.

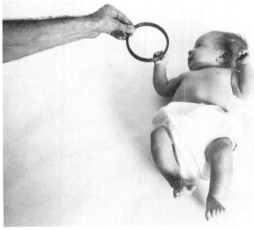 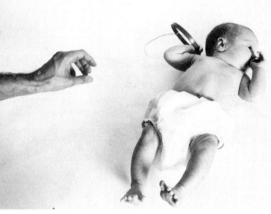

The 4-to 8-week old infant will automatically grasp objects placed in his palm. But if you brush an object against the baby's fingertips instead of placing it in his palm, you can activate an "avoiding" reflex, and his fingers will stay open instead of closing around the object.

When babies show excitement at seeing objects they want to touch, their hands sometimes show both opening and closing movements. In time, the reflexes that open the hand and the reflexes that close the hand give way to more precise and useful patterns of voluntary grasping.

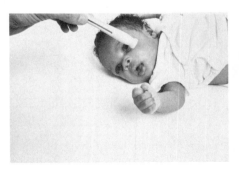  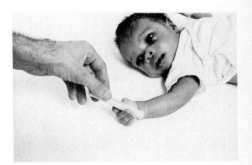

This simple form of play gives him experience touching different kinds of objects. It also gives him another way to be close to people.

Touching and Holding

Birth - 3 Months

**Between 6 Weeks and 3 Months, Reflex Grasping
Is Replaced by Voluntary Grasping**

By 6 to 8 weeks, your baby's hands are open more often, and the grasp reflex is diminishing. He no longer grasps everything that is placed in his hand. He often holds on to objects for 30 seconds or more, particularly if they are light in weight and easy to hold.

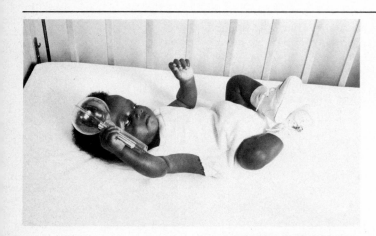

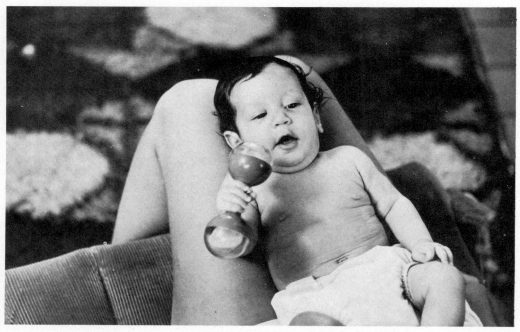

Some parents worry about the fact that infants now hold on to objects less securely and for shorter periods of time than they did during the first month of life. The early form of grasping was involuntary, and it is now being replaced by voluntary grasping. Although voluntary grasping is clumsy at the start, it is important to understand that it allows the baby to hold on to things that she *wants* to hold on to — and this is a great step forward in her ability to become an active explorer of the environment. Voluntary grasping gives her great pleasure, and it gives you a chance to encourage her development by showing your own pleasure when she takes hold of objects successfully.

180

Touching and Holding

Between 6 Weeks and 3 Months, Reflex Grasping Is Replaced by Voluntary Grasping

A baby's arms and hands are able to move most freely when his body is well supported. Your baby can have some of his most successful early experiences with grasping when you hold him. Hold him so that his floppy head has a place to rest, and so that his arms and hands are free to move. Your support will encourage his arms to move and his hands to grasp things. Reaching and grasping are fun for your baby. And the more playful and happy you are when you help her, the more she enjoys learning these new skills. Be prepared for some tugging on your hair, glasses, nose, and ears. They are very convenient and attractive targets.

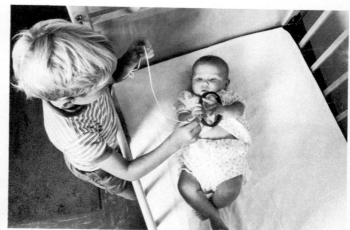

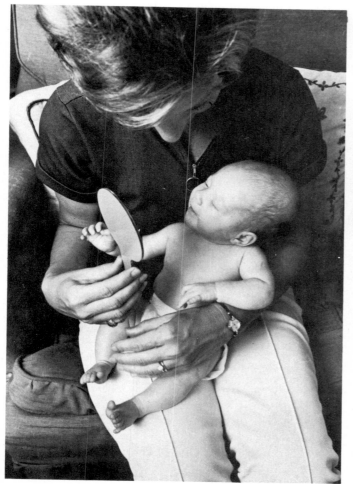

At the same time as your baby is getting better at holding objects, her interest grows in mouthing them and looking at them. Her first efforts to bring an object to her mouth will also bring the object into view, and she will glance at it briefly and even follow it a bit with her eyes. As reaching, grasping, and holding improve, it is easier to amuse her, and it is easier for her to amuse herself. Play begins to blossom, and with it a tremendous increase in her opportunities to learn.

Touching and Holding

Swipes at Objects with His Arms and Hands

Between 2 and 3 months of age, most babies are looking up as they lie on their backs, and their arms and hands are moving more freely than before. A baby this age is able to swipe at objects suspended about 1 foot above his face. During such swiping, the hands are often closed, and the extended arm and fist become skillful at finding their target. This form of play helps your baby practice reaching. His grasping improves at the same time. Soon he is able to reach for and grasp an object swiftly and accurately. Meanwhile, the swiping and batting movements give your baby a great deal of pleasure.

The best objects for a baby to swipe at are large, lightweight, and decorated with colors and patterns that he likes to look at. This toy is a 10-inch cardboard cube, painted with faces and other patterns. It is suspended from a crib mobile support by an 8-inch elastic cord. The elastic cord allows the cube to move up and down as well as spin around when the baby hits it, so he can see the different patterns on different sides. Babies enjoy batting and swiping at the cube for long stretches of time — often 10 minutes or longer. There are no infant toys designed especially for swiping and batting, so you will have to exercise some ingenuity. Try using a colorful breakfast cereal box; and if you don't want to search for elastic cord, a short piece of string will do nicely.

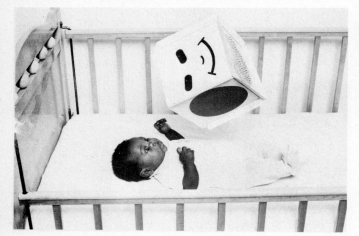
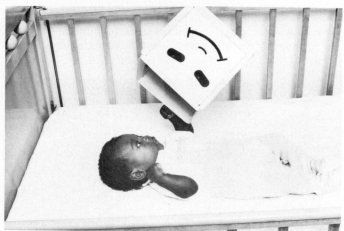
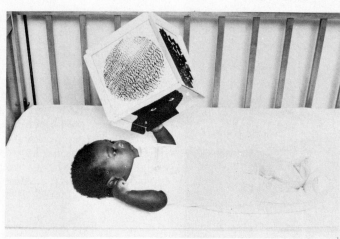

Touching and Holding

By 3 Months Your Baby's Hands Are Open Most of the Time, and She Is Eager to Have More Objects to Touch and Hold.

By 2 to 3 months your baby's hands are usually open. In fact, her whole body is straightening out from the curled-up positions she preferred earlier. She kicks more, and moves her head to take in more sights. This increase in body movement is a signal that she's ready for more experiences. The third month is usually a good time to provide new objects to touch, hold, and look at.

Touching and Holding

Plays with Hands and Feet

Babies are constant, active explorers. They want to look at, touch, and handle *all* of the interesting things near them. It isn't surprising that hands and feet become favorite objects for exploration — after all, they are always close by, and they move about in the most fascinating ways!

When babies first begin to look at and handle their own hands and feet, they probably regard them as just another group of objects to be explored. They don't yet seem to understand that these objects are part of themselves. When hands and arms fall out of sight, a young baby makes no effort to see where they have gone, and he doesn't try to lift them back into view.

Slowly he begins to understand that he can control the comings and goings of his hands and feet. He drops them out of view, brings them back into view, makes them disappear again, and even looks for an arm that has moved out of sight.

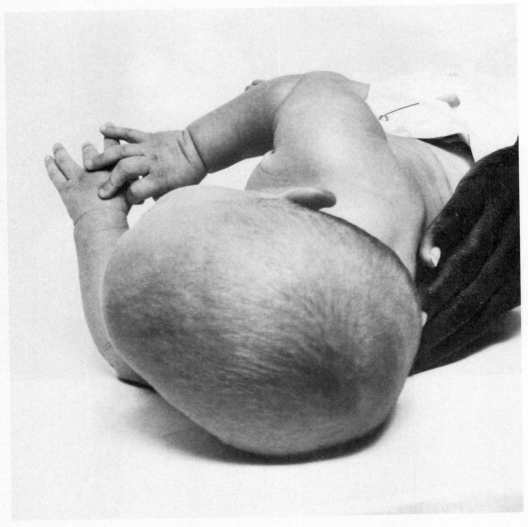

Touching and Holding

Plays with Hands and Feet

By 5 to 6 months, he has good control over the movements of his arms and hands. At this stage the baby's hands explore not only each other, but all of his other body parts as well: feet and toes, hair, nose, ears, and genitals. These explorations of the body parts, including the genitals, is normal, healthy behavior.

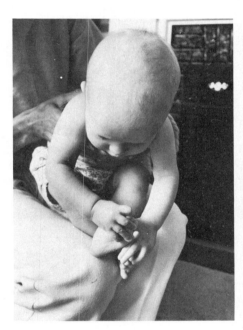 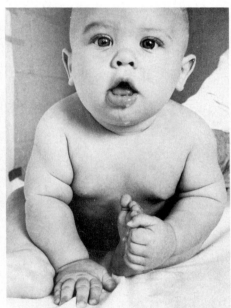

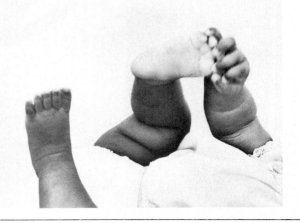

Touching and Holding

Brings Most Objects to His Mouth

Babies use their mouths to get information about the shape, texture, and hardness of objects, as well as taste. The mouth, like the hand, is an organ of touch. Lips and tongue move over objects, just as fingers do, in an effort to understand the qualities of the objects that make up the infant's world. The desire to bring objects to his mouth is 1 of the reasons your baby reaches and grasps so much.

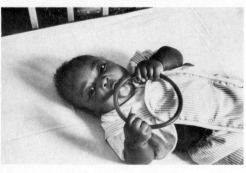

Touching and Holding

**Looks, Reaches, Grasps and Mouths Objects in a Swift
and Accurate Sequence of Movements**

Between 3 and 6 months, babies learn to explore objects
more efficiently. Their earlier reaching, grasping, handling, and mouthing are now linked together into smoothly
coordinated *sequences* of movement.

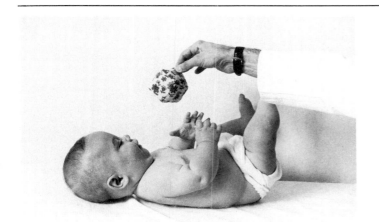

From 3 to 4 months, a baby usually moves both arms
toward an object, and often grasps it between 2 hands. It
is easier for him to do this if you hold objects right in front
of him instead of holding them off to one side or the other.
When a toy is just out of reach, his hands may grasp each
other instead.

Touching and Holding

3 - 6 Months

Explores 1 Object at a Time

Although the 4-to 5- month-old baby can reach for and grasp objects quite well, she is able to give her attention to only 1 thing at a time. If you hand her an object while she's already holding one, she will either ignore the second, or let go of the first in order to take the new one.

Touching and Holding

Reaches in Different Ways for Different Kinds of Objects

By 5 months, babies hold their arms and hands in different ways, depending on the shape, size, location, and hardness or softness of the object they are reaching for.

Touching and Holding

3 - 6 Months

Reaches in Different Ways for Different Kinds of Objects

By 5 months of age, infants spend less time looking at objects beyond their reach, as if to say, ``Why bother looking at things I can't get at? I'll spend my time looking at the things I can get my hands on!``

Babies now begin opening their hands as they reach for objects, and they open their hands wider when reaching for big objects than when reaching for small objects.

The 5-month-old baby reaches for familiar objects very quickly, and he positions his arm and hand in ways he has learned will give him the best control. When he is handed a new object, he pauses to figure out how he should position his arm and hand, and then he begins to reach.

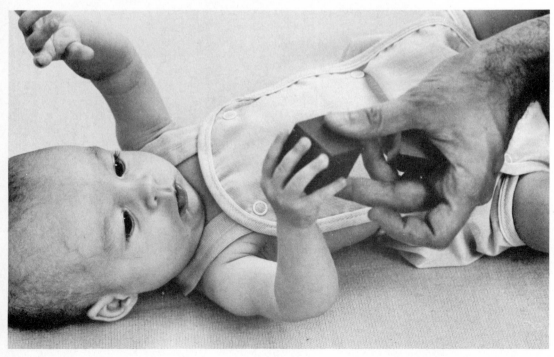

Touching and Holding

Increases His Use of Fingers to Touch Hold and Examine Objects

In earlier months, your baby held objects in his hands in a rather clumsy way, pressing them against his palm with his fingers. It was hard to manipulate objects well with this grasp, and objects often fell out of your baby's hand before he was through playing with them. Now he begins to grasp them between his fingers instead of pressing them into the palm of his hand. Doing this enables him to hold things more securely, and, more important, to manipulate them *thoroughly*.

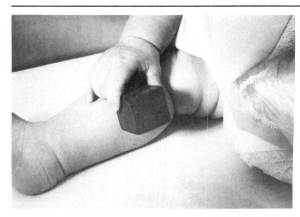

Your baby now concentrates on finding out what objects are like. The ability to use his fingers more skillfully increases his opportunities to explore the qualities of objects — their size, texture, shape, and the separate parts they're made of. The fingertips have nerves that give information about whether objects are hard or soft, wet or dry, sticky or non-sticky, rough or smooth. Pressing and twisting give information about whether objects are flexible or rigid. The ability to hold one part of an object still while moving another part helps your baby learn how many parts an object has and whether the parts are similar.

Touching and Holding

**Moves Arms Up and Down and Side to Side:
Hitting, Waving, Patting, and Shaking**

Between 4 and 6 months, your baby is able to move his
arms up and down. He often strikes things against hard
surfaces and other objects. When he doesn't hit anything
with the object he is holding, his movements look like
waving. Sometimes he moves his hand up and down
against an object. If his movements are forceful, it looks
as if he is hitting the object. If his movements are gentle,
it looks as if he is patting it.

When up and down and side to side movements first
appear, your baby will use them no matter what she is
holding. However, you can add to her interest by providing objects that make clear, easy-to-hear sounds when
they are shaken or waved.

Touching and Holding

Babies Learn to Predict How Heavy Objects Are

An infant 6 to 7 months of age grasps all objects firmly, whether they are heavy or light. Each time he's handed a new object, his arm tends to drop a bit because of its weight. The tension in the arm is quickly adjusted, and the object is brought back up to the desired position. When the same object is handed to the baby over and over again, the same thing happens — the arm still tends to drop. The baby is not able to predict the weight of the object and prepare to hold it so his arm won't drop. By 9 months the situation changes. Then, after grasping a new object a few times, the baby makes the proper adjustments in the tension of his arm, so it no longer drops when the object is handed to him.

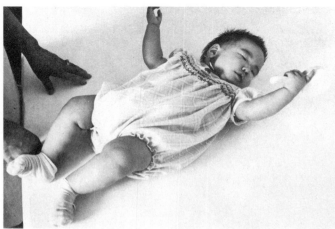

Touching and Holding

Manipulates Objects in Many New Ways

Your baby now handles things in many new ways. She can tear, pull, push, crumple, squeeze, rub, slide, poke, twist, scrape, and fold.

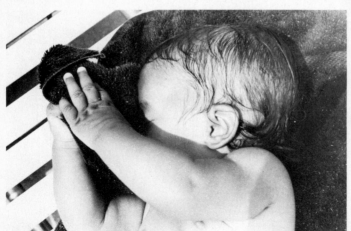
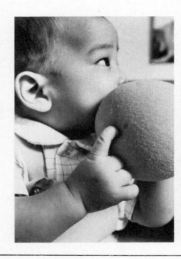

Touching and Holding

Manipulates Objects in Many New Ways

At this stage of development, babies enjoy playing with things that change shape while being handled. Paper and cellophane are great favorites. These not only change shape, they also make nice sounds. You'll have to supervise this play because paper and cellophane tear into small pieces that your baby may try to swallow.

Touching and Holding

Manipulates Objects in Many New Ways

Babies this age also like to explore pieces of cloth and fabric. Like paper, fabric easily changes shape and readily responds to many ways of handling. In addition, most fabrics are less likely to be torn into small pieces that your baby might try to swallow. Still, it's a good idea to supervise this play. Your baby might ball up a piece of cloth and fit it in her mouth.

If you like, occasionally give your baby pieces of different fabrics to explore. Choose those with interesting textures, such as corduroy, flannel, terry cloth, fake fur, velvet, and the like. Make sure each fabric is colorfast and safe for chewing.

Of course, your baby will explore almost any cloth within her reach—even if it's her father's new necktie!

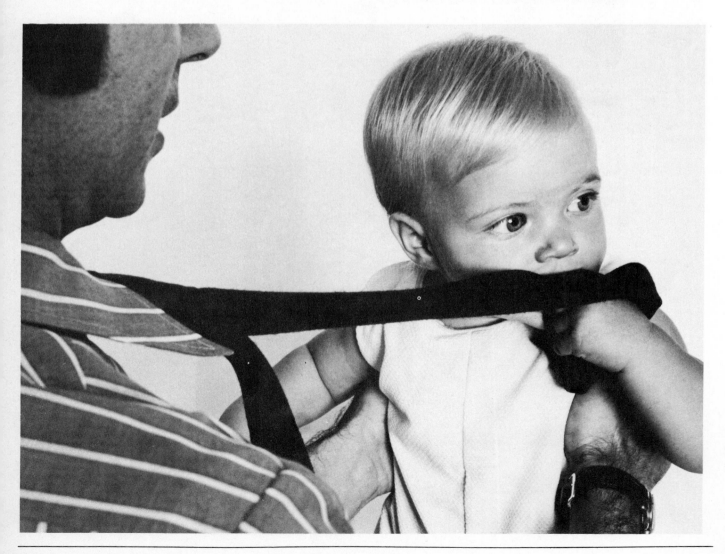

Touching and Holding

Objects Are Now Handled in Ways That Differ According to Their Size and Character

A baby's interest in the way things *look* and *feel* is increasingly giving way to interest in how things work. At this stage, babies enjoy playing with things that have several parts, especially parts that move. Early explorations of relationships between objects can be undertaken with a set of nesting cups, with small blocks, and with 1-piece clothespins that babies can put into a plastic tub and empty out again. Your baby will be increasingly interested in the objects you use to care for her. She will also be more attentive to the ways you use her playthings, and she will begin to imitate the things you do with them.

This baby is trying to fit one cup inside another.

More complicated exploration of objects takes more concentration, and your baby won't like interruptions any more than you do when you're in the middle of something. She may now object strongly when you try to take away an object she is busily exploring.

This baby has learned to put a block inside a cup — and now she discovers it will come out again when the cup is tipped.

The more an object changes when a baby plays with it, the more enjoyment it provides.

Holding her own feeding bottle is more than another example of increasing ability to use arms, hands, and fingers together. It is also a step toward increasing independence.

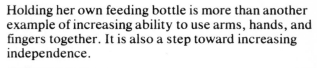

Uses Objects as Tools

When babies use objects to bang and hit, they are learning that objects can be used to make things happen. These are the earliest experiments with a vital human skill — the ability to use tools.

Tool use is as much a reflection of the baby's developing intelligence as it is a reflection of developing motor abilities. Using tools requires 2 important mental abilities — having a goal in mind and using objects in ways that help to achieve that goal.

 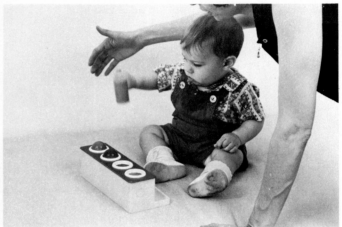

Our principal tools are our hands. They let us manipulate the objects that surround us so we can shape the environments we live in to suit our needs, our interests, and our imaginations.

Touching and Holding

Uses Objects as Tools

The objects we hold expand the tool functions of the hand. The early hitting and waving movements of babies develop into mature skills of the sort that allowed these workmen to make their barrels.

From: **L'Encyclopédie, ou Dictionnaire Raisonné des Sciences, des Arts et des Métiers.** Paris, 1751. Reprinted in: Charles Coulston Gillespie (Editor), **A Diderot Pictorial Encyclopedia.** New York: Dover Publications Inc., 1959

Transfers Objects from One Hand to the Other

A baby's ability to pass an object from hand to hand is another step toward independent but coordinated movement of the arms and hands. This ability also prepares the way for transferring an object from the preferred hand to the other hand so that a second object can be grasped.

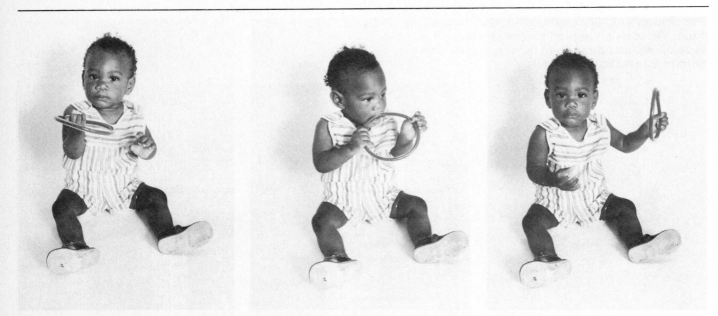

Increasingly independent movements of each hand allow your baby to hold 2 objects at once. At first, she rarely uses the 2 objects in combination. However, by 9 months of age, she holds them together to compare them visually, and she will touch them together, bang them together, try to fit them together, and try to put one inside the other. In general, she will try to do more with the 2 objects than she can do with either one alone. Between 9 and 12 months, many babies can take a third, and even a fourth object. They often store objects in one hand, in their laps, or on a nearby surface so they can grasp something new with their free hand.

Touching and Holding

9-12 Months

**Uses a Cup with Less Spillage,
and Attempts "Self-Feeding" with a Spoon**

Some parents find it hard to let their baby handle her own
feeding spoons and cups because she is slow, clumsy,
and messy. But, to the extent to which you are able,
allowing your baby opportunities to help feed herself can
contribute to her independence and self-esteem.

This baby shows the same interest in her feeding cup that
she shows in her toys. Through months of practice, she
has learned to use it with skill and confidence.

 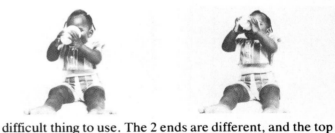

At 6 months, a baby grabs his feeding spoon because it is
another interesting shiny object. At 9 to 12 months, he
grabs it so that he can try to feed himself. He has begun to
understand its purpose, and he has gained the self-
confidence to try using it. Of course, a spoon is a rather
difficult thing to use. The 2 ends are different, and the top
and bottom sides are different. And, as if that weren't
enough, every time something new is put in the spoon, it
has to be handled in a slightly different way. No wonder
learning to use it well takes a long time.

  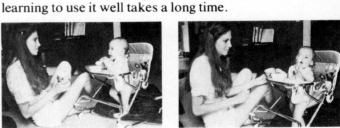

Some of the grip positions that 10-to 12-month-old babies
use to hold a spoon are shown in these drawings.
Through months of practice, babies learn to stop using
grip positions (a) and (b) because these don't allow good
control of the spoon. They learn to use positions (c) and
(d) because these positions allow a baby to bring a spoon
to his mouth with greater success.

Adapted from: Kevin Connolly,
"The growth of skill," in
Roger Lewin, editor, *Child Alive!*,
New York: Doubleday Anchor Books, 1975.

 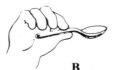

A   **B**   **C**   **D**

Touching and Holding

Holds Small Objects between the Tips of the Thumb and Index Finger

At around 9 months, your baby is much better at grasping small objects. He learns to approach them with thumb and index finger alone. By the end of the first year he will be able to grasp them between the tips of his thumb and index finger. A closely related skill consists of the ability to use the index finger alone, to point, poke, and pry.

This baby is learning to pick up small objects. He is pressing the raisin between the tip of his thumb and the *side* of his index finger. He will soon be able to hold it between the tips of both his thumb and index finger—a position that allows him to manipulate such small objects without dropping them.

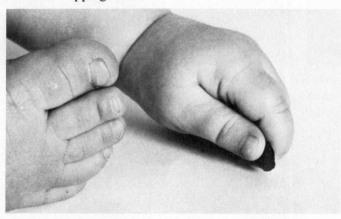

You can help the development of these skills by letting your baby handle "finger foods"—small pieces of fruit, cheese, crackers, chopped foods, raisins, grapes and so forth. You can also make sure he has some soft playthings to poke at with his index finger.

Touching and Holding

9 - 12 Months

Shows Objects, but Usually Doesn't Let Go of Them

During the last quarter of this first year of life, your baby usually extends and shows you a toy when you ask her to. Sometimes she does this without being told. Extending an object toward another person is almost always interpreted by adults as an offer to take the object. Well, you have a surprise in store! When you act on your instincts and reach out to take the object, your baby may be surprised or even annoyed. She had no intention of letting it go. Imagine, you are already facing a "generation gap" problem! The best way out of this is to make it into a game — a gentle "tug-of-war" — which most babies will enjoy, especially if you let them win.

Touching and Holding

Drops and Throws Objects

No one knows all the reasons why babies take such a liking to throwing things to the floor. But we do know 2 of the reasons why babies like to drop and throw things. First, they are learning how to let go of things when they want to let go of them, and they enjoy practicing this new skill over and over again. And, when they first start dropping things, they realize that different objects move in different ways, and make different sounds when they land. So dropping things also becomes a way of learning more about the properties of objects and how things work.

Within limits, picking things up and handing them back to your baby can be an enjoyable game. But when the game becomes tedious or annoying, you can stop returning them, allowing your baby to empty her crib of small objects and letting them pile up about the room until a convenient time to gather them again. Just make sure that some larger things are left for her to play with, and that some of her favorite toys are tied by strings, so that she still has plenty to do after all of her dropping and throwing is finished.

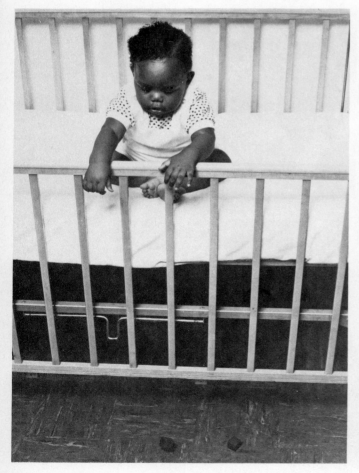
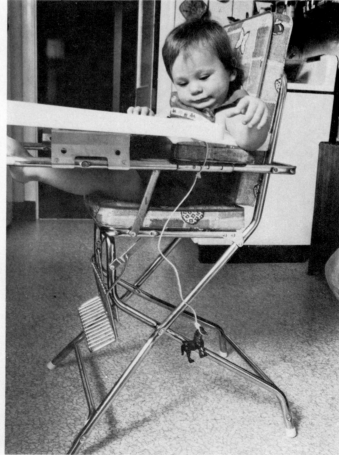

Touching and Holding

A Baby Uses Objects to Assist the Growth of Understanding

In the final 3 months of the first year, more and more of a baby's handling of objects seems designed to help the growth of understanding. Fitting one thing inside another is a first lesson in understanding "bigger" and "smaller." It is also a lesson in understanding that things which fit inside one another can disappear, and then reappear.

When a baby pulls on a string to get a toy, we are seeing growth in his ability to influence his environment, as well as an opportunity to learn "cause and effect" relationships between a tug on the string and the availability of the toy.

In earlier months, you saw your baby occasionally put one thing inside another. Sometimes this happened almost by accident. Now dropping objects inside containers and taking them out again becomes an important form of play. It occupies your baby's attention for long periods of time. You and your baby can take turns dropping things into containers. You can also help her discover different ways to get the things out again.

Touching and Holding

**A Baby Uses Objects to Assist the Growth
of Understanding**

It is harder to put plastic cups inside one another than it is
to drop little blocks into a large plastic bucket. But
toward the end of the first year, your baby will be able to
put one cup inside another cup. At first she may need a
little help.

Small wooden blocks continue to be interesting because
they can be brought together in different ways, and used
for simple construction projects. By 1 year of age,
some babies are able to put one block on top of another,
and have it remain there. It is usually a somewhat
crooked tower because even though she knows what she
wants to do, once the second block is properly placed on
top of the first, she may not be able to let go fast enough
for it to remain in place. This problem corrects itself as
her ability to release things improves. At this stage it
may be easier for her to stack plastic cups. They are
larger than blocks and easier to handle.

Objects contribute to the growth of understanding in
forms of play, such as

    swinging objects tied to strings

    taking lids off, and putting them on

    standing things up, and knocking them over again

    swinging cabinet doors back and forth

    turning light switches on and off

    pressing a lever to get a ''jack-in-the-box'' to appear

    opening and closing books that have thick pages

    turning doorknobs.

Between 9 and 18 months, infants spend almost half of
their waking hours inspecting and manipulating objects.
The physical environment becomes a laboratory in which
the infant labors to enlarge her understanding of the laws
that govern experience. Objects are the equipment for
her ceaseless experiments.

Touching and Holding

A Baby Uses Objects to Assist the Growth of Understanding

Of all the objects that infants enjoy experimenting with, water holds a particular fascination. Perhaps this is because water can react in so many ways. Bath time provides a wonderful opportunity for exploration — and washcloths, sponges, soap, things that float, and things that squirt all help to widen opportunities for exploratory play. When a baby is not in the tub, her interest in water is still keen, and most babies discover that a supply of water is ready at all times— in the toilet bowl. This is a particularly tempting place to play after your baby learns to pull herself to a standing position. You can, of course, provide some attractive alternatives. Sturdy, generous-sized, and inexpensive plastic containers are easily available, and they can be used to provide water-play experiences almost anywhere.

Your baby will also be developing her understanding of the proper uses of objects. She will try to put a shoe on her foot, and she will hold out her arms and legs in an effort to help you dress her.

As your baby engages in more and more exploratory play, it is important to supply new and challenging objects. Once an object has been thoroughly explored, babies become bored with it — at least for the moment. You may want to put some of your baby's toys away for awhile so she can be surprised when you give them back again. Many babies prefer the toys used by their 2-and-3-year-old brothers and sisters to their own toys. When such an interest is shown, it is helpful if you can get the older children to share some of their toys with the baby. A good way to do this is to ask the older children to help you find some new things the baby might like to play with.

Your job as the manager of your infant's environment during these early years of active exploration has 2 important aspects. One aspect involves ensuring that your child has experiences that are sufficiently varied and challenging. This is the aspect we have discussed the most. The other aspect involves anticipating and avoiding objects and situations that threaten your infant's safety. Baby-proofing the kitchen and bathroom requires particular care.

Touching and Holding

9 - 12 Months

Your Examples and Encouragement Strongly Influence the Way Your Baby Handles Objects

By the end of his first year of life, your baby can handle objects with great skill. In addition, he is now attentive to the ways you handle objects, and likes to imitate the things you do, especially the things that please you. You will be surprised to see how quickly your baby will do something he has never done before, once you have shown him how it is done, and encouraged him to copy you. Playing now involves much more cooperation between the two of you.

This baby watches carefully while her mother builds a tower out of plastic cups. She then takes her turn at trying to do the same thing.

This baby has held a truck before. He has put it in his mouth, and he has waved it and banged it. But he doesn't roll it on the floor, imitating the actual motion and sound of a truck, until he is shown how.

Crude attempts at scribbling are now possible. But first you will have to show your baby how to hold a crayon.

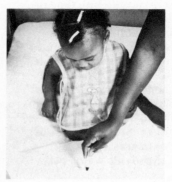 

Some of the other things babies do once they are given good demonstrations are: wearing a "necklace" of beads, hugging a doll, putting clothes on a doll, "walking" a toy animal, and wrapping things up.

208

4. Seeing

Visual Abilities of the Newborn Baby

When does a baby begin to see? As soon as he is born. Newborn infants distinguish light from dark and perceive at least several colors. They look at faces and other objects; they prefer simple patterns to solid colors; and they move their eyes to follow a slowly moving object.

During the early weeks of his life, your baby will stare at lights, windows, and bright walls. This baby is looking at the light from a small flashlight.

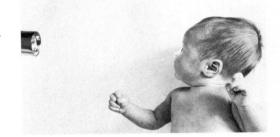

If a light is too bright, your baby will blink his eyes. This is 1 of the reflexes that help babies to be comfortable in a world they cannot yet control.

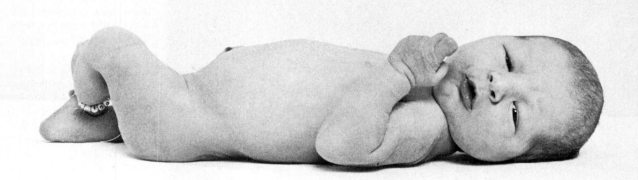

Visual Abilities of the Newborn Baby

A newborn also looks at your face and at simple patterns. At this age he cannot get a clear image of things if they are too close or too far away from his eyes. He usually sees objects best if they are somewhere between 8 and 12 inches away.

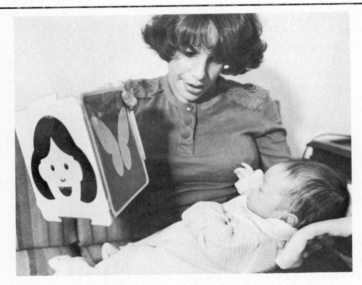

In the first few weeks, your baby will move his eyes to follow an object when you move it slowly in front of him. These eye movements are not very smooth until 3 to 6 weeks of age. If he is very interested in the object, he may also move his head.

Your baby also has a reflex that protects her when an object moves too close to her face. She pulls her head back, and holds her arms and hands between the object and her face.

Even a 1-to 4-day-old infant gets bored looking at the same thing for too long. In 1 experiment, newborn infants were shown a pattern with large checks for 60-second periods of time — again and again — until they looked at it much less than they had been doing. Then they were shown a pattern with small checks. Their attention picked up immediately and their looking time increased.

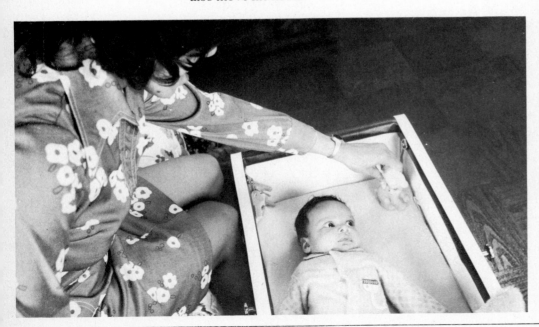

Seeing

Parents Can Influence the Ways Their Babies Look at the World

Here are some ways you can help your baby to enjoy looking at the world around her:

1. Handle her in ways that help her to be alert and interested in you and the objects that are nearby.

2. Bring interesting objects close enough for her to see clearly.

3. Carry her to objects that she can't see well without your help, like interesting wallpaper, and flowers in the garden.

4. Let her see how interested *you* are in looking at things, and point out some of the interesting things you are looking at to give them special emphasis.

5. Show your pleasure when she looks at objects carefully, and talk to her about the things she looks at.

6. The more you share your own visual experience, the more visual interest she will show on her own.

Looking around is one of the most important ways very young babies learn about their environment. Varied visual experiences hold a baby's attention and provide him with opportunities for learning to see things clearly; to tell the difference between one thing and another; and to understand what he is looking at. Many forms of handling increase his visual alertness and decrease his tendency to be bored and listless.

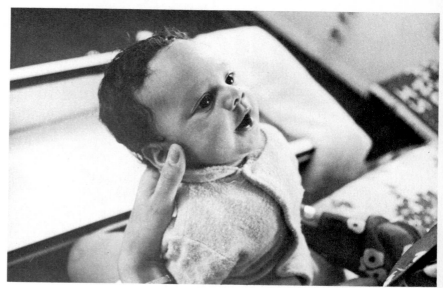

Seeing

Parents Can Influence the Ways Their Babies Look at the World

Picking up a baby and holding him against your shoulder
is 1 of the most effective ways of increasing his visual
alertness. Even a crying baby will usually quiet down,
open his eyes wide, and look about if held to your
shoulder.

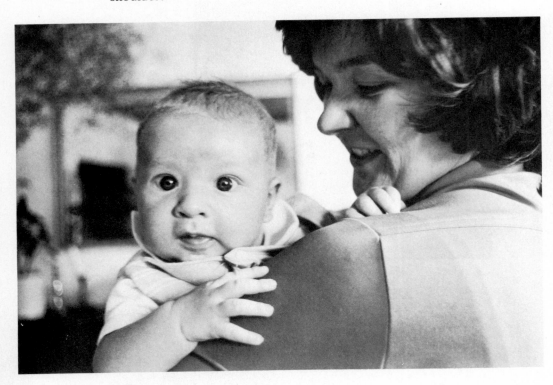

Seeing

**Looking at Objects Produces Changes
in a Baby's Body Movements**

When babies are a few weeks old, they begin to stare at
objects more and more. When this first starts to happen,
your baby stops his body movements for a little while,
and gives his entire attention to looking. When he has had
more experience looking at objects, he also shows excitement when he sees something that interests him, and his
arms and legs begin to move.

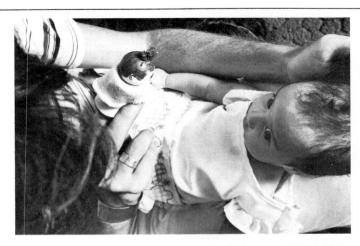

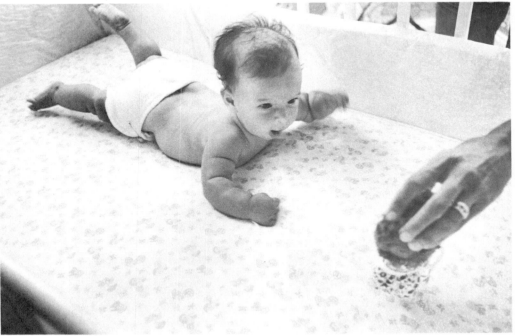

Enjoys Looking at Slowly Moving Objects

After 6 weeks of age, your baby is more alert and spends
more time following moving objects with his eyes.
Between 6 weeks and 3 months, he learns to follow moving objects quite accurately, even when they are held
several feet in front of him and are moved fairly rapidly.

The 6-to 10-week-old baby will look at almost any object
you move in front of his eyes. By 3 months, your baby
will take a quick look at a new object, but he won't keep
looking at it unless he is interested in it — even if you
hold it directly in front of him.

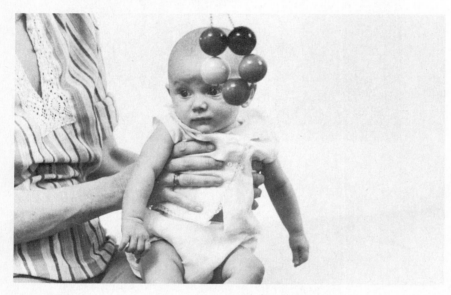

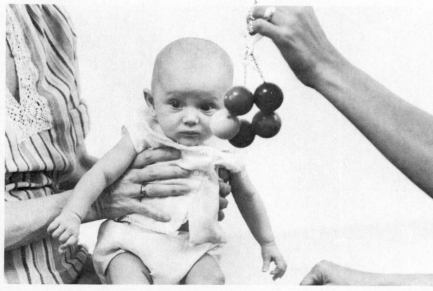

Seeing

Enjoys Looking at Slowly Moving Objects

This baby is looking at a large ring tied to a string. The baby follows the ring with her eyes as it is moved slowly from one side of her head to the center. This simple game gives her eye muscles practice in moving together smoothly.

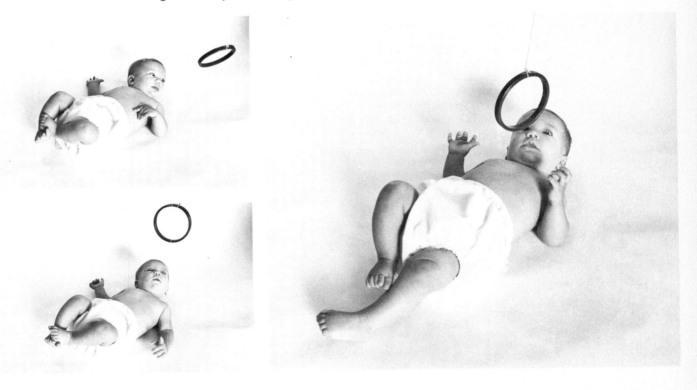

If your baby doesn't notice an object you are holding, you can jiggle it, tap on it, or use an object that makes a sound, like the bell this baby is looking at.

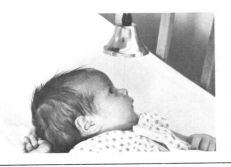
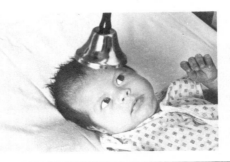
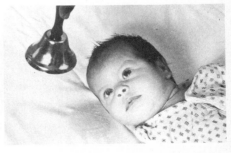

Seeing

Enjoys Looking at Faces

Babies only a few days old will look longer at a simple drawing of a face than at bright colors.

Experiments in which babies look at simple drawings of faces show that they look at them in different ways as they develop. The 1-month-old baby tends to look at the outside features of the face — the hairline, chin, and ears. The 2-month-old baby tends to look at the inside features of the face — the eyes, mouth, and nose. Between 1 and 2 months you may notice that your baby first looks at the outside of your face — moving his eyes from your hairline, down to your chin. Then he looks at the inside of your face — bringing his eyes back up from your chin to your eyes. When he looks at your eyes, he may break into a smile. At first this is more likely to happen if you smile also, and if you talk and move your head at the same time.

Your baby's preference for real faces grows during the first 3 months of life. By 3 months of age, he may still smile at a picture or drawing of a face, but he is far more likely to smile at a real face.

Seeing

Enjoys Looking at Faces

At first, episodes of eye-to-eye contact between you and your baby are brief. Later, he will stare at your face and other faces for longer periods of time. However, even the early, fleeting episodes of eye-to-eye contact are a form of social behavior. This is an exciting new experience for your baby and for all the people who want to be close to him.

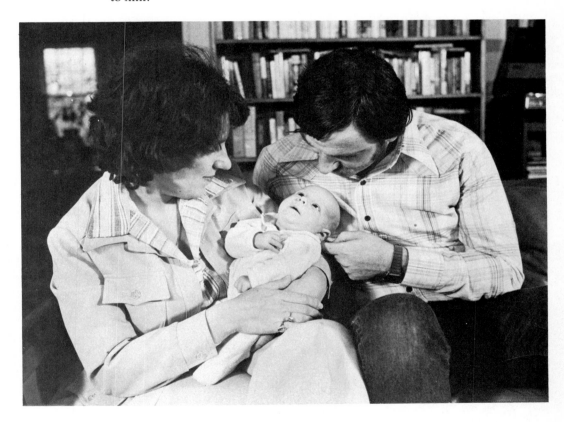

Seeing

Enjoys Looking at Faces

Eye-to-eye contact is an enjoyable early form of play,
and a parent quickly learns that touching and holding the
baby, as well as making sounds, add to their joint
pleasure in looking at one another.

Babies like to look at objects that are similar to things
they've seen before but different enough to arouse their
curiosity. Faces have the ability to keep changing
expression without changing so much that we can't
recognize them. This probably contributes to the special
interest babies have in faces.

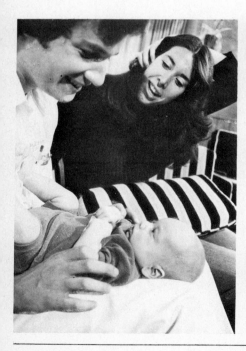 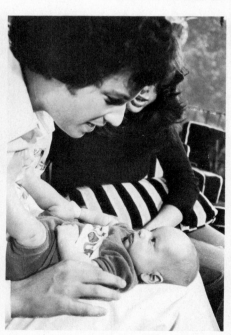 

Seeing

Enjoys Looking at Patterns

We tend to associate bright colors with childhood, and many parents are careful to see that the things they buy for their baby are colorful, because color adds cheerfulness to an infant's room. However, young infants are more interested in looking at patterns than they are in looking at colors. Patterns such as checkerboards, bull's-eyes, large geometric shapes, and simple outlines of animals and other forms attract a young baby's attention. Patterns interest babies most when they are printed in dark colors, such as black, blue, red, and green, against light backgrounds.

You can draw simple patterns like the ones in these photographs, or you can cut simple patterns from magazines. Make sure your patterns are large and bold. If you use colors, use dark colors such as red, green, and blue — so they will stand out against the lighter background of the paper or cardboard you put them on.

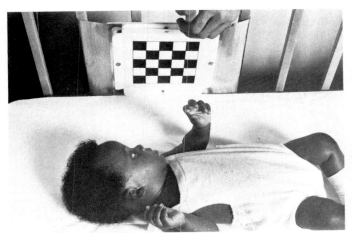

The preference of babies for looking at patterns over colors was first demonstrated by Dr. Robert Fantz. He measured the length of time infants looked at different test cards. Some of the cards had simple patterns on them, such as a face or a bull's-eye. Others were painted with solid colors — white, yellow, and red. He found that infants a few days old looked longer at the face and the bull's-eye than at the colored cards. The same preferences were shown by infants 2 to 6 months old.

Seeing

Enjoys Looking at Patterns

From 2 to 3 months of age, babies begin to prefer pictures that have 3-dimensional qualities and they like to look at 3-dimensional objects more and more.

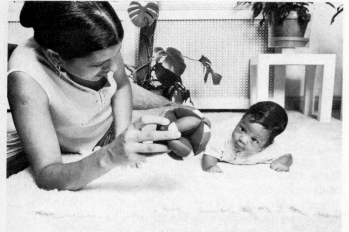

In fact, the 2-to 3-month-old baby enjoys looking at pictures so much that it is not too early to show her books that have simple and bold illustrations.

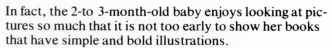

Although babies a few weeks old have visual preferences, they will look for some time at most of the things you hold in front of them. From 2 to 3 months of age, they become more discriminating, preferring to look at some things much more than others. Your baby prefers some pictures more than others not only because she can now examine complex patterns better than she could before, but also because she is developing as an individual with tastes of her own.

Seeing

Babies Become Excited when They See Objects They Will Soon Be Able to Grasp

By 2 months of age, babies are looking at objects in a very "hungry" way, as if they just can't wait to touch and play with them. Their excitement is communicated by their entire bodies. They not only stare at objects intently, their shoulders also hunch forward toward the object, their arms and legs make jerking movements toward the object, and even their tongues sometimes point toward the things they want to get at. If the object being looked at is moved, the baby shifts his body to keep it in sight. There is a build-up of tension and excitement as if to say, "I know what I want — but I can't get at it yet by myself." In part, the baby's movements communicate his *interest* in the objects around him, and in part they communicate his urgent *need* to have adults hand him the things he wants to hold.

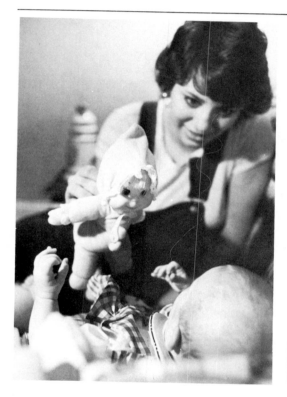

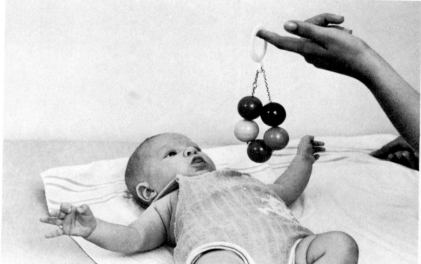

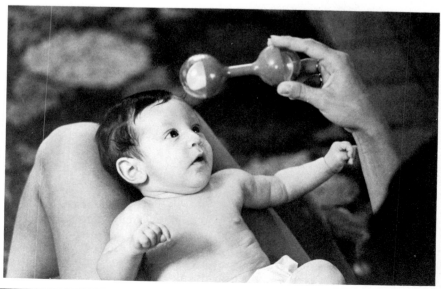

Seeing

Looks at His Hands for Long Periods of Time

Sometime between 1 and 2 months you will notice your baby give an occasional glance toward his outstretched arm and hand. Soon he will begin looking at it for longer periods of time until finally he begins staring at it with the same concentration he has shown when looking at lights, slowly moving objects, faces, and patterns.

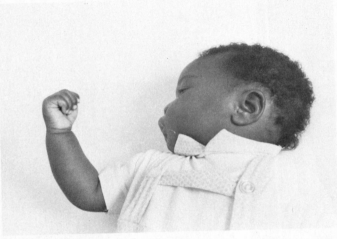

No one knows why a baby becomes so interested in looking at his own arms and hands. Perhaps it's because they are often in the baby's line of sight.

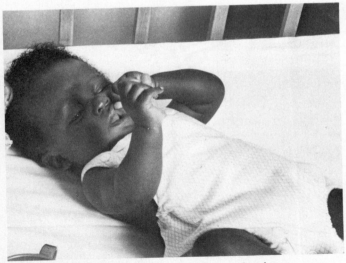

As the hand opens more, and the fingers begin to move about, the "hand show" becomes increasingly interesting to watch.

These experiences help to coordinate the movements of the baby's eyes with the movements of the arm and hand.

Seeing

By 2 to 3 Months, Babies Can Keep an Object in Focus from Several Feet Away to 4 to 6 Inches in Front of Their Eyes

When you hold your index finger directly in front of your eyes and then move it as far away as you can, your image of the finger remains clear. The ability of the eyes to move closer together as an object being looked at gets closer to the face is an important part of being able to keep it in clear focus. Babies are learning to do this between 2 and 3 months, and by 4 months they do it as well as adults.

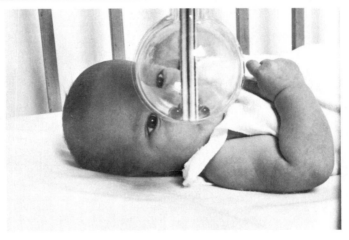

When you move a familiar and interesting object toward your baby's face, you will now be able to see her eyes move closer together as the object gets closer to her face. She is learning how to keep the object in focus no matter how close or distant it is.

A baby now enjoys watching an object as you lift it higher and higher above his head, and then lower it again.

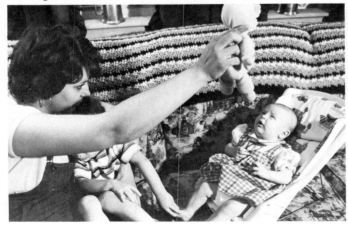

Seeing

**By 3 Months Babies Examine Objects Carefully,
and They Recognize Familiar Things**

Three-month-old babies look at objects with great intensity and for long periods of time. When an object your baby enjoys looking at comes into view, notice how quickly he becomes alert and gives his attention to it. Sometimes he will raise his arms as a way of showing interest in an object. He may become very alert and interested when you bring a favorite object, such as a feeding bottle, into view.

Seeing

**Your Baby Now Watches What Is Going on
in All Parts of the Room**

As your baby becomes able to see things clearly at a distance, and as her curiosity grows, she appreciates being "where the action is." She wants to be in the rooms where the other people are and in places where lots of things are going on.

Seeing

Babies Like to Look at Some Colors More than Others

We have recently learned more about how babies see colors. Researchers are making use of the fact that babies get bored with sights that don't change to find out whether babies can tell colors apart.

In 1 experiment, 4-month-old babies were shown a colored light. When they became bored and stopped looking at it, the experimenter changed it. If the light was simply changed to another shade of the same color, the baby showed little interest. But if the light was changed to another color altogether, the baby definitely spent more time looking at it. The babies in this experiment could tell the difference between blue, green, yellow, and red.

Besides seeing colors much as we do, babies also have color preferences like ours. Another experiment showed that 4-month-old infants looked longer at blue and red lights than at green and yellow lights. The experimenters went on to ask adults to rate the lights according to how pleasant they were to look at. Without knowing what the babies had done, the adults rated the blue and red lights more pleasant to look at than the green and yellow lights.

Of course, these experiments tell just part of the story of how babies see and respond to colors. Like the rest of us, babies have some interest in all colors, and they also develop individual color preferences.

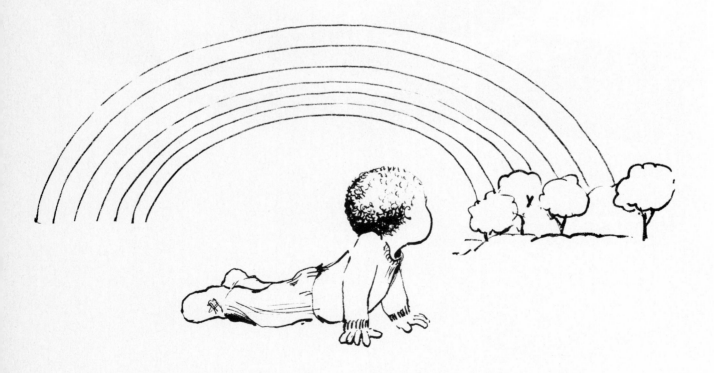

Seeing

Babies Enjoy Looking into Mirrors

A mirror is one of the most exciting things babies can play with. They are delighted to see their own images and the reflections of other people. When your baby sees his own face, he becomes particularly excited. He may smile or laugh and experiment with other changes in expression. He may reach toward the mirror and touch it or pat it. Sometimes he kisses it, and he may even look behind it to find the "other baby." He also makes sounds that express his interest and pleasure.

When does the baby realize that he is looking at his own face? Most people who have watched babies younger than a year old playing with mirrors feel that the babies don't yet know they are looking at themselves, and when babies look behind the mirror to find the "other baby," it's quite clear that they don't yet understand what is really going on. Recently, an ingenious experiment has shown when babies realize they are seeing themselves. A small colored spot is put on the baby's nose. If — while looking in a mirror — he reaches up to his *own* nose to touch this strange new spot, he must realize he is looking at an image of *himself*. Some babies do this as early as 15 months of age.

Why are mirrors so fascinating to babies? We can only guess at the answer. The fact that the baby sees a face probably accounts for a large part of his interest. We have already discussed the interest shown in faces by even very young babies. The fact that the scene in the mirror is responsive to what he does is probably an additional source of pleasure and interest.

Many of the mirrors in your home can be safely used for play under close supervision. And there are now a number of unbreakable mirrors that have been made specifically for babies to play with when alone.

Unbreakable mirrors can be used in almost any setting, and they can be conveniently carried along on trips as well.

Seeing

Looks at Small Objects

During the early months of life, your baby attended to large, nearby objects. Now he will be giving increasing attention to objects that are small. You can provide him with opportunities to practice by holding close to his eyes some of the small objects he shows an interest in. His ability to look at small things, and even reach out and grasp them, greatly expand the range of objects available to him for exploration.

This baby is looking at the small plastic balls that move about inside his rattle.

These babies are looking at small objects as if they want to reach for them. Sometimes they do reach for them and touch them in a rather cautious way. Just as he learned about large objects, your baby first comes to know small objects through sight, and only then combines his looking with handling.

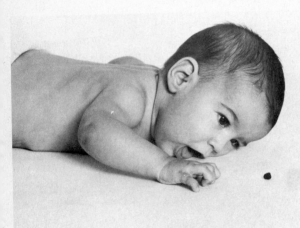

Seeing

As Reaching and Grasping Improve, Babies Spend More Time Looking at Objects They Want to Hold

From 3 to 6 months there are remarkable improvements in the baby's ability to reach and grasp. Almost any object within reach will be looked at and then grasped.

As your baby's reaching and grasping movements become more skillful, she will spend less time looking at her hand as it reaches out. This is particularly true for objects she is familiar with.

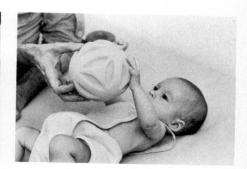

From 3 to 6 months of age, a baby becomes very good at recognizing objects that are graspable — even when they are out of reach. In addition to staring at them, she begins to reach her arms out toward them. But you will often have to help bring objects your baby stares at close enough so she can reach them.

Seeing

Babies Enjoy Looking at Facial Expressions

We have already discussed the great interest babies show in drawings and photographs of faces, as well as in actual faces. From 3 to 6 months your baby will show more and more interest in your facial *expressions* — and he will, in turn, make use of an increasingly wide range of facial expressions to communicate his interests and feelings to you.

Speaking to your baby becomes easier and more enjoyable now, because of the close attention he pays to the changes in your facial expression when you make sounds. He will often make sounds in reply. These early "conversations" help the baby to learn speech sounds. They also help him to pay close attention to another fascinating aspect of faces — their ability to communicate by sound as well as by appearance.

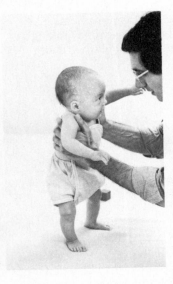

Seeing

**Babies Come to Enjoy More Complex
and Realistic Pictures**

As their visual abilities improve, babies like to see more
challenging pictures. They enjoy looking at pictures that
have more details and that are more realistic in character.
Photographs now interest them more than simple
patterns.

Seeing

**More Time Is Now Spent Closely Examining
Objects with Eyes and Hands**

As your baby learns to handle objects with increasing skill, her eyes and hands work together to carefully examine the appearance, size, shape, and feel of everything within reach.

This baby has noticed a small, clear plastic block — possibly because it reflects light and magnifies. Every time he changes its position, he sees something new.

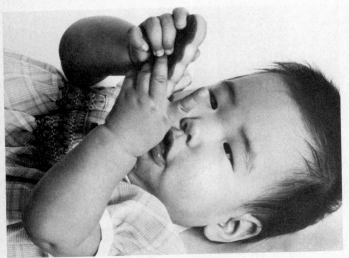
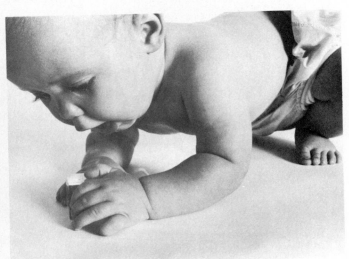

This baby is exploring the ball with a tried and true method — feeling it with his mouth. But that isn't a very good method for getting to know about something so large. Now eyes and hands can take over to examine it more thoroughly.

Seeing

Fascinated by Tiny Objects

The ability to see very fine details improves throughout
the first year of life. When such new sensory abilities
develop, babies like to use them repeatedly, just the way
they like to practice new motor skills. So you will see
your baby looking at smaller and smaller objects. She
becomes fascinated by the smallest things, such as
cracker crumbs or a loose thread on the carpet.

Seeing

Learns to Understand Depth

A baby's ability to understand depth has been studied using the device shown in the photograph below, designed by Dr. Richard Walk and Dr. Eleanor Gibson. It is a well that has a shallow portion and a deep portion. Both portions are covered by a thick sheet of glass. Infants 1 to 3 months of age show no fear when they are placed on the glass directly over the deep side. They can't yet perceive the depth and the danger that goes with it. But 7-to 9-month-old babies *do* show fear when placed on the glass over the deep side — and they refuse to crawl across the glass from the shallow side to the deep side even when their mothers encourage them.

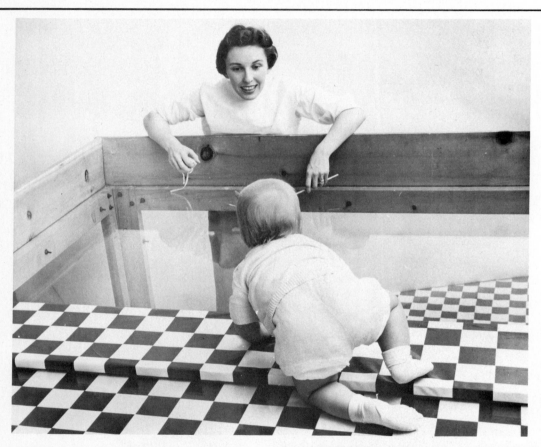

Your baby develops his sense of depth by crawling around and combining what he sees with the changes in positions of his body. But during the first year of life, his awareness of the danger involved in crawling over steps and other ledges is inconsistent. Therefore, you can't trust his developing sense of depth to keep him from crawling over a ledge and hurting himself.

Seeing

Loses Interest in a Toy if It Is Covered Up

When you hand a 5-to 6-month-old baby an interesting toy, he takes it from you very quickly and plays with it. But if you bring the toy into the baby's view and then cover it with a cloth, he shows no interest in it at all. He may even be surprised to see the toy again when you lift the cloth. It looks as if an object that is out of the baby's sight is also out of mind.

In recent years Dr. T.G.R. Bower and other researchers have been testing the ''out of sight, out of mind'' idea — and they find things aren't quite that simple.

If a baby is shown an interesting toy and the room lights are turned out before he begins to reach, he has no trouble grasping the toy in the dark. The toy is still very much in mind, even though it can't be seen.

But if the toy is covered by a transparent cup, the baby does lose interest in it, even though it can be seen.

It seems that the baby loses interest in a toy when it is covered up because he hasn't yet learned that things can be *inside of* other things.

By about 8 to 9 months of age, babies *keep their interest* in a toy even after it is covered with a cloth — and they will lift the cloth to get their toy back.

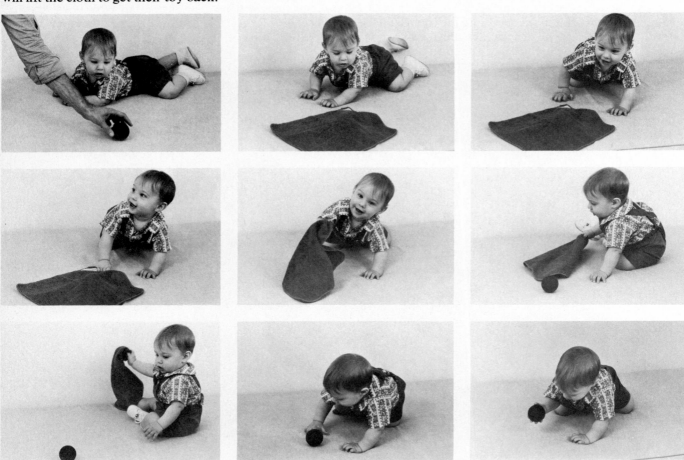

Seeing

Enjoys Looking at Other Children Playing

Babies now enjoy looking at scenes as much as they enjoy looking at people and objects. They show particular interest in other babies and young children at play. Once again, the eyes give clues about your baby's changing interests. The way she looks at children playing reveals her growing interest in social experiences. It is a preview of the expanded social life that will unfold during the second year of life.

Seeing

Crawling Is Often Interrupted to Look at Interesting Objects

The ability to crawl makes many more objects available for examination. You will often see your baby interrupt her crawling when a new object comes into view. She may just stare at it awhile — and then start moving again. Or she may pause to examine it more closely with eyes and hands together.

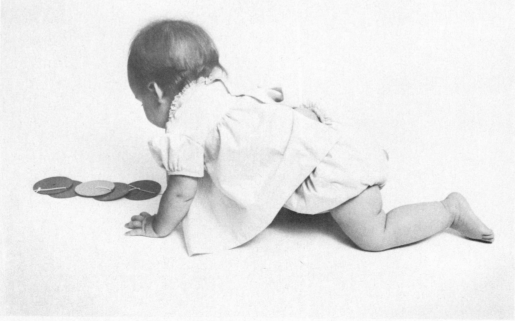

Wants to Get Back Toys that Have Fallen Out of Sight

From 6 months on, your baby has been showing more and more interest in looking after objects that have fallen from view. At first she looked briefly in the direction of the fall and then quickly turned her attention to something else. But as her understanding of how objects move through space grows, she becomes more persistent in wanting to get back things that have dropped out of sight. She seems to realize that they must still be nearby. The question is — where?

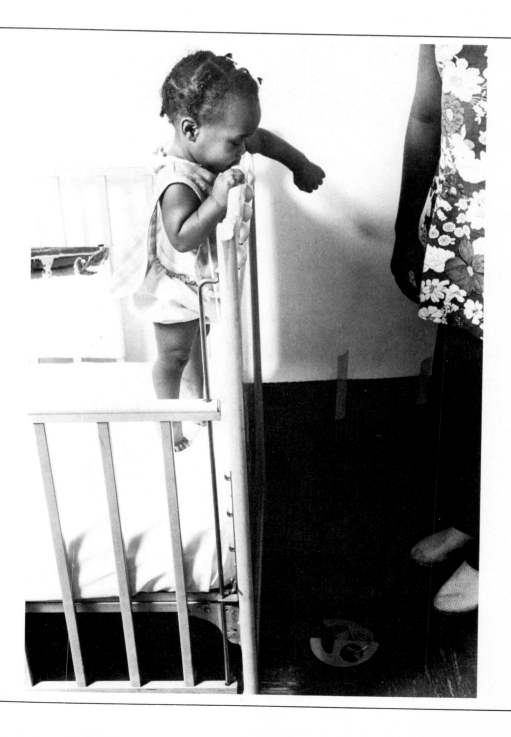

Seeing

Interested in Books that Are Easy to Handle

The baby's close visual inspection of complex patterns and her ability to manipulate objects skillfully with both hands contribute a great deal to her growing enjoyment of books.

5. Hearing

Babies Can Hear before They Are Born

Your baby can hear before he is born. The womb is a noisy place. The mother's heartbeat, her digestive noises, and the rush of blood through the vessels that go from mother to baby and back again all reach the baby through the fluids in which he lives. He can also hear his mother's speech. Hearing these sounds may help him to develop the ability to listen.

Hearing

Newborn Babies React to Sounds Differently when They Are Awake, Sleeping, Feeding, and Crying

When she is awake and alert and she hears a sound, your baby may move her arms and legs or even her fingers. Her eyes may also open wide or she may blink. A really loud sound will startle her.

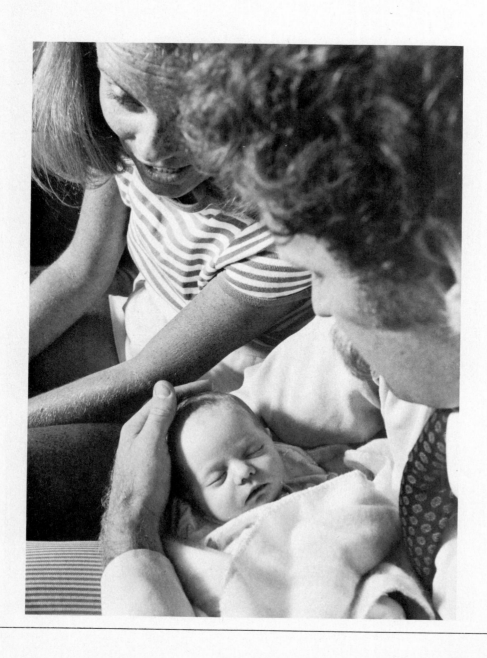

Hearing

Newborn Babies React to Sounds Differently when They Are Awake, Sleeping, Feeding, and Crying

When your baby is nursing and she hears a sound, she may stop sucking or she may suck even harder.

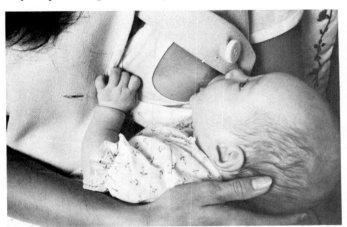 

If your baby is getting ready to cry and her arms and legs are waving about, speaking to her may calm her down. Steady noises from an air conditioner or a vacuum cleaner in another room may keep her quiet for a long time.

Hearing

Birth - 3 Months

Babies Look to See Where a Sound Comes From

Early in life, some babies will begin turning to see where sounds are coming from. At first they may not look in the right direction.

Babies also know very early that voices go with faces. In 1 study, 3-week-old babies were put in a special seat facing the mother, who was on the other side of a window. The mother talked to the baby in any way she liked. Her voice reached the baby through a loudspeaker placed just above her mouth on the baby's side of the window. After

some time, the mother's voice was suddenly made to come from another speaker located off to one side. The babies made faces showing that they were upset by this switch. They seemed to know that the sound was now coming from the wrong place.

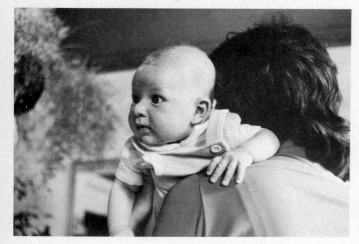
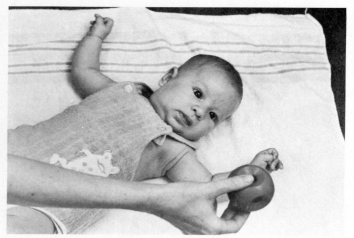

244

Hearing

Babies Respond Differently to Different Sounds

Early in life, babies begin to do different things when they hear different sounds. Very young babies notice only sounds that are of ordinary loudness and sounds that are really loud. They react to these loud sounds by a change in activity or facial expression. If you think that your baby is not hearing loud sounds, ask your doctor to have his hearing checked in a hearing and speech clinic.

A high-pitched noise, like a whistling kettle, may make her "freeze" or cry. For many birds and animals, high-pitched calls are warning calls and cause an instinctive reaction of fear. High-pitched sounds, like a police siren or fire engine noise, make *us* freeze, too.

Your baby is likely to cry when she hears another baby crying. Perhaps it is the high pitches in another baby's sounds of distress which start her off.

Babies can tell us a great deal about what they like to hear when they are given a chance to control the situation. They would rather hear sounds that keep changing than sounds that stay the same. They like music better than steady noises. In 1 experiment, babies sucked on a nipple which was hooked up to a recorder. The recorder showed how long each suck was and how long the pause was between sucks. When music was played to the babies during their sucks, and a steady noise was played during the pauses between sucks, the babies gave longer sucks than before. When a steady noise was played during the sucks and music was played during the pauses, the babies gave longer pauses than before. Your baby will enjoy your singing and the sounds of musical toys very early in life.

Hearing

Babies Listen to Speech in a Special Way

Speech also has very complicated sound patterns. Most everyday sounds are much simpler. Yet babies pay special attention to speech and even to the differences between one speech sound and another. They particularly like it when the speaker uses "singing" pitches.

The baby's interest in speech has been demonstrated in a number of ingenious ways. In 1 study, a 3-month-old boy found that he could turn on a tape recording of his mother talking by kicking a lever at the end of his crib. He kept on kicking after that. Later on, the rules of the game were changed so that he had to make sounds to turn the tape recorder on. At that point he stopped kicking and began to make many sounds. He did whatever he had to do in order to hear his mother talking.

Hearing

Babies Listen to Speech in a Special Way

Babies move in a special way when they hear speech. Slow-motion films show that they wave their arms and legs to keep time with the speech they hear, even if it is in a foreign language. They behave like an adult who nods his head and moves his body as he listens to a speaker making a point. The babies' movements show that they are sensitive to the rhythms of speech long before they can understand the words.

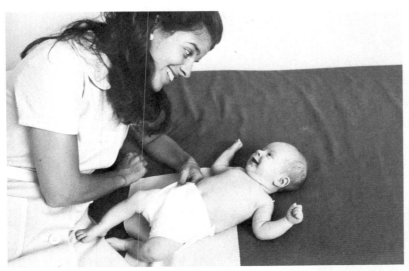

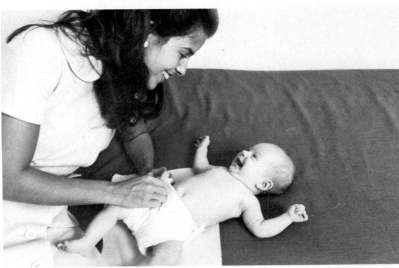

Hearing

Sounds Have More Meaning for Your Baby

Your baby begins to know that sounds mean something. When she hears you working with pots and bottles in the kitchen, she knows you are preparing food and looks for it eagerly. When she hears you getting up in the morning, she stops playing with her mobile or toys and cries for *you*.

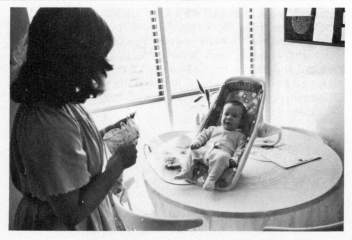

Speech is still the most interesting sound for her. She knows that speech sounds go with people. When she hears talking she becomes excited and looks for people. At 4 or 5 months she notices the difference between the lower voice of her father, the higher voice of her mother, and the very high voices of children. It is as if she knows that these high and low voices go with different people.

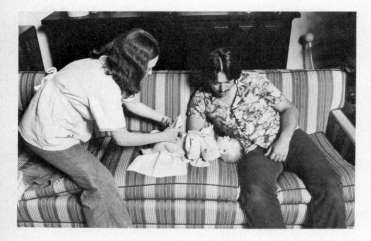

Hearing

He Knows the Differences between Angry and Happy Tones of Voice

Your baby will now react differently when he hears different tones of voice. Sharp, angry voices may cause his face to pucker up, ready to cry. A pleasant voice will make him smile. He is beginning to know how you feel from the way your voice sounds.

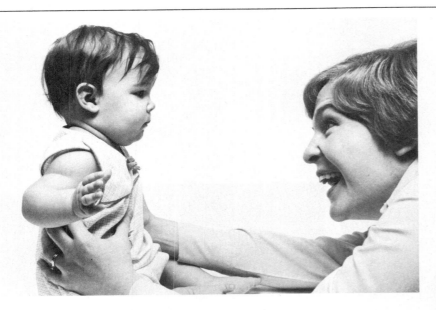

Hearing

**Babies Hear the Differences between One Speech Sound
and Another**

By 4 months, or even earlier, babies can hear the differences between speech sounds like *ba, pa, da,* and *ga*. In a series of research studies, these speech sounds were played to babies while they sucked on a nipple. When a baby heard a single speech sound *ba,* he became interested and sucked faster. But after he heard it for a while, he lost interest and his sucking became slower. When the new speech sound, *pa,* was played to him, he became interested again, and sucked faster. After the baby lost interest in hearing *da,* his interest increased and he sucked faster if he heard *ga*. This is how the researchers learned that he could tell the difference between *ba, pa, da, ga,* and other speech sounds, too. It is much easier to get babies to listen to the differences between speech sounds than to the differences between simple tones.

Hearing

3 - 6 Months

Your Baby Is Getting Better at Finding Where Sounds Are

Your baby is getting better at finding where sounds come from as she grows older. At 6 months of age, she will even try to locate soft sounds, like whispers and the rustling of paper. By then she has become more interested in finding soft sounds than loud sounds.

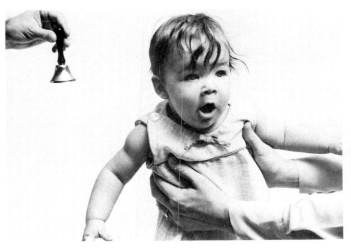

Hearing

He Likes to Hear Himself Talk

A baby, like an adult, enjoys hearing himself talk. He shows his pleasure by repeating the sounds he hears himself making. He also likes to play with sounds, making them longer and shorter, higher and lower, softer and louder.

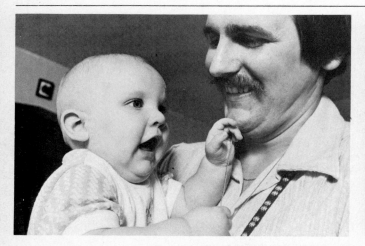

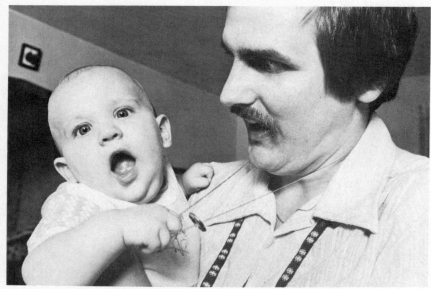

Hearing

Babies Like to Be Talked to in a Special Way

Adults talk to babies in a special way. You will find that you speak more slowly to your baby than you do to adults and that you use exaggerated tones and emphases. These tricks of speech probably help your baby to pay attention. They are also fun for her. So is the sound of children talking. It seems that babies enjoy voices which sound like their own. Mothers and fathers naturally make themselves sound more like children when they talk to babies.

Hearing

Your Baby Sometimes Ignores You when You Talk

Now it is sometimes difficult for you to get your baby's attention by talking to her. This doesn't mean that she is deliberately ignoring you. She's simply absorbed in playing, mouthing toys, and watching interesting movements. But she is aware of what you are doing and will check on you from time to time. She may begin to fuss if you leave the room, or she may try to get your attention if you move away. It is all right for her to ignore you when *she* is busy, but she may not like it if you ignore *her*.

Her ability to pay close attention to interesting objects and events is the first sign of increasing independence. This independence should be encouraged. When she is older, the things you say will have more meaning for her. She will begin to pay close attention to you when you talk about objects and events.

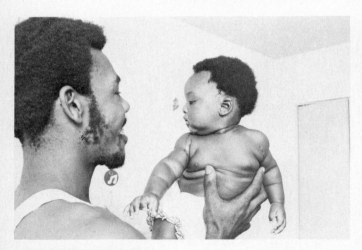

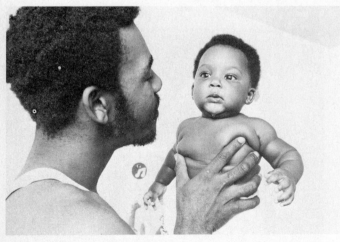

Hearing

**He Knows the Sounds That Go with Familiar Toys
and People**

Your baby now plays with many more toys. He knows
that different toys make different noises. If he shakes a
bell, it rings; if he bangs a spoon, it makes a lovely sharp
sound on his high chair. He will come back to his toys
again and again to make the sounds he likes to hear.

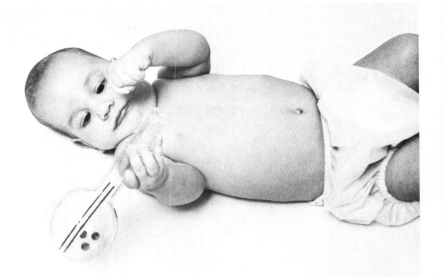

Your baby will now be surprised when the sounds of toys
don't come out as she expects them to. One baby was
really surprised when she threw her bottle down from
her high chair and didn't hear it hit the floor. Her mother
had caught it in mid-air. The baby looked over the edge of
her chair as if to say, "What's going on down there?"

Your baby now recognizes your voice. When he hears it,
he will look for you. If he is tired, uncomfortable, or
afraid, he will cry for you. Your voice and face will
usually comfort him.

Hearing

Babies Can Hear the Differences between Different Sentence Tunes

Sentences have different "tunes" as well as different words. Some have the rising tunes of questions, others have the falling tunes of statements. Try saying these 2 sentences aloud and you'll hear the difference: 1) "Do you really see *that?*" 2) "*Yes,* I see it." Still other sentences have the tunes of exclamations, like "What a surprise!" Your baby is now becoming aware of the differences between sentence tunes but she doesn't yet understand what they mean.

In 1 study babies heard a sentence with falling tunes — "See the cat" — over and over coming from a loudspeaker. Suddenly the sentence was changed to have the tune of a question — "See the *cat?*" The babies showed that they noticed the difference by changes in their movements and by looking toward the speaker.

Hearing

Babies Enjoy Music

Babies are able to show their enjoyment of music more and more. They may rock themselves, wave their arms, and after 9 months of age, some babies even hum and sing out when they hear music. They try to turn on musical toys. By the second year of life they try to dance to music, shuffling round and round as if they had 2 left feet.

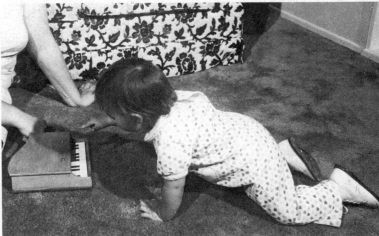

Singing is still a good way to help your baby get to sleep. She will also enjoy sitting on your lap and feeling you move in time to music while you sing.

Hearing

Babies Begin to Learn Games Like "Peek-a-boo"

Babies love to play games like "peek-a-boo" and "pat-a-cake." They like to hear the words that go with these games because they have nice tunes to them. Between 6 and 9 months they enjoy having their hands moved for them as you say "pat-a-cake," or seeing your face come back from behind your hands as you say "peek-a-boo." Later they get to know the tunes very well and begin to clap their hands the minute you say "pat-a-cake."

Hearing

She Copies Your Sounds

Your baby imitates you if you make the sounds she knows, like *hi, oh oh, or dada.* If you sing a musical tune along with these sounds, she will like it even better.

Imitating helps her to learn new words. When she imitates, she is listening to you and to herself. She tries to match the two as well as she can. Even when they don't appear to be listening, babies change their voices and the sounds they make because of what they hear other people saying.

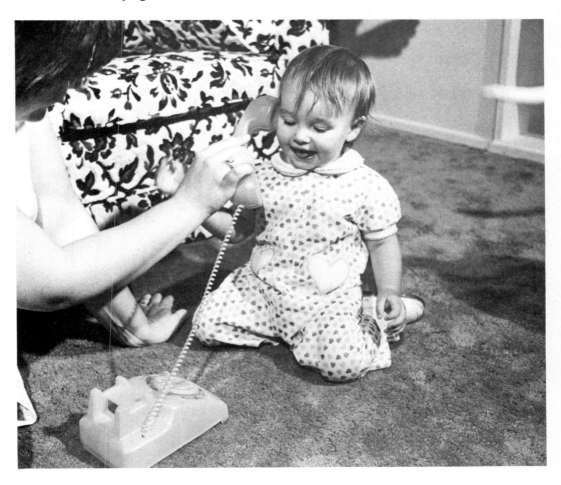

Hearing

Your Baby Likes to Hear New Things

Your baby will now enjoy new listening activities. He likes to hear the names and sounds of animals in picture books and enjoys new rhymes and stories.

In 1 project, year-old babies were allowed to choose what they listened to by pushing certain levers. They could choose a short conversation played over and over or a long conversation played over and over. At first, they liked the short conversation, but after learning how the levers worked they seemed to become bored with the short tape and began to listen to the long tape instead. They didn't like hearing the same story repeated so soon, any more than we would.

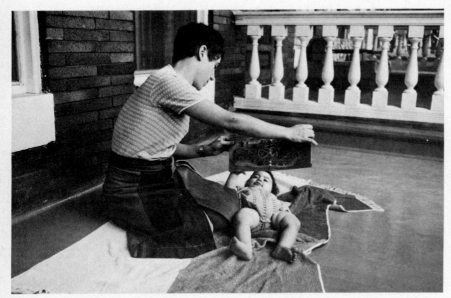

Hearing

He Knows His Own Name and the Names of Familiar People

Your baby now knows his own name. Before, he would turn around if you called him, but this was because of your tone of voice. You might just as well have said, "Hey, you there." Now he is beginning to have an idea that he has *a name of his own*.

By the end of the first year, a few babies also learn the names of familiar people, animals, and toys, and begin to use them often.

Hearing

Babies Try to Do What People Ask Them to Do

At the end of the first year, some babies will try to follow commands from adults. Your baby may look for something, perhaps not the right thing, when you say, "Where's Daddy?" or "Where's the clock?" He may lift up his arms when you say, "*So* big." or "Baby is *so* big." He can give some meaning to the different tunes of these sentences but not always to the words they are made of.

In the second year of life he will point to objects and pictures and give them to you when you ask him. He will learn the names of his body parts: eyes, mouth, and nose. He will even point to them on a doll. He won't do this every time you ask him, only when he feels like it. And just when you want him to show off for a friend, he may act as if he had never heard of body parts.

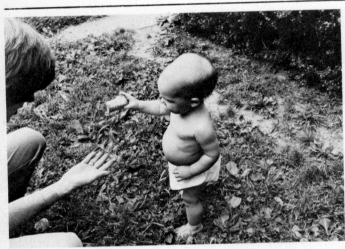

Hearing

She Understands More than She Can Say

Your baby now understands more and more of what you say to her. She also understands more than she can say herself. You can help her to understand by pointing and looking at what you are talking about, and by your facial expressions. It is not hard for your baby to guess that you want her to come if you reach out to her as you say, "Come here, Baby." Also, she hears the same words many times over in the same situations. This helps her to figure out what they mean.

Hearing

She Understands More than She Can Say

Your baby also understands the meaning of "No." Later she will go up to a forbidden object and touch it while saying "No, no, no, no" to herself, shaking her head at the same time. She will not at first know the meanings of "Yes" *and* "No." When she answers questions like "Do you want a cookie?," she may say "No" when she means "Yes."

At the beginning of her second year she will "kiss the baby" and "look at the light" when other people ask her to, not just you. Although a word never sounds *exactly* the same from one speaker to the next, she learns that each slightly different version of a word means the same thing. This is not as easy as you might think. The most ingenious efforts to build machines that can understand words coming from more than 1 person have failed.

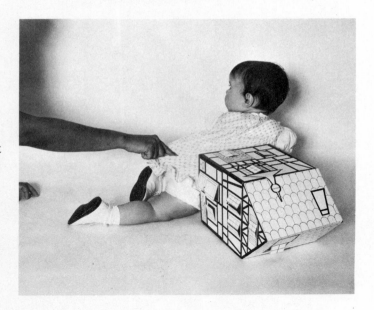

The best way to talk to your baby is the way that is most natural for you. When your baby was very young, it didn't matter much what you said to him so long as you sounded bright and lively. You probably asked him a lot of questions and then answered them yourself: "You feel a little blue today, don't you? Yes, I think you're really upset with the world today," and so on. Now he is able to share his games and his interests with you. It is natural for you to talk with him about the things he points to, reaches for, or shows you. It is fun to talk about what he is doing and what you are doing. Try not to talk too fast, say too much, or use big words. But don't make a special effort to be a teacher. Just do what comes naturally, and have fun!

6. Making Sounds

**Newborn Babies Have No Control Over the Sounds They
Make, but They Do Have an Inborn Readiness to Communicate**

A newborn baby burps, swallows noisily, and smacks his lips in feeding. He yawns, and grunts, and sighs as he moves about. He cries when he becomes tense. But he has no control over his sound making.

Babies soon begin to use sounds, especially crying, to let their parents know how they feel. It seems they try to communicate in other ways too.

High-speed films of babies and their mothers made during the first few weeks of life show that as a mother talks to her baby, the baby looks at her and gestures toward her with his hands. He even works his mouth, as if he were trying to talk to her.

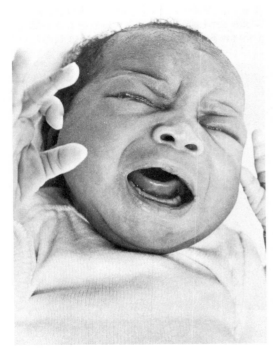

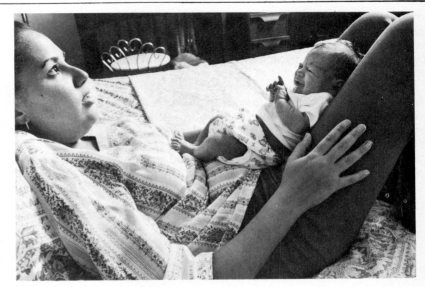

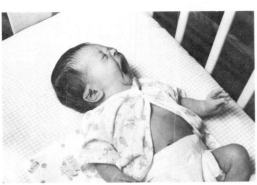

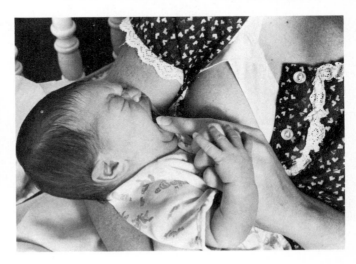

Making Sounds

Babies Learn that Crying Brings Mother

Your baby learns that crying is a way of securing attention when he needs it. If he is not too distressed, he will pause from time to time in his crying, as if to find out whether you are on your way to help and comfort him.

One way of quieting your baby when he is crying is to talk gently to him, or to make a long *ah* or a *bzzz* or *mmm* sound. When he is overtired, your baby will sometimes be hard to comfort and you may have to let him cry himself to sleep.

Several studies have shown that after the first few days, a mother is able to pick out her own baby from other babies by the sound of his voice and his particular way of crying. You probably learn to recognize your baby's voice because you listen so carefully for his cries and go to him quickly when he does start to cry.

A mother who is breast-feeding may find that her milk begins to flow when her baby cries. This is another sign of the bond that forms between a mother and her baby.

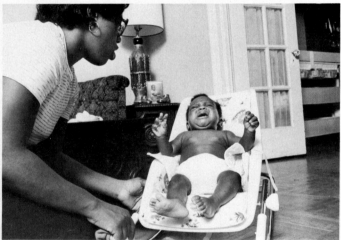

Making Sounds

A Baby's Pain Cry Is Different from Her Hunger Cry

From very early in life, probably the first week, your baby will cry differently when she is hungry and when she is in pain.

When she is hungry, your baby will gradually work up to a full cry, often stopping to suck for a moment as her movements accidentally bring her fists or blanket in contact with her mouth. Once she is really worked up, there will be long stretches of regular, rhythmic crying, in which each cry is followed by a sharp and noisy gasp for air.

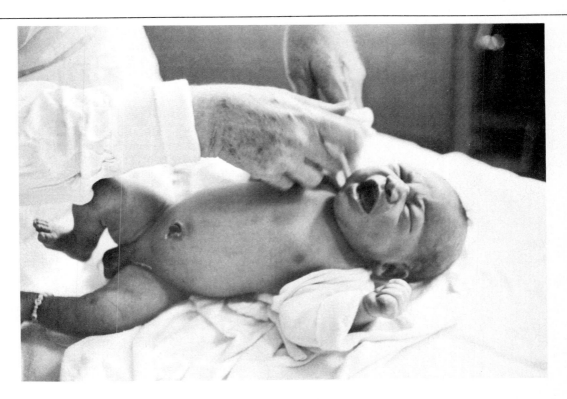

If your baby feels a sudden sharp pain, for example, when he is given an injection, his face may turn darker. He will let out one long yell which will be followed by an even longer spell of breath holding. After that, his crying will gradually subside. Crying from pain that lasts longer is often very high in pitch and sounds like shrieking. You are more likely to be alarmed and to come running when your baby cries in pain than if he cries in a more steady way from hunger, being tired, uncomfortable, or bored.

Making Sounds

Babies Make Sounds When They Hear Sounds and See Faces

Even as early as 2 to 4 weeks of age, your baby will suddenly make short *ah* sounds when he is looking into the face of someone who is holding him close and talking.

Babies as young as this will call out only if they see a face *and* hear a pleasant sound at the same time.

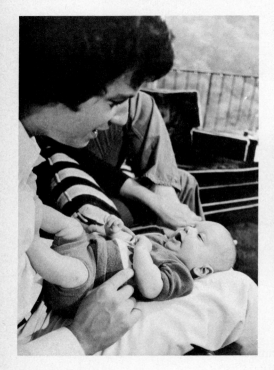

This baby is paying attention to the face of a toy bear which is held close to him. The toy bear contains a music box that is playing the "Teddy Bears' Picnic" song. All of a sudden the baby lets out a loud *ah* sound.

Making Sounds

Your Baby Has a Large Tongue

The baby's tongue is very large compared with the size of his mouth. So he has to breathe through his nose, except when his mouth is open very wide while crying. For the very young baby, there is not much room for the tongue to move. It is always hitting against the roof of the mouth or the back wall of the throat, or moving in and out of the mouth making faint clicking, buzzing, and smacking sounds. As he grows older, the shape of the inside of his mouth will change and it will become much bigger.

Now faint sounds that are made by the tongue in this way can be triggered by any excitement or activity, such as being with people he enjoys, being moved about, or just changing his position.

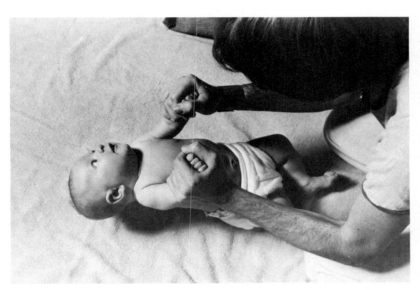

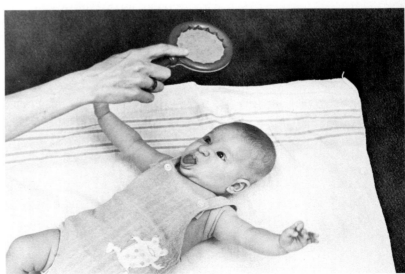

Making Sounds

She Coos and Gurgles

Your baby will begin to make cooing sounds at about 6 to 8 weeks of age. Her first cooing will sound very much like the less tense and strained sounds which she makes at the end of crying, as you pick her up, rock her, comfort her, or offer her the nipple. She will coo as she looks at you and smiles. She is more likely to gurgle and coo when you talk to her and when you smile and nod your head. At first she will not wait for you to stop talking and then answer, but will keep right on talking along *with* you.

It is important for you to talk to your baby when you change her or pick her up and cuddle her. After a while she will learn to take turns talking with you. Her cooing back to you, like her looking and smiling, makes you feel closer to her.

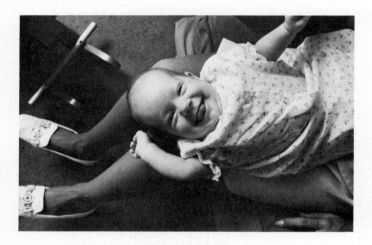

Because she is happy and excited, little pops, hums, gurgles, and buzzes keep getting in the way of your baby's cooing sounds. Now you can hear them easily, because her voice makes them sound louder. These pops and gurgles will eventually become the *p*'s, *b*'s, *t*'s, *d*'s, *m*'s and *n*'s of real speech.

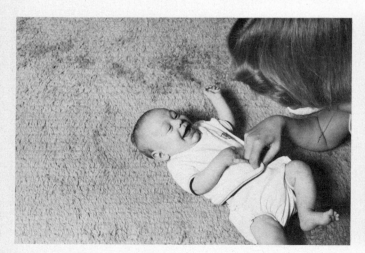

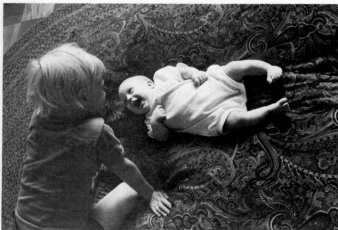

Making Sounds

He Becomes More Expressive

At 3 months your baby begins to make sounds more frequently and in a greater variety of situations, for example, when you take away a favorite toy or when he is reaching for something that catches his attention. He expresses a wide range of feelings: interest, amusement, excitement, and surprise.

If you smile, chuckle, and touch your baby when she "talks," she will "talk" all the more. You may find that if you do all these things when she makes a *particular* sound, she will make that sound more often. But she also has her *own* ideas about what sounds to make. The very next week she may come out with an entirely new sound which you had never expected her to make. These surprises make her talking more fun for you.

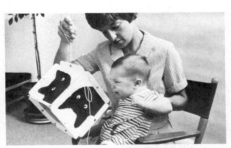

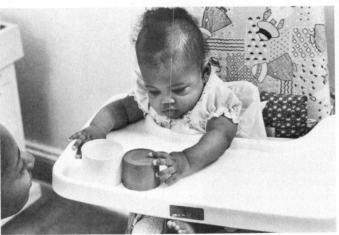

Making Sounds

Your Baby Makes Long "Speeches" when Looking at Interesting Things

At about 3 months of age, your baby will begin talking longer and longer as he looks at interesting things, for example, a mobile, a blade of grass, or the branches of a tree moving in the wind. There are no *p*'s or *b*'s or *d*'s or *m*'s in this talking, only *ah*'s and *ya*'s. At first he goes on and on with these sounds only as he winds down from crying and notices something of interest. But very soon he makes these long "speeches" without crying first, when he is already having a good time.

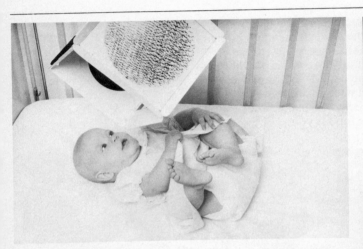

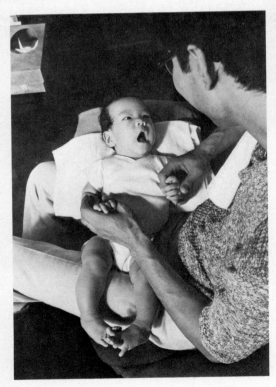

He may be especially talkative when he wakes up in the morning and looks around his crib at all his toys. When he is talking to his toys and other interesting things, he will make the same kinds of sounds that he makes when he is talking to you. But he talks to his toys without stopping, as if he knows not to expect an answer. Now, when he is talking to you he often stops to watch your movements and facial expressions and to listen for your response.

Making Sounds

Your Baby Chuckles and Laughs

At 3 months of age, your baby may chuckle when she is happy. Her chuckling will gradually begin to sound more like laughing. At about 4 months of age, she will begin to laugh loudly. If your baby gurgles when she is happy she will gurgle when she laughs. If she squeals when she is happy she will squeal when she laughs. At first she will laugh when you do something out of the ordinary that she can hear or feel, for example, when you make funny sounds with your mouth, or blow on her belly, or tickle her.

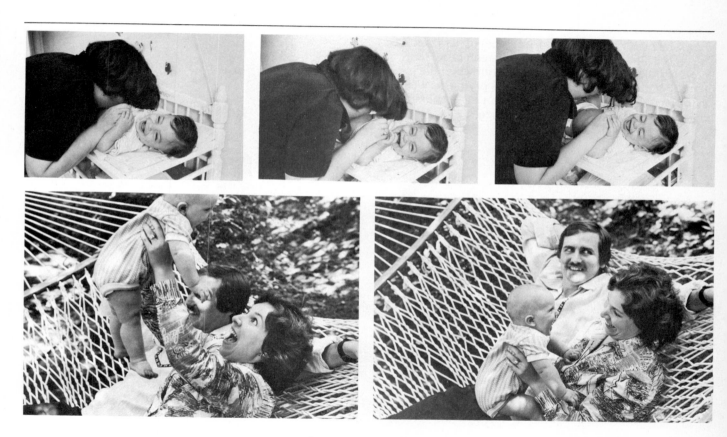

When she is older she will laugh at a surprising event, for example, a bottle falling over and rolling about on the floor, or when you play games: pretending to bite on her arm, holding her up in the air, or bringing your hand toward her with a "spider crawl," then poking her in the ribs. It is as if she enjoyed the ridiculous contrast between a threatening gesture and the smiling face and happy sounds of the loving person who plays with her. Her laughter relieves the tension built up by these games.

Making Sounds

She Experiments with Making Sounds

Between 4 and 5 months of age, your baby will begin to experiment with sounds. If she hears herself squealing, it may become her favorite sound. Or, she may suddenly notice a gasping sound she makes while sucking in her breath and continue to practice that. Other sounds she may use in play include growling, blowing bubbles with saliva (or cereal), and gurgling at the back of her mouth. All of these sounds may be drawn out and made to last 1 or 2 seconds, or even longer. Sometimes they will be combined with one another.

For a while she may use a favorite sound of hers, such as gurgling or blowing bubbles of saliva, a great deal more than any other. This sound may come out when she is frustrated, upset, and even when she is crying, as well as when she is having fun. It is as if she can't help making *that* sound every time she uses her voice.

When your baby first makes these favorite sounds and you imitate her, she may stop and stare at you as if you were doing something strange and surprising. Later when you do this she will enjoy your imitation of her sounds and will repeat them back to you.

Making Sounds

Babies Make Sounds with Objects in Their Mouths

Between 5 and 6 months of age, your baby may vocalize most when he has something in his mouth: a toy, a crust, a spoon, or even his fingers. He will soon discover that he can use these things to change his sounds in interesting ways. He will spend a good deal of time over many months exploring different possibilities of this kind.

Making Sounds

Your Baby's Sounds Are Becoming More Like Speech

You will notice that at about 6 months of age your baby begins to babble, using mostly *ba, da, ma,* and *na* sounds. At first she will make these sounds one at a time. Then she will begin to string them together, saying, for example, *da da da da da* or *ba ba ba.* ___

Making Sounds

Babies Talk Differently to People and Things

At about 6 months of age, your baby will begin to talk quite differently when he is playing with *toys* and when he is looking at *people*.

He makes his latest *ba* and *da* sounds while playing with toys, usually when waving, shaking, or banging them. When he is given an unfamiliar toy he may be so overcome by its newness and so absorbed in finding out how it works that he is quite silent for a while. After he has given it a thorough going over, he will start babbling again as he plays with it.

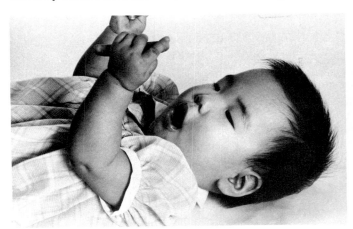
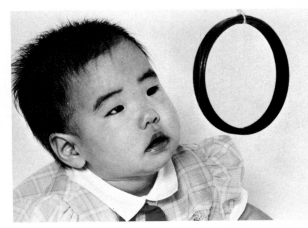

Making Sounds

Babies Talk Differently to People and Things

When he talks to people, he makes simpler sounds, like a long *"aah,"* to call for attention or to scold you for not coming to feed him sooner. He may use *ma* and *na* sounds when things go wrong and he starts to fuss.

This baby wants to grab his mother's glasses and is yelling as he reaches for them.

This baby is having a good time playing with her mother and is calling for the game to go on.

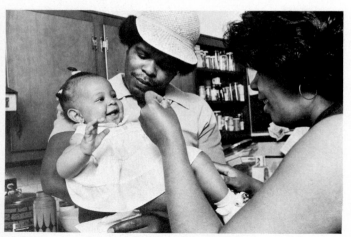

It is interesting that in many countries a word like *mama* or *nana* is used as a name for mothers, who have traditionally been the ones to comfort the baby, calm him down, and attend to his needs. Words like *daddy, papa,* or *tata* are used for other important adults in the baby's life, who also play with him and talk to him.

Making Sounds

Your Baby Stares at Your Mouth when You Talk

At 6 months of age, your baby may begin to stare at your mouth rather than your eyes when you talk. He may feel your mouth, and even put his fingers in it. It is sometimes difficult to get him to imitate your sounds at this time, although he may open and shut his mouth in imitation without making a sound. He may also feel his mouth and then yours as if comparing them. All of these actions show that he is becoming very interested in *how* you talk.

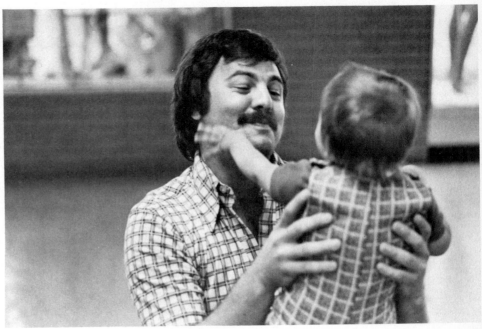

Making Sounds

She Imitates Her Own Sounds when You Say Them Back to Her

Between 6 and 9 months of age, your baby will begin to repeat her own sounds after you. She will only imitate the sounds she is used to saying on her own like *dada* or *baba*. At first it will be easier to get her to repeat sounds if she has just said them herself. Later on you may be able to start the game up by making some of her sounds when she is quiet. After a few weeks of playing this game she may become quite enthusiastic about it, decide to take the lead, and make sounds for *you* to imitate.

She now enjoys singing a few notes. She may try to imitate your singing or familiar tunes she hears on TV.

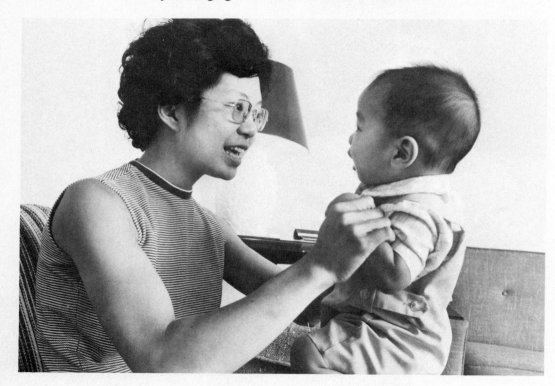

Making Sounds

6 - 9 Months

Babies Use Their Voices to Get What They Want

Now your baby will use her voice in a quite determined way to get what she wants. Sometimes she may just want to get and hold your attention. She may greet you and try to have a pleasant conversation with you. If you are talking to other adults she will try to join in.

At other times she may shout, demanding to be picked up, fed, or given a toy you have just taken from her. Or she may scream in frustration and anger. Her hand gestures and facial expression as well as her voice will usually make clear what she wants and whether she is angry or having fun.

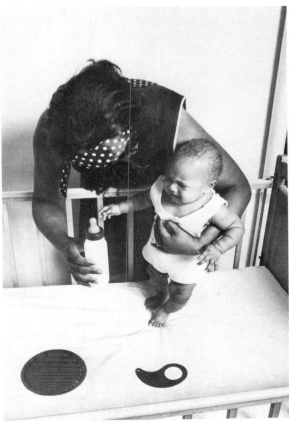

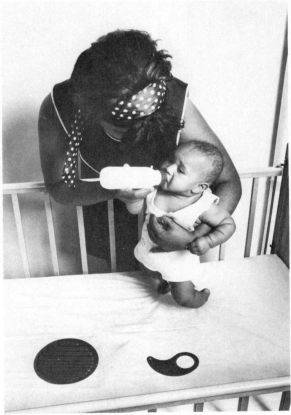

Making Sounds

Babies Begin to Make More Difficult Sounds

At about 9 months many babies begin to make sounds like *s* and *f* or *ts* (as in "hats"). In order to make these sounds a baby needs to be able to control his mouth much more skillfully than for *ba* or *da* or *ma*. He has to make a narrow funnel in his mouth, between his upper teeth (which have now come in) and his lower lip, or between his tongue and the roof of his mouth. He has to keep this funnel from closing, so that he can blow air gently through it. He will almost always make these sounds when he is carefully examining the details of a toy. These more difficult sounds are not as likely to be used in his first words as the easier sounds, *ba* or *da* or *ma*, but they continue to be favorite sounds for the rest of the year.

Making Sounds

Your Baby Makes More Complicated Speeches

Just before he is 9 months old, your baby may begin to use different syllables, all in the same breath, for example, *badawayaya.* His sounds become even more complicated toward the end of the first year of life. The tunes of conversational speech begin to be added to these groups of syllables. Sometimes they sound like complete sentences: questions, demands, or statements. You may have the feeling that your baby is talking to you in a foreign language, but sometimes you think you can catch real English words among the nonsense sounds.

Babies from many different countries talk in exactly the same way. They do not yet use the sounds or the tunes of any *particular* language. This kind of talking may be drawn out longer and get even more complicated after 1 year of age.

Making Sounds

Babies Babble to People as Well as Objects

Your baby will still babble a lot as she plays. It will sound as if she is talking to herself about new things she finds to explore and about her toys and what she does with them. Sometimes, now, she will turn to look at you while making these very same sounds, as if to comment about things she has discovered. She will enjoy it if you answer her back, as if you understood her. She will feel that you are playing with her and she may continue the ''conversation'' with you.

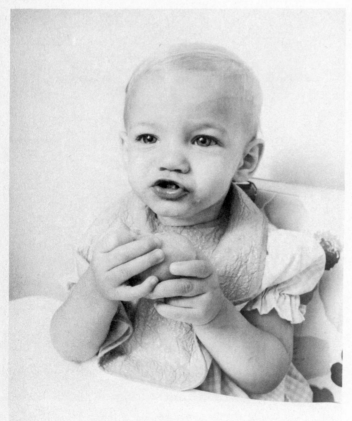

Making Sounds

**Your Baby Makes Different Sounds for
Different Wants and Needs**

Before the end of the first year of life, your baby will begin to make different sounds to communicate different needs. He may use 1 group of sounds to ask for things he wants. These are often short, simple words with an *m* sound in them, for example, *mi, imi, ma, ama,* and so on. Gradually, in his second year, these may all merge into a single word, like "more," or "mine." Another class of sounds may be used regularly to indicate dislike of some food or activity, for example, having his face washed. Still another class of sounds may indicate pleasure and surprise, for example, at seeing a balloon for the first time. All of these words help him to express his needs and his feelings to the people he knows.

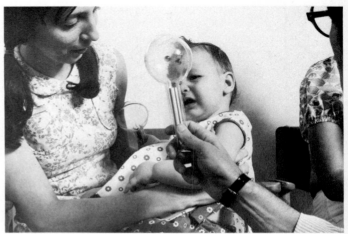

Making Sounds

He Imitates New Sounds

Between 9 and 12 months of age, your baby will begin to imitate new sounds and words which you say for him. He no longer repeats only the sounds he has made first. His imitations will begin to sound like your words, but with great variation from one try to the next. At first he won't realize that the words you say to him in this game have any meaning. He will be most likely to imitate your words if you accompany them with some playful actions which he can also imitate, like banging.

This mother is bouncing her 1-year-old baby up and down and saying "Bye Baby Bunting." The baby bounces himself when his mother stops. Sometimes he says *ba ba* as he bounces.

Making Sounds

She Talks Most when There Is Plenty of Action and Everyone Attends to Her

In this period your baby will enjoy having lots of activity going on around her. She will laugh and talk a lot when you play with her or take her to new places. As soon as you come into the room she may try to get you to pay attention to her and join in her play. If she is accustomed to other children, she may talk most when they play with her.

If you are in the room with her and strike up a conversation with another adult, she is now less likely to *interrupt* you than when she was younger. Instead, she may now stop talking and *follow* your conversation.

In 1 study, babies of 10 to 12 months were put in a playpen with a tape recorder beside it. By pressing 1 of 2 levers, they could listen to music or to their mother's or their father's voice. They preferred the voices to the music. When they listened to the voices, they talked less themselves.

Making Sounds

Babies Make Their First Word-like Sounds

Some babies go on making long speeches of nonsense words in the second year of life. They are sociable babies who want to tell you how they feel about things and events. Other babies don't spend as much time making speeches and give them up altogether at about 1 year of age. Instead they concentrate on speaking single words.

Your baby will pick up words like "bye bye," "oh! oh!" and "hi" by listening to you. You can include these words in the games you play together. Whether your baby prefers talking in long sentences of nonsense words, or in single words that are like some of the words you use, she will use her speech to keep you interested in her.

Throughout her first year and a half of life, your baby is constantly combining and re-combining sounds, tunes, and words with one another in new and interesting ways. It is this capacity for combining and re-combining that enables her to learn to talk. But she still has to find out what the sounds, words, and tunes of her native language should be. You and your family and friends are the ones who must give her that information by talking with her as much as you can.

At the same time, your baby must learn about her world and what goes on in it, so that she knows what it is you are all talking about. The more chances you give her to explore, and the more you talk to her about the things she experiences, the more rapidly she progresses in learning to talk and learning the meaning of words.

In the first part of the second year of life, your baby slowly begins to add more words, perhaps about 1 a month. Some of these words may be dropped after a time and never used again. It is only at about 18 months of age that most babies realize that words really do stand for things, for important people, for food, and for actions. They then begin to ask about names, for example, by saying "Wa sat?" or "This?" They now begin to learn words at a much faster rate. Among the first words you can expect your baby to learn (apart from "mommy" and "daddy") are ball, dog, and car. These words are all names of objects that move and act in interesting ways. He uses the *same word* to communicate *different messages*. For example when he says "ball," he sometimes means "Let's play ball." At other times when he says "ball" he means "That's a ball," and so forth. He may use gestures to help you understand the different things he is trying to say when he talks in single words. Very soon he may put his single words into little phrases such as "more ball," "hi, dog," or "no car." These phrases help him to say more about what he wants, what he is interested in, and how he feels about important things in his life.

PART FOUR: PLAY AND LEARNING

1. How Your Baby Learns

The answer to the question of how babies learn is just beginning to emerge, but the issue is so important we would like to give you some idea of what has been discovered.

Less than 10 years ago, there was little evidence that babies under 6 months had much capacity for learning. Today the situation is dramatically different. There is now strong evidence that learning can occur in the very first days of life. One scientist, Dr. T. G. R. Bower of the University of Edinburgh in Scotland, goes so far as to say that "the newborn can learn better at that point in his development than he ever will again." This explosive growth in understanding of the newborn's learning abilities has been generated by new scientific methods which allow the newborn to show what he likes to pay attention to, what he gets tired of, and what he prefers.

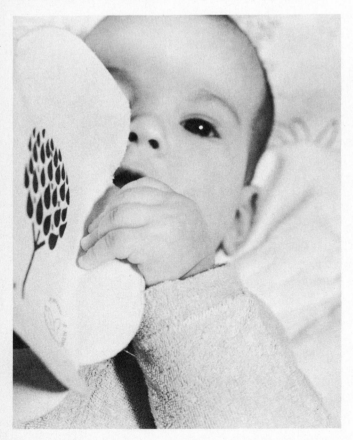

Babies Are Naturally Curious and Motivated to Learn

In recent years it has been discovered that babies have an *inborn curiosity,* and are willing to work hard for the chance to experience things that interest them. For example, Drs. Einar Siqueland and Clement De Lucia at Brown University set up a machine that displayed illuminated pictures of geometric patterns, cartoon figures, and human faces. They hooked the machine's controls to a pacifier held in the mouths of babies as young as 3 weeks, who were propped up in an infant seat in front of the machine. Within a few minutes the babies learned to regulate what they saw by sucking — when they sucked hard and continuously the picture was bright, but when they let up, the picture became dimmer. In other situations, sucking on the pacifier brought a fuzzy picture into focus or made soft music or human voices louder and easier to hear. In every situation, even the youngest babies were willing to put a great deal of effort into their sucking in order to see the pictures clearly or to hear the music or voices.

Newborns Have a Tremendous Appetite for Novelty

It has also been shown that even the youngest infant has a memory. He gets bored with repetition of a familiar experience and has a tremendous appetite for *new* experiences. For example, in the experiments just described, babies began to suck less vigorously after they'd looked at the same picture for a few minutes. It occurred to the researchers that the babies might be getting bored with the picture. But it was also possible the infants were just getting tired of sucking. So Dr. Siqueland set up a new situation. When a baby stopped sucking while looking at a familiar picture, a new picture was flashed on the screen, and he began to suck vigorously again! It seems he was bored with the old picture, and his interest and curiosity were rekindled by the new one.

In a similar study, babies from 1 to 4 days old were shown a picture of a checkerboard again and again. At first they were fascinated, staring at it intently. After a while, however, their interest began to decline noticeably. If a checkerboard with squares of a different size was then shown, their interest was renewed.

The length of time they looked at a new checkerboard depended on how different it was from the old one — they looked longest at those most different.

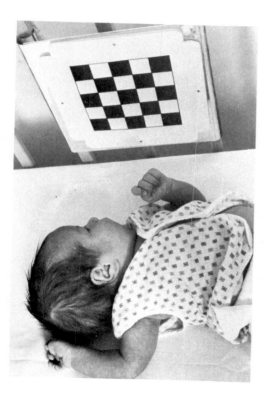

When your baby looks at something that interests him, his eyes fix on part of it, focus, then shift to another part of the same object and focus again. Vision is a newborn's most important source of information, and he's beginning to understand the world by forming memories of what he sees. He "files" these and when he looks at a new object, or at an object he's seen before, he checks to see if he already has its image on file. If he doesn't, he takes a little extra time to register what he sees.

Your Baby Learns to Recognize You in His First Month of Life

The fact that infants can *remember* things they've experienced and seek out *new* experiences, accounts for their learning potential. By the time your baby is 2 to 4 weeks old, he's learned to recognize the most important part of his new world — his parents. Dr. Genevieve Carpenter of St. Mary's Hospital Medical School in London, placed babies as young as 2 weeks in an infant seat inside an enclosure with an opening close to the baby's face. The baby's mother placed her face in the opening and spoke to the child for about 30 seconds. Then a woman the baby had never seen before did the same thing, using exactly the same words. Even the youngest babies had already learned to recognize their mothers. They watched their mothers with fascinated attention but tended to avoid looking at the stranger.

The discovery that these young babies pay more attention to familiar people than to unfamiliar ones seems to contradict what we said earlier about the baby's tendency to be bored by the familiar and fascinated by novelty. However, where people are concerned, familiarity seems more likely to make a baby feel secure than to bore him.

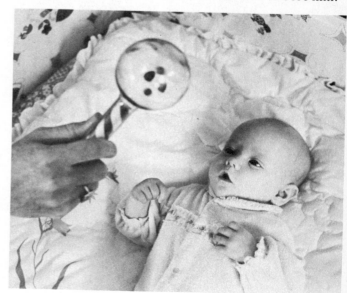

How Your Baby Learns

A baby learns by following her natural appetite for new experiences and for responses from people and from objects. A baby learns through play. What is your baby doing when she plays?

Exploring

Your baby will spend many hours exploring, carefully examining and studying the properties of objects, people, and places, trying to make sense of what she sees. She wants to see everything and tries her best to touch or mouth everything.

From her first few weeks, your baby will delight in following a moving object with her eyes.

She will hold on to it for as long as she can.

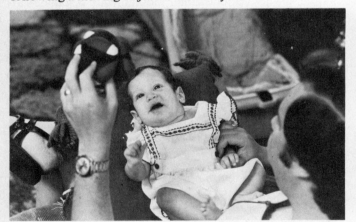
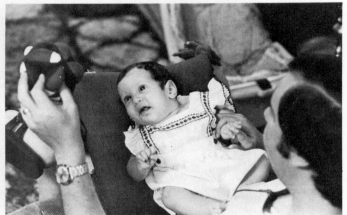

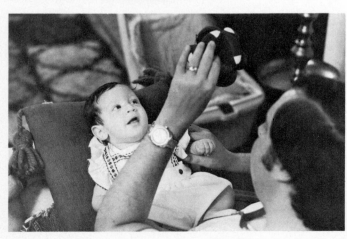

And will welcome it back when it reappears.

Once she is able to use her hands to reach for objects and grasp them, at about 3 to 4 months, she uses these new tools and her mouth to further her efforts to understand the world. She uses her

teeth

mouth, and

hands.

**How Your Baby
Learns**

In fact, your baby's hands will challenge almost anything.

He will tug on beards

pull earrings

pop bubbles

pat donkeys

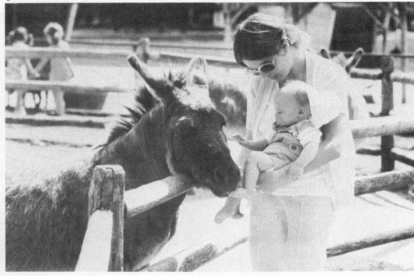

catch falling water, and

even grab for your eyes
if you're not careful.

He will learn that some things taste good

some roll

some have wet noses

some are hard to pull off, and

some come as a surprise.

When you give your baby a new toy,
he will look at it

wave it

roll it

pull it

chew it

smell it

squeeze it

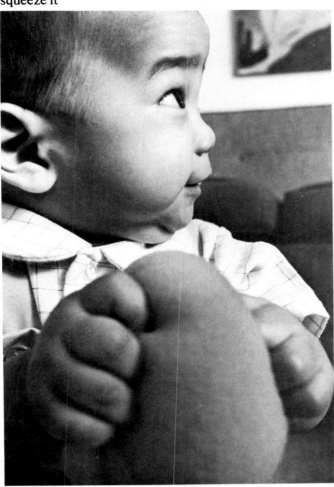

turn it

kiss it, and

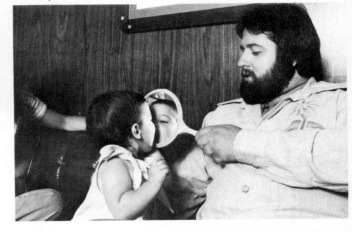

handle it in many different ways, to learn as much as he can about its properties.

How Your Baby Learns

Repeating and Mastering

Each time your baby begins to handle objects in a new way, you'll see him repeat the activity again and again. This is his way of practicing a new skill. His drive to practice new skills is strong. It has to be. It takes a lot of effort to learn to reach, grasp, sit, stand, and walk.

Notice how this baby works at reaching this mobile.

He swipes at it

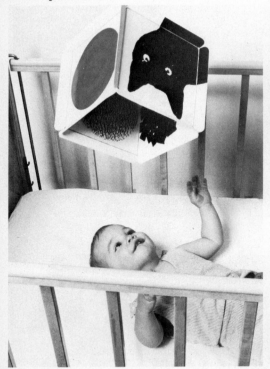

until suddenly he makes contact with it.

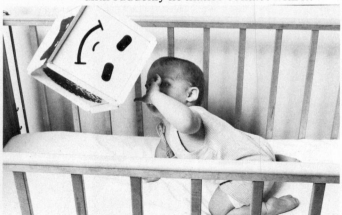

He pulls it down to play with it.

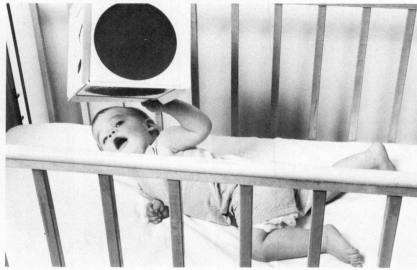

His efforts are slow and clumsy

Soon he'll be able to reach right out and grab it.

but he concentrates hard, and slowly, but surely, his reaching and grasping skills improve.

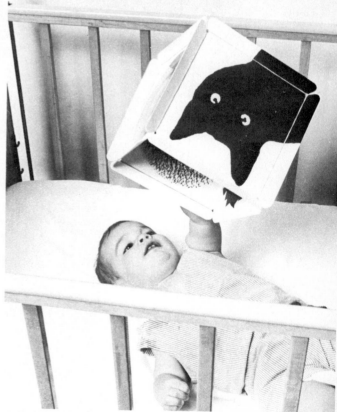

Finally he masters this new activity, and will no longer need to concentrate as hard as he did before. Now he'll enjoy batting and pulling more and more.

How Your Baby Learns

This baby is ready to master feeding himself — a first try at independence.

He lets his mother know by grabbing the spoon.

He refuses her efforts to help him.

When given a chance to feed himself, he's a bit sloppy at first.

Some food spills, but what a great beginning!

He thanks his mother for giving him the opportunity.

Gradually he masters this new activity, and shows how pleased he is with himself by the expression on his face.

**How Your Baby
Learns**

Here is a baby who has already mastered crawling and pulling up on things. Now he's putting these two skills together in order to accomplish a new feat — climbing.

Although awkward in the beginning

he practices going up 1 or 2 steps and returning.

Soon he'll be able to go up quickly on his own, and

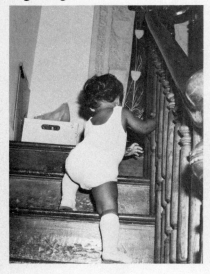

may even be able to go up and come down before you can catch him.

Problem Solving

Your baby explores objects to satisfy her curiosity about how they operate. She will work for long periods of time in her search for an answer.

The mother in these pictures is giving her baby a chance to learn about a lid and a pan.

First the baby examines the pan

to figure out how it works.

To make it more exciting for herself, she puts 1 of her toys in the pan.

With a pretty good aim, she lowers the lid.

However, she sees that it doesn't quite fit

so she works at it

until she pushes it into place.

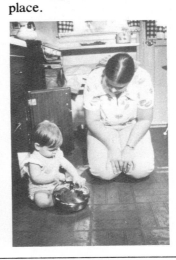

**How Your Baby
Learns**

Occasionally, these "experiments" can be trying for you, as when your baby practices her ability to let go of things she's grasped by dropping them over the side of her crib or high chair. Try to keep in mind how important this practice is for her and that she's *not* dropping her toys to irritate you. Later in the Play and Learning section we suggest tying strings to your baby's toys, so she can learn to reel them back by herself.

An older baby will often deliberately set a difficult task for herself and will sometimes persist until she's solved the problem. For example, infants in 1 laboratory setting were supposed to find a variety of hidden objects. Later, their mothers reported the babies spent hours at home practicing "hiding" objects and "finding" them again.

Imitating
Early in life, a baby discovers the joys and rewards of imitating his parents and others. He carefully watches how his parents respond to him, how they react when they are happy or sad, and what they do when they are working and when they are playing.

He learns a great deal by simply observing and imitating. He gains such skills as

waving bye-bye

kissing

using a telephone, and

playing games.

Mimicking gives your baby practice in matching his own movements to those he sees.

When he is playing games with you, your baby is learning an important rule for relating to other people — taking turns. When this mother blows on her baby's face

it comes as a pleasant surprise.

Her baby tries to blow back.

Mother blows again.

Baby waits her turn, blows back, and gets better with every try.

What fun it is!

How Your Baby Learns

Using Objects in New Ways

Toward the end of his first year, your baby begins to figure out what objects can do. He learns to use objects as tools. The spoon that was once a teether now becomes a musical instrument.

He knows how to use his cup for drinking. Now he discovers it

can be used as a pull toy, or a place to hide his blocks.

And he can substitute his shoe for a car.

He is showing more and more signs of creativity.

Putting It All Together

Your baby's play helps him get acquainted with the world of people and objects. Most important, it's the way he learns how he fits in. The more you play with your baby, set the proper atmosphere, and provide the right toys, the more he enjoys play and learns from it.

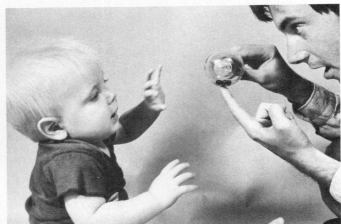

2. Your Role in Play

With this emphasis on how a baby plays, and how she learns through play, it's easy to overlook *your* role in your baby's play and learning. How parents contribute to play is more easily seen if we think of play as being of 2 types: independent play and social play. A baby needs both kinds of play: she needs to have opportunities to explore on her own, and she also needs playful interaction with you and other playmates.

Independent Play

Independent play concerns exploration of the environment by your baby when she's alone. Just like adults, babies *need* to spend some time alone — to explore and manipulate and experiment by themselves. And learning how to play alone helps create independence as well as the ability to provide one's own stimulation. These independent playtimes are more rewarding when you provide interesting environments for your baby to look at, and materials to play with.

Most babies seem to spend about 60% of their free waking time just staring at the world around them. You can make your baby's visual explorations more stimulating by making her crib, room, and home rich places to look at. In addition, you can add variety by taking your baby on errands and outings where she can see different environments and meet new people. The chapter on Designing Your Baby's Environment will give you many specific ideas.

In addition to interesting environments to look at, babies need toys and other objects to explore. A study by Drs. Leon Yarrow, Judith Rubenstein, and Frank Pederson of the National Institute of Child Health and Human Development, found that the variety of responsive play materials a baby had to handle was directly related to his motivation and intellectual development. Responsive play materials are those that change shape, make interesting sounds, and invite the baby's continuing efforts to "do something" with them.

Just as important as the *kinds* of play materials is the *way* they are presented. The way you offer toys has an influence on how your baby plays with them.

When a baby is given a new toy, he first plays with it in ways he already knows. With trial and error and further exploration, he may discover some new uses. With *your* help, the number of possible uses can be greatly increased. For example, your baby may discover that a set of cups can be inspected, chewed on, poked into, and maybe used for drinking. When you play together, he can also learn that the cups can be stacked into a tower, taken apart, and fit inside each other.

It's also up to you to help your baby "choose" her toys — old ones as well as new. A plaything that excited her last month may be of no interest now, perhaps because she's bored by playing with it so often. If your baby loses interest in a particular toy, put it away and offer it again in a few weeks. By that time, your baby may have learned new skills that make it seem like a new toy, or a tool to use with other materials.

And remember: you are almost always a favorite "toy."

In addition to playing with toys, your baby needs opportunities to explore objects in the world, especially in your home and yard. You can help by making those places safe for her excursions. Ideas on baby-proofing can be found in the Designing Your Baby's Environment chapter.

Social Play

Independent play is only part of the story. Your baby also enjoys playing *with* you and other playmates. Social play is not only a rich learning experience; it's also of direct importance to independent play. Studies show that the more a baby is played with, the more he will play by himself. And play is a baby's way of learning.

It is believed that play begins in the atmosphere of affection and stimulation that are part of your natural caregiving. All the time spent with your baby is a form of play. Before you can begin to play "games" together, you should establish a comfortable and secure relationship. This process begins with the closeness you feel during feeding, changing, bathing, and cuddling. Such pleasant contact puts the two of you "in touch" with each other, and communication is essential for social play. In fact, establishing this communication is an early form of play itself. So, while performing these routines, you can make them more interesting by looking directly into your baby's eyes, talking, singing, playing with his arms and legs, and massaging his body. Your hands are very good communicators. A pleasant touch tells your baby that you care about him, and that you're caring for his needs.

2

Your Role in Play

The best time for social play is when your baby is alert, usually just after a nap or bath. In addition, your baby must be feeling sociable. There are times that your baby will enjoy being left alone, even when he's alert. After all, there are times when *you* like to be alone also. No matter how enthusiastic and playful you may act, your baby plays with you only if he's in the mood. For the first month or so, these times will be fairly rare. Playtime together usually lasts only a few minutes before he falls asleep again. As he grows older, and begins to stay awake for longer periods of time, your opportunities for playing together will increase.

Often your baby will be the one to begin playtimes together — so be aware of those cues he gives to let you know *he* wants to play: smiling at you, making sounds to catch your attention, extending his arms, holding out a toy, throwing things for you to pick up, and so forth.

Finding Other Playmates

There will undoubtedly be times when your baby is eager for social play and you are either too busy or just not in the mood. At these times, you shouldn't feel that parents are the only playmates who can suffice. Older brothers and sisters can be wonderful playmates—and may even teach your baby games you might not have thought of. Also check around your neighborhood. Most teenagers (boys as well as girls) jump at the chance to play with a baby. What about people whose own children have grown up, or people who are retired? And don't forget your favorite babysitters. You don't have to be going out to want their services. Finding your baby a group of other playmates gives him an opportunity to learn about new people, and gives you a chance to be alone when you need to be.

Can You Overstimulate Your Baby?

We talk about the importance of play and stimulation in helping your baby to develop his abilities. Some people worry about going too far. Can a baby be overstimulated?

You won't overstimulate your baby if you are on the lookout for signals she uses to tell you she's had enough. Your baby will repeatedly turn her head away, fuss, make unhappy faces or sounds of displeasure, refuse to hold toys, or push away from you. At such times, you

shouldn't be offended. It doesn't mean that your baby has grown tired of you — just tired of playing. Your attention to your baby's signs is the key point. Look to her for advice.

You can help avoid these potential situations by following some common sense rules:

1. Give your baby only a few toys at a time.

2. Let your baby play with a particular toy as long as she wants.

3. Try to match games and toys to her level of development.

4. Avoid "pushing" your baby into learning a new game or skill before she is ready.

5. Pay attention to your baby's moods.

Also, understimulation is far more common than overstimulation. Most parents don't have as much time as they would like to spend with their babies. This is another reason why finding additional playmates is a good idea.

Now On to Play!

The remainder of the Play and Learning section contains 2 kinds of suggestions — first, some for making the environment more interesting to encourage independent play, and then, some for activities for playtimes together. Not all of our ideas will appeal to every baby — everyone, even a baby, has personal preferences. But we have provided a rich resource so you can choose things that appeal to you, and that you think your baby may enjoy. As a rule of thumb, "If it isn't fun for both of you, forget it." And since your baby will undoubtedly have other caregivers and playmates, you may want to ask grandparents, babysitters, and other friends of your baby to read this section, too. It may give them some welcome ideas.

3. Designing Your Baby's Environment

One role you have as parents is that of Environmental Designer. Your baby has a strong motivation to explore, and it's up to you to provide him with interesting settings and objects. We know that babies like novelty and variety, which are important for their stimulation. We also know that babies spend much of their first year exploring the world around them. So, *give your baby a world worth exploring!* A rich environment is not only more interesting, it increases his opportunities to learn by playing, especially when he plays alone.

When we speak of a baby's environment, we include
   the room where he sleeps
   his furniture
   his playthings
   his home, and
   the outside world.

This chapter contains ideas for making each part of your baby's environment safe, more enjoyable, and more responsive to his explorations.

Designing Your Baby's Environment: His Room

Lighting

A bright, cheerful room is more likely than a dark, drab one to stimulate a baby to explore visually and to play with her crib toys, especially when she's alone. However, many parents (and babies) prefer a dim light to a bright one for naptimes and for middle-of-the-night feedings. By replacing the wall switch for the overhead light with a dimmer switch (available at hardware stores and 5 & 10's), you can very easily control the light level.

Windows

By putting your baby's crib where she can see out a window, but not within reach or in direct sunlight, you present her with a safe world of interesting sights. A few colorful bottles on the window sill or a stained glass decoration hung from the frame make the view even more attractive. And a simple birdfeeder outside, or some seed on the ledge, will provide a flurry of activity for her to watch.

Walls

To make baby's walls more interesting, you can cover them with colorful wallpaper,

paint a mural

make and display a wall hanging,

spell his name in large wooden letters, or

decorate with pictures.

Pictures
In their first year, babies like colorful, simple shapes and bold features. You don't have to limit his picture gallery to posters designed for children. Many babies enjoy a visit to the art museum. You can create one in his room with the inexpensive reproductions of famous paintings that are available in museum shops. Animal scenes, landscapes, and portraits are especially appropriate. Or try your own hand at art. Homemade paintings and collages add a personal touch. And since babies like variety, change your display whenever the mood hits you.

When hanging things on the wall, keep your baby's eye level in mind. For the young baby, pictures should be displayed near mattress height. Raise them to crib rail level when she starts to look actively about when lying on her back, usually around 3 months. For the older baby, you might also hang some pictures and an unbreakable mirror at baseboard height. She can explore those when playing on the floor.

Other Ideas
Plants are wonderful for making a room more colorful. A small lamp shining up through 1 or 2 hanging pots casts fascinating shadows on the walls and ceiling.

Wind chimes hanging near a door or air-conditioning vent make pleasant and interesting sounds.

Since most babies enjoy listening to music, and it can be effective at soothing them to sleep on fussy nights, you may want to include a radio or inexpensive record player.

You can also make his changing table more interesting by setting it near a window, or hanging pictures on the wall next to it.

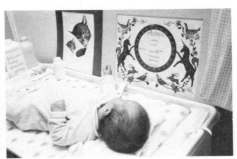

Choosing Furniture

Furniture for a baby should meet 3 main requirements —
it should be: **1.) simple** (free of unnecessary dirt-catching
decorations), **2.) rugged,** because most items will really
get a workout, **3.) safe,** with no exposed hardware that
could cut your baby or pinch his fingers. A smooth finish
is easiest to keep clean. Large items should be very stable, because your older baby may use them for pulling
himself to a standing position.

Sources of Information on Buying

There are many baby products you may wish to own,
both for your convenience and for your baby's enjoyment. Detailed information about choosing baby
products is currently available in 2 books, which you
may wish to consult before making your selections:

Consumers Union Guide to Buying for Babies

Sandy Jones's *Good Things for Babies*

For information on obtaining these references, see the
Further Information section of this Guide.

Where to Report Hazardous Baby Equipment

The government uses information from parents to help
design safety standards for monitoring and upgrading infant products. The agency responsible for this activity is:

U.S. Consumer Product Safety Commission
Washington, D.C. 20207

Their safety hotline (toll-free in the continental United
States) is: 800-638-2666. Maryland residents only,
call 800-492-8363.

Choosing a Crib

We give cribs special consideration since nearly all
parents buy them. A crib is more than a place to sleep:
it's an exercise yard and a play area for the playtimes that
come right before and after sleeping. Because of the relatively large amount of time your baby spends there, we
suggest you choose a crib carefully.

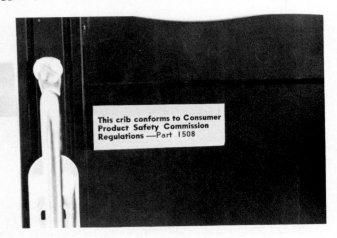

When purchasing a new crib, *make sure it bears the
Consumer Product Safety Commission (CPSC) safety
compliance sticker.* This is a hanging or stick-on label
that should be on both the crib and the carton. The label
states that the crib meets the CPSC requirements for full-
sized cribs (actual wording varies according to the
manufacturer). This tag is your assurance that the crib
meets the latest government safety regulations: the slats
are close together, so a baby can't accidentally slip
between; all metal hardware is safe; locks and latches are
secure from accidental release; and the crib is a standard
size so that the mattress has a snug fit. If there's too
much space between the mattress and the side of the bed,
a baby may become wedged in, and smother.

Features to Look for:

1. Adjustable mattress height. A high mattress is easiest
   on you when your baby is very young. When she
   begins to stand up, lower it to the bottom position.

2. Teething rails on the top of the crib sides. Make sure
   they're firmly attached.

3. Large casters that roll easily.

4. Ease of assembly. There will be times when you'll want to fold up the crib in order to move or store it.

If you inherit an older crib:

1. Make sure the finish and hardware are in good condition. If you repaint, use non-toxic paints.

2. If you can insert 2 fingers between mattress and crib side, the mattress is too small. Replace it, or wedge a rolled-up blanket or towels into the space.

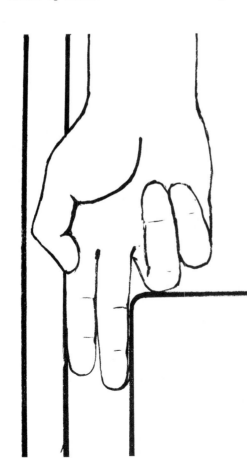

3. Use bumper pads if the slats are more than 2-3/8 inches apart. These should surround the inside of the entire crib, and be held in place with at least 6 straps. It's a good idea to use bumper pads on ALL cribs. They protect your baby from bumping his head when he begins rolling over. Remove them when he's old enough to pull himself to a standing position. Otherwise he can use them as a "ladder" for climbing out.

4. Make sure top rails are free of cracks or splinters.

Crib Safety

1. Always be sure crib sides are securely locked in place.

2. Set the mattress at its lowest position as soon as your baby can pull himself to a standing position.

3. Don't leave any toys or other articles in the crib that your baby can use to help himself climb out.

4. Don't keep your baby in the crib once the height of the side rail is less than three-fourths of your baby's height.

5. Replace any damaged teething rails. They can cut your baby's mouth.

6. Always wash new blankets before putting them in the crib, to get rid of balls of fluff.

3

**Designing Your Baby's
Environment: Toys**

Choosing Toys

Your baby doesn't play with toys just to while away the hours. Toys are a very important part of her learning: about size, texture, shape, and the ways things work. So look for objects that provide opportunities for exploration and stimulate in a number of ways. The most interesting playthings are those that say to your baby "Pick me up and do something with me," rather than toys that say "Admire me."

For the first year, your baby will look at, reach for, grasp, and handle toys in a variety of ways. In addition, she'll put them in her mouth and strike them against other surfaces. So toys should be safe, attractive, easily grasped, washable, and strong.

The following guidelines will be helpful.
1. General Safety
First and foremost, ANYTHING your baby plays with must be safe! For this first year, make sure his playthings:

    are too large to swallow
    have no sharp edges or points
    have a finish that's safe for mouthing
    are practically unbreakable.

When you buy toys:

Make sure every box or label indicates that the toy is made from non-toxic materials.

Stuffed toys should have strong seams and covers too thick to be easily torn or bitten through. And make sure facial features (especially eyes) can't be pulled off. Painted or embroidered eyes are the safest.

The noisemaker in a squeak toy should either be internal, or so strongly attached that even you can't pick it out.

When you go shopping, it's a good idea to open the box and inspect a toy before you buy it if possible. Otherwise check it out when you get home — and if you feel it *is* unsafe, return it. Go through these same inspections with toys given as presents. Potentially dangerous toys should be taken back to the store or thrown away. You may temporarily hurt Grandpa's feelings, but that's much better than exposing your baby to possible harm. In fact, this is a good time to educate your family and friends about toy safety — they'll understand you're doing it for your baby's benefit. In addition, examine his toys periodically to make sure they're in good condition.

2. Attractiveness
Babies are most attracted to bright colors: bright reds, blues, greens, yellows, and oranges. Those pastel pinks and blues adults tend to find so pretty do little for babies. And noisemakers should be loud enough to be easily heard, but not so loud as to be frightening. Remember, your baby explores toys by looking at, listening to, and touching them. Her collection should include objects which invite 1 or all of these types of play.

3. Age Suitability

Your baby most enjoys those toys which match her level of development. As a general guide, early toys should have strong visual appeal. Between 3 and 6 months she will begin grasping and exploring with her hands, so they should be interesting to the touch as well as the eyes. From 6 to 9 months give her toys with different parts and moving pieces to explore. And near the end of the year, she'll also like toys that stack, nest, and move in interesting ways when handled.

You don't need to strictly follow the age recommendations printed on many toy boxes. They can be helpful in a general way, but aren't always accurate. Babies often enjoy toys before or after the recommended age.

4. Versatility

As a general rule when you buy toys, look for those that stimulate exploration in a variety of ways and places. The best toys encourage many different kinds of play. In general, hand toys that are small enough to be grasped easily, colorful, and safe for mouthing, can be played with in the crib, playpen, infant seat or swing, and on the floor. Such toys are really economical, since they continue to be interesting for a number of months. Your baby spends much of this first year experimenting with the different ways an object can be handled, so it makes sense to choose toys with a multitude of uses.

5. Cost

Look for high quality construction. Toys will get a lot of use. And shop comparatively. Don't always assume that a high price means a good toy, or that everything a particular company makes is the best available. You have to decide this yourself, using the suggestions we've made.

Comparative shopping also means pricing the same toys at different stores. You'll be surprised at some of the price differences.

Even if you follow these recommendations, this does *not* ensure your baby will like every toy you choose. Everyone has his own taste. You may think a toy is terrific, but your baby may just yawn and toss it aside. If this happens, either wait awhile before giving it to him again, or save it as a present for a friend's baby.

The Toy Manufacturers of America has prepared a useful pamphlet on selecting and using toys, called **The World of Children's Play and Toys,** by Dr. Brian Sutton-Smith. You can request a copy by writing:

Toy Manufacturers of America, Inc.
200 Fifth Avenue
New York, New York 10010

3

Designing Your Baby's Environment: Toys

Household Items as Toys

Toys are more than just those nicely packaged objects that sit on store shelves, anything your baby enjoys playing with can be her toy. So look around your house. You already have a variety of wonderful objects that can make her environment much more stimulating. For example, the kitchen is a splendid source of interesting objects.

And remember, your baby's first playthings, and often the most important ones, are parts of your body and his own.

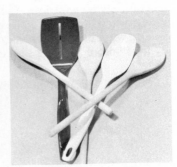
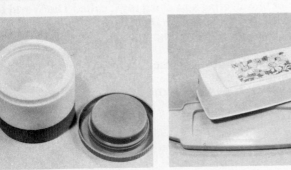

316

Making Her Crib or Cradle More Interesting
Since your baby explores primarily with her eyes for the
first few months, make her cradle or crib an interesting
place to explore!

For a change, substitute patterned crib sheets for the
traditional white. Either buy them, or decorate plain
sheets with fabric cutouts.

Even babies a few weeks old enjoy looking at pictures
hung at mattress height. Paint them yourself, or cut them
out of magazines and glue them onto cardboard. Use
bright colors and simple shapes.

It's a good idea to change these crib toys every few
weeks. A good toy to hang for the entire year is an
unbreakable mirror.

When your baby prefers to lie on her back and look up,
hang a mobile or make a seeing tray.

And occasionally let your 2 - to 3-month - old wear a pair of
booties with jingle bells attached. Her kicks will become
more interesting to her.

A Change of Scene
Besides giving your baby a frequent change of scenery in
her crib or cradle, give her a change of setting. The
easiest way is to lay your baby in different places in her
crib during the day so she can see the same sorts of objects from slightly different directions.

Besides pictures, you can hang other things from the
crib side:

    a patterned necktie
    colorful hand toys
    fancy ribbons and bows, and
    a patterned kitchen towel.

Sometimes roll her crib into a different room.

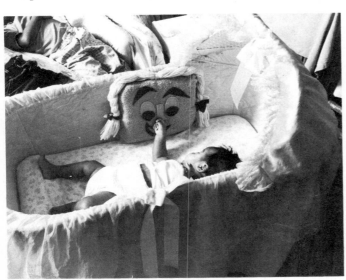

Designing Your Baby's Environment : Your Home

There are 2 pieces of equipment that allow your young baby to explore more of her home.

Wind-Up Swing

Many young babies enjoy sitting in a wind-up swing. (You might have to prop her up with pillows.) Not only does it let your baby look around the room, but the gentle swinging motion is relaxing. Some swings have a bassinet attachment, which is good for naps.

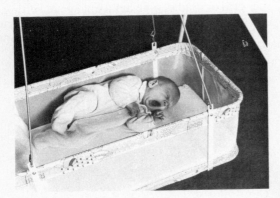

Infant Seat

An infant seat is excellent for letting your baby see what's going on around her. Set it on the kitchen table or counter so she can watch you prepare meals, eat dinner, and do the dishes (many babies are fascinated by running water). Sit her in front of a screen door or floor-length window for a glimpse of neighborhood activity. And many babies love to watch rain showers, snow storms, and other weather phenomena.

For safety's sake, whenever you carry your baby in her infant seat, cradle it in your arms. Holding it by the handle is much clumsier than you might realize. And discontinue its use as a seat when your baby becomes very active. Most infant seats tip over far too easily.

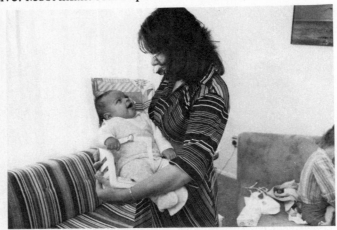

Changes in His Crib

After a few months your baby becomes much more active — waving, kicking, and squirming around. Now's the time to make some changes in his crib environment:

Remove any light cardboard pictures — he might rip or chew them up and try to swallow the pieces.

Raise his mobile so it's out of reach. He still enjoys looking at it, but most mobiles are too fragile for handling.

Take away any hanging toys that aren't safe for grasping and mouthing.

And add some new features:

Hang up a cradle gym — he'll like something to reach for, hit, grasp, and pull.

Hang a noisemaker over his feet. Your baby may like something to kick as well as things to grasp. A soft chime toy, stuffed animal with a noisemaker, or even a cardboard box with a bell inside might be welcome.

Or you can stick a suction-cup toy on the crib end.

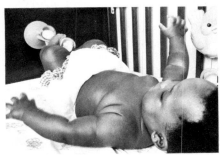

Also on the market are a number of crib toys that move or make noise when the baby pulls a handle or string.

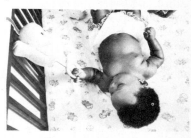

Useful Equipment

Three items help your growing baby explore his home.

Hanging Jump Seat

Give your baby a chance to see the world from a different point of view. A hanging jump seat holds him in a standing position and lets him exercise his legs. And many babies love the bouncing motion, especially since they produce it themselves. Make sure the doorways you hang this in are too wide for your baby to bump against the frames. And don't use a jumper until your baby is strong enough to hold his head up without help.

**Designing Your Baby's
Environment: Your Home**

Walker

Like the jumper, a walker holds your baby upright. In addition, it allows him to move around the room under his own power. A walker with a round base is the safest kind —it's much more stable. To protect your baseboards, wrap the bottom of the frame with felt window weather stripping. It's better not to let your baby play in his walker unattended; he might back into a sharp object, or tip over.

Playpen

Here's an item as useful for parents as for babies. A playpen is excellent for giving your baby changes of environment when you're too busy to share them with her. You can roll it into almost any room, and even outside on the porch or in the yard. Just be sure to keep an eye on her from the window. In addition, a playpen is a fine gymnasium. The solid floor is a good base for practicing rolling over, sitting alone, and crawling; and the top rails are perfect supports for taking the first steps. A playpen is an excellent portable bed, for visits with friends, or an afternoon nap outdoors. And it's a safe indoor playground for the crawler when you just *have* to leave her alone for a few minutes, to run to the laundry room, take a quick shower, or finish preparing dinner. Your baby will like it more if you make it an enjoyable place to play. Decorate the playpen with the same types of pictures, hanging toys, and cradle gyms that she enjoys so much in her crib.

Many baby care books recommend that you set the playpen in the same room where you're working so your baby can watch you. But many parents we've talked to have found this is not a good idea. Since people are easily the most interesting part of the environment, your baby naturally would rather play *with* you than *watch* you. But placed in another room, where he is not distracted by familiar people, a baby will usually play quite happily in a playpen.

A playpen is fine for short periods, but don't depend on it too much; it can become a prison. Your baby needs opportunities to explore your home. In addition, as with any piece of equipment, each baby has personal preferences. If yours happens to dislike a playpen, jumper, walker, or whatever, it's better not to force it on him. For this reason you might want to borrow items or get them secondhand.

Your baby's new ability to crawl gives him a new independence. Now he can explore his environment more actively — and more on his own. *He* seeks out things to explore, rather than waiting for you to bring them to him. And he'll try to explore things you would never bring him — like the electric outlet and lamp cord! So now your job as Environmental Designer is more than giving your baby a variety of interesting objects and settings; it's making your home SAFE for his new ways of exploring, by baby-proofing it.

Baby-proofing Your Home
Baby-proofing can seem like a nuisance at first — but it's worth it. Babies have a natural curiosity, and every home is rich in fascinating things to learn about. And no matter how hard you try, you just can't keep an eye on your baby at all times. Turn your back a few seconds and she may be into the dog's dish. Even when you closely supervise all excursions it's best to baby-proof. Accidents have a way of just happening. So, when you baby-proof, you're doing it not only to protect your house from destruction at her inexperienced hands, you're also protecting your baby from dangers she's too young to understand. Her curiosity can draw her to an inviting staircase or to those bright bite-size pennies that have slipped under your dresser. She's too young to tell the difference between a safe plaything and a "Hands Off" item.

To begin your baby-proofing, get down on your hands and knees. This gives you a better idea of how your baby sees things, and it may highlight some dangers you could overlook. Anything you notice that she shouldn't touch should be put out of reach or made safe for her explorations.

What are some potential dangers?
Small Things. Clear your floors of all small objects he might put in his mouth and try to swallow: pins, buttons, tacks, coins, paper clips, nails, screws, matches, even balls of fluff that accumulate on your carpet and especially under furniture. Check the knobs on your television, stereo, and radio. If small ones can be pulled off, replace them with controls too large to fit in his mouth. They are available in stereo and electronic stores.
Things on Tables. Remove any untouchables from your low tables, such as glass figurines, china bowls, cigarette lighters, and especially ashtrays. Babies just love sticking cigarette butts in their mouths. And be careful with burning cigarettes. On dining tables, it's a good idea to use placemats rather than hanging table cloths. Secure lamp wires against your baby's tugging by wrapping them around table legs, or fastening them to the undersides of table tops.
Electrical Things. Cover any unused outlets with safety caps from the hardware or variety store. Be careful to keep small appliances, such as fans, hairdriers, and kitchen items out of the reach of his crib, playpen, walker, and high chair.

Hot Things. If your radiators don't have covers, block them with large pieces of furniture. It's a good idea to cover heating ducts with guards. They are available at appliance stores.

Sharp Things. Make sure knives, scissors, razors, pencils, pens, and sharp tools are always out of reach.

Wastebaskets. Babies love to get into trash cans, but they usually contain all sorts of hazards: small objects, broken glass, used razor blades, spoiled food, and so forth. It's best to buy at least 1 large garbage can with a locking lid to use for your dangerous throw-aways. Empty your wastebaskets frequently.

Plastic Bags. These are super-dangerous, because they can smother a baby very quickly. Destroy IMMEDIATELY those thin plastic bags your dry cleaning comes in. Tie them into knots or throw them in the outdoor trash. They should never be used as a waterproof cover for his mattress or playpen pad. Your baby might pull up his sheets and find the plastic. Keep plastic food storage bags and plastic food wrap out of reach as well.

Stairs. It's a good idea to install safety gates at both the top and bottom of your staircase. Remember to put a safety gate at the top of your basement stairs.

Plants. Few things are more attractive to babies than plants. The trouble is that house plants are heavy, not very stable, and covered with not-so-edible leaves in pots of not-so-edible dirt. Put small plants out of reach, and be sure to watch your baby when she's around floor plants.

Here are some safety considerations for specific rooms:

1. Nursery
Remember about crib safety!

Be sure all appliances (fan, vaporizer, etc.) are safely out of reach.

Shield radiators and heating ducts.

Make sure he can't reach plants, curtains, venetian blind and window shade cords, and other pieces of furniture from his crib.

If you baby-proof his room, a gate across the doorway turns the nursery into a giant safe playground.

2. Bathroom
Because of the slick floor and all those hard fixtures, the bathroom is *not* a safe place to play. It's a good idea to keep the door securely closed or locked from the outside when not in use. A simple hook and eye is fine.

In case he just might wander in, keep scissors and razors out of reach, and put ALL medicines and cosmetics in high cabinets, such as the one over the sink. Many cosmetics are poisonous.

3. Kitchen
Keep his high chair away from hot surfaces.

Move ALL poisons (and this includes nearly every cleaning agent) to an overhead cabinet. If you can't, put them all into 1 cabinet and LOCK IT UP!

If your baby can reach up and open drawers, make sure they can't be pulled all the way out.

Make sure low drawers don't contain dangerous objects, such as sharp cooking utensils, knives, forks, and cooking thermometers.

Keep your baby away from pet beds and feeding bowls.

The Indoor Playground

Now that she's crawling, your baby will probably use your entire house as a playground. You've made it safe; here are some suggestions for making it fun:

A row of pictures at baseboard height makes a hallway more interesting for the crawler.

1 or 2 lower shelves in the family bookcase are good for storing his books—real ones as well as old catalogues, magazines, and mail advertisements. He can reach them himself, and they may distract him from pulling *your* books out and dumping them on the floor.

A bookcase rather than a toy box in the nursery makes it easier for your baby to choose her own playthings.

Large pillows on the floor are fun to crawl over.

An empty cardboard box or grocery bag turned on its side can be a fascinating house to crawl into.

And some of the best places to play are the living room, with all those knobs and handles on cabinets and desks; in front of the floor-length mirror in your bedroom; a closet full of shoes; and, best of all, the kitchen.

Playing in the Kitchen

With all those drawers and cabinets just waiting to be opened, and full of such treasures, the kitchen is probably the Number 1 play area.

A cabinet he's allowed to explore will be much appreciated. You don't have to fill it with his toys. Use it for storing those safe kitchen objects he'll want to play with:

> plastic cups, bowls and all kinds of containers

> pots and pans

> muffin tins and bread pans

> aluminum pie plates.

A low drawer is endlessly fascinating when filled with plastic cooking spoons, measuring cups, coasters, spatulas, and similar items.

Until he's at that label peeling stage, canned goods are excellent for pulling out, putting back, stacking like blocks, and rolling on the floor.

The high chair can be a fun place for your baby to play while waiting for her meals. A suction-cup toy on the tray is good for batting. She also might like to play with some hand toys or kitchen items. When your 8-to 12-month-old begins dropping or throwing these, tie them onto the high chair with string, and show her how to retrieve them. A wooden or plastic cooking spoon is a fine drumstick, and the tray a good drum. Maybe give her a spoon and empty plastic bowl, so she can practice feeding on air — it's less messy than applesauce. Paper is fun to handle. And so is a damp washcloth, both to chew and to practice how to wipe her own face.

As excellent a playground as it is, the kitchen can be the scene of many accidents. Always be alert to possible dangers. The kitchen floor is not a good play area for your baby when you're preoccupied with cooking. Things might spatter and spill, and you might not notice her underfoot when moving hot foods from one place to another.

House Tour

The first part of this chapter concentrates on ways to make your baby's surroundings safe and stimulating, especially for exploring on her own. However, traveling with an experienced companion can be a wonderfully rewarding way to explore a new environment. So . . . be your baby's guide! The first place you can explore is your home.

Both you and your baby may enjoy making a walking tour of your house a part of your daily routine. As you carry her from room to room, stop frequently to observe the scenery and talk about interesting objects she might like to see: things on the top of your dresser; posters, pictures, photographs, and hangings on the wall; a carving on the top of the banister; knicknacks on the living room bookcase; plants; a centerpiece on the dining room table; articles on your desk; toothbrushes in the bathroom; clocks; candlesticks on the mantlepiece . . . . Take time to look out windows and describe things outside. And of course, be sure to stop at every mirror.

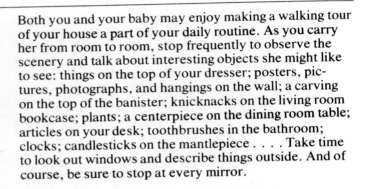

Your 4-month-old and older might like to touch as well as look. So pause on your tours to let her feel the softness of your bedspread, or water rushing over her hand in the sink, or the texture of a wall hanging. Let her handle those safe objects she takes an interest in: the hairbrush, your key ring, a door knob. These house tours are excellent opportunities for beginning to teach your baby about the names and textures of different objects.

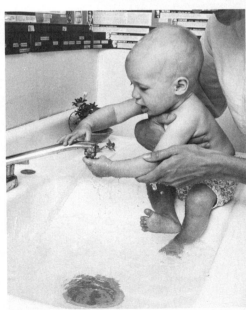

Yard Tour
In nice weather it's fun to spend part of your day together
outside. You may want to take a daily yard tour, just as
you tour your house. The yard has many interesting
things to explore: a hedge, leaves, blades of grass, trees,
an acorn or small flower, a garden, and animals.

Because there is usually so much activity around you, it's also fun to spread a blanket on the grass and watch cars going by and other children playing outdoors. Sitting under a large tree is especially nice; most babies enjoy listening to the rustling of the leaves, and watching the play of light and shadow when branches sway in the wind. Of course, a picnic lunch is nearly always a welcome treat — and so is an afternoon rest together on the blanket or in a hammock.

Two things you may want to consider getting for outside playtimes with your 6-to 12-month-old are a sandbox and a plastic or rubber wading pool. These can help make summertime a lot more fun.

**Designing Your Baby's
Environment: The Outside World**

Outings

You shouldn't feel confined to house or yard when you have a baby — and neither should he. There are many products which make it easy to take your baby on outings, where he can see different things and, best of all, meet new friends. You'll also be doing the world a service. Babies bring out the best in the people they meet.

Places to Go

Take your baby wherever there are people to watch and interesting things to look at:

Walks around the neighborhood. Besides the pleasure of being out in the fresh air, these walks allow you and your baby to make new friends and see old ones. You'll be surprised how many people will want to follow her growth and progress.

The grocery store is almost every baby's favorite place to visit. All the design devices used by manufacturers to attract *your* attention to their products will also interest your baby. And a supermarket has lights and colors and people and noise and music.

Shopping malls

Department stores, particularly the mirrors

Toy stores

Pet shops, especially those with brightly colored birds and tropical fish.

Besides joining you on errands, most babies enjoy all types of outings. They especially like places that usually attract families, since your baby likes to see other children. Such places include:

The zoo

Museums (especially with your baby in a back carrier, since the pictures are hung at adult height). Besides art museums, there are children's museums, transportation museums, fire museums, museums of natural history, etc.

Plant conservatories and greenhouses

Outdoor concerts, arts festivals, fairs, and carnivals

Special seasonal exhibits (such as Christmas displays)

Parades

Picnics in the park

The swimming pool or beach.

Remember that on longer outings, a baby needs protection from strong sun and high temperatures. His sweat glands don't work too well at first, and his skin hasn't had a chance to build a resistance to bad sunburning. When you're going to be in the sun for any length of time, make sure he wears a hat, and use a SUNSCREEN lotion on his skin. Be sure to check the label; many suntan lotions sold for adults don't contain a sunscreen.

At the pool or beach he'll need shade: under an umbrella or a tent made from blankets. Even with this overhead protection, the glare from the water can burn, so don't stay out in the sun for more than a few hours at most. And it's better to avoid the hottest part of the day (between 11 AM and 2 PM).

Designing Your Baby's Environment: The Outside World

Equipment
There are a number of devices that make outings with your baby easier.

Carriages
Best suited to a young baby. A carriage is useful for relaxing walks around the neighborhood, and as a bed for outdoor naps. Here's a model from the 1930's:

Strollers
For any age, depending on the type. The standard stroller, with rigid frame and canopy top, is wonderful for taking your baby on long walks. One with an adjustable back will be the most useful. For the younger baby, lower the back so she can lie down; the 3-to 6-month-old can sit

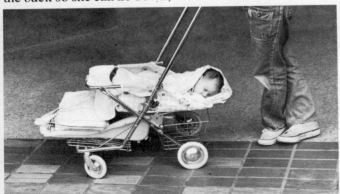

in a semi-reclining position; for the older baby, who can sit well alone, raise the back to the regular sitting position. An umbrella type can be used from about 3 months on, since it "cradles" the baby in a semi-sitting position. Because it's light, and easy to fold up and maneuver, an umbrella stroller is good for crowded places and for taking your baby on errands. However, it's less comfortable than a standard stroller for longer walks, since it affords the baby relatively little freedom for moving his arms and turning his head to look about.

Carriers
For any age, depending on the type.

Sling
A sling, which supports your baby on your hip, is best suited to his younger months. Using a sling is better than holding him in your arm when you're carrying other things or need a free hand for other tasks.

Snuggly-type

This is a cloth carrier with 2 zippered pouches: a small one which provides head support for the younger baby, and a larger one for carrying an older baby. A snuggly can be worn in front or back, depending on your baby's weight and age.

Backpacks

A back carrier with a rigid metal frame can be used when your baby has gained good control over the muscles that support his head (usually around 6 months). Some have a support piece that enables them to stand up alone. This makes it easier to put on by yourself, and allows the carrier to be used as a feeding chair or stand-up sleeper.

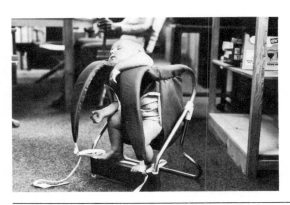

Carseats

A safe carseat is a MUST for automobile travel — even on short errands. Manufacturers are constantly upgrading their products based on safety tests conducted by the government and concerned safety groups. We suggest you write either:

Physicians for Automotive Safety
500 Union Avenue
Irvington, New Jersey 07111

or:

Consumers Union
Mount Vernon, New York 10550

for their most recent recommendations.

Traveling with Your Baby
Being the parent of a new baby shouldn't make you feel
you have to skip your vacation, or any long trips you may
have been wanting to make. Most babies are very accom-
modating travelers, especially when you keep these
helpful hints in mind:

Whatever way you travel (car, plane, train, or bus), it's
convenient to carry a separate case for your baby's
necessities, to have them at your fingertips. The case
should include:

a change of clothing

disposable diapers

pre-moistened towelettes

lots of tissues or paper towels (for cleaning up messes)

a few regular diapers (for bibs, pads, and to protect
surfaces when you change his other diapers)

first aid items, including a pain reliever, a
thermometer, and a nasal aspirator

care items

food.

And to help make traveltime playtime, take along a bag
of tricks. What should go inside? A few new hand toys,
some old favorites, maybe a portable mobile. Avoid toys
with many small pieces — they're too easy to lose. And
bulky toys take up more room than they're worth.

Car Travel

When traveling by car:

Always use a safe carseat.

A picnic lunch can be even more fun than eating in
restaurants.

For safety, keep the back window ledge free of objects
that might fly around when you make a sudden stop.

Public Transportation
When traveling by plane, train, or bus:

When you buy your tickets, ask about special services
for babies. Some companies lend you a bassinet or
other type of carrier. This can save bringing unnecessary
equipment. Also, see what accommodations they have
for preparing food.

Carry his personal case with you rather than putting it
in the baggage compartment.

On a plane, it's a good idea to feed your baby during
takeoff and landing. The sucking helps reduce the
pressure on his ears.

Baby's Schedule
If at all possible, try to stick to his regular feeding and
sleeping schedules when you travel. With all the newness
and excitement of a trip, consistency in these routines
can be comforting.

4. Exercising Your Baby's Body

We all know that physical stimulation can be pleasurable for both parents and baby, and that infants need a certain amount of cuddling, cradling, and rocking for proper development. Physical play can also put your baby in a receptive mood for further interaction and many different games. Therefore, massages and exercises are often a good warm-up for other play sessions. Finally, physical stimulation is very important for communication and learning.

The Touch of Love

One of the best ways to communicate with your baby is by touching. A baby's skin and body are very sensitive, and the way he's handled through this first year gives your baby messages about those who care for him. An infant gets impressions of the person who touches him in much the same way we form opinions about other adults based on a handshake or embrace. Expressing your love through tender holding and physical play will tell your baby about your feelings, and give him a sense of warmth and security.

The process of getting in touch with one another begins the first time you hold your baby, and continues through the regular handling and closeness experienced during daily caretaking routines. Your normal day already includes a great deal of this time together. However, if you're new parents and have had relatively limited experience with babies, it's easy to overlook ways to add variety to your regular physical stimulation.

Massages

One way to add variety to your baby's physical stimulation is to give him a massage. A perfect time is right after his bath, or while changing his diaper. Gently stroke or rub your baby's back, stomach, arms, and legs. Your warm hands are great, but occasionally you may want to add some variety by wearing a cotton glove or soft mitten, or by using:

    a cotton ball

    a feather

    a piece of soft fabric, or

    a *soft* paint brush.

Watch your baby's reactions to see what type of things he likes best.

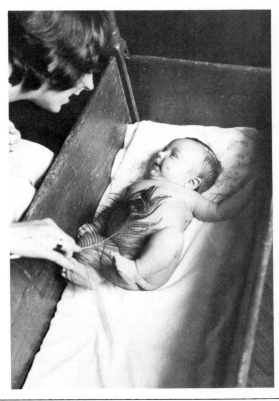

Exercising Your Baby's Body

Baby Exercises

Your baby won't be strong enough to really move about on her own for a number of months — but she doesn't have to wait that long to exercise her limbs and body. You can help, starting around the first month.

In most cities, there are organizations which hold both prenatal and postnatal exercise classes. Many encourage mothers to bring their babies, and part of each class is devoted to exercising together. Check with your local YWCA or the International Childbirth Education Association (P.O. Box 5852, Milwaukee, Wisconsin 53220) for information on classes in your area. Besides the fun of exercising, these give you the opportunity to meet other new parents and provide your baby with a new environment.

Exercising your baby involves more than just aiding her muscle development; at the same time she's learning about you through your facial expressions, voice, and touch. Your movements should be gentle and gradual; be careful not to jerk your baby into position or cause any strain on her body. Exercises will be more fun for your baby if you enjoy them, too, and let her know it. And be sensitive to her feelings. Your baby will tell you which exercises she enjoys and which she doesn't.

Do as many or as few of these exercises as you both desire at any 1 playtime. Many babies enjoy a few repetitions of each movement before going on to another. At first you'll probably be a little clumsy, but don't get discouraged. As with any new skill you learn, it takes practice. Exercises are even more enjoyable when you sing favorite nursery rhymes, and move your baby to the rhythm.

For the Early Months

1.
While holding your baby's leg with one hand, with your other hand gently twist his foot inward

and outward

and then up

and down.

2.
You can help her do knee bends: both at the same time

or left

and then right.

3.
Help your baby "ride a
bicycle."

4.
And then gently roll him
over and do frog kicks.

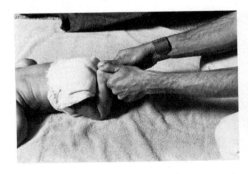
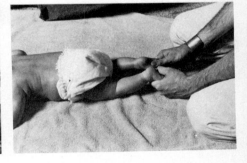

5.
To exercise her arms: bring
your baby's hands together

then cross her arms over
her chest

and straighten
them out to the sides.

**Exercising Your
Baby's Body**

For the Early Months
6.

Stretch her arms up   and down   and then one each way (and alternate).

  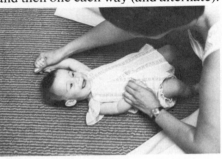

7.
You can also combine
arm and leg stretches.

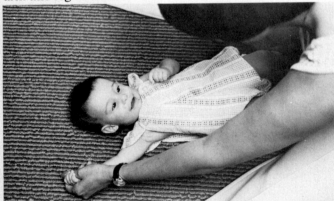 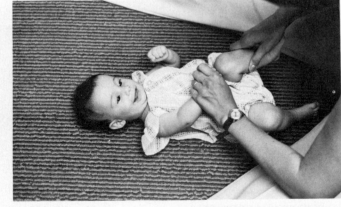

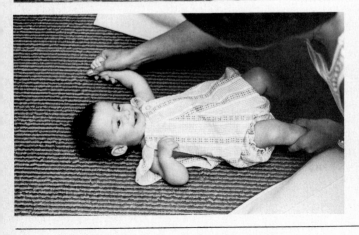 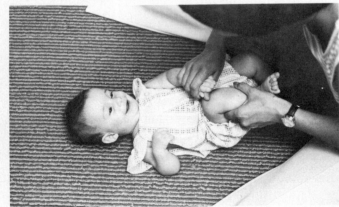

Adding More at 5 Months
Now your baby's greater
strength permits more
strenuous exercise.

1.
You can help with first
push-ups. Lift his legs a
few inches from the floor,
and encourage him to
straighten his arms and
push.

2.
To exercise his stomach,
hold your baby by the
waist and "roll" him back
and forth over a round
pillow, or beach ball.

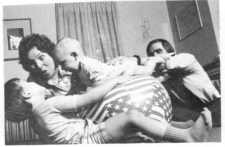

3.
From the floor,

pull to a sit-up

and to a stand-up.

Let her practice
deep-knee bends.

Adding More at 5 Months
4.
He can also do sit-ups and
"fall-backs" in your lap.

5.
For all sorts of thrills, give
your baby an airplane ride
(there are a number of
ways).

And More at 8 Months
New exercises become possible as your baby approaches
the walking stage.

1.
Try doing sit-ups from the *other* end. Go only as far as his
natural flexibility allows!

 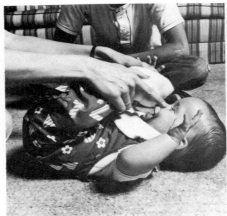 

2.
Now your baby might try
push-ups when you hold
his ankles.

3.
When he's quite steady at this, walk him like a
wheelbarrow.

4.
And, of course, she'll enjoy
walking the more usual
way, too.

**Exercising Your
Baby's Body**

Rides

Physical play and exercise needn't be confined to the exercise pad. The rhythm and sensation of moving through space is also a wonderful experience, so give your baby rides.

Whenever you feel like it, carry your baby in a front or backpack for walks around the neighborhood, on errands, and even around the house. These are also excellent opportunities for treating your baby to a range of settings.

At around 6 months, when she's developed good control over her neck muscles, you can introduce a number of new rides. She may like swinging in a large plastic basket, riding on your shoulders, or taking a flying walk. While holding your baby in a standing position with your hands under her arms, walk a few steps and then, "One . . . two . . . three . . . UP!"

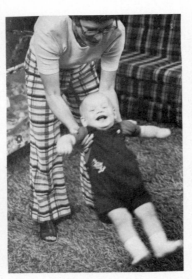

Using a small blanket, pull your 2-month-old around her crib, and your 3-month-old and older across the floor. Watch out for bumps.

Your 3-month-old also might enjoy a "Camel Ride." This is much safer than riding on your back, because he's near the floor, and you can see him at all times.

He might also enjoy swinging, either alone in a safe kiddie seat, or maybe together with you.

Using Her Crawling Muscles

These games take advantage of your baby's developing ability to move around by herself. There are 2 main ways you can help your baby with her crawling:

1. Getting her started.

2. Making it more fun.

You've already been helping your baby prepare, through your massaging, exercising, carrying her about, and giving her opportunities for large body movements in your physical play. Cap it off with a chance to practice. Of course she'll probably make crawling motions while in the crib or playpen; in addition, put her stomach-down on the floor. Then let her flail about. When you have the time to participate, a push against her feet may provide the added traction she needs to get going.

You can make crawling more fun by giving your baby something to crawl toward: a toy shaken out of reach, a favorite piece of finger food, or just your outstretched arms (often the favorite encouragement).

She might like to crawl after a slowly rolling ball or a string toy you pull along the floor.

"Chase"

The game of "Chase" is good for this age group, so get down on the floor with her and crawl after each other. Sometimes she'll enjoy pursuing *you*. And when the roles are reversed, your "I'm gonna get you!" noises will usually bring squeals of laughter.

"Obstacle Courses"

When your baby is a good crawler, make his trips a bit more challenging and interesting. You're a most enjoyable obstacle course: let him crawl all over you, sneaking under your knees, snuggling up under your arm, stopping to explore your clothing or jewelry. For variety, make an obstacle course out of pillows or cushions, with a surprise toy behind each barrier. This is usually more fun if you lead the way. Or fashion a series of tents and tunnels for him to crawl through. Boxes with the ends cut off, a blanket draped over 2 chairs, or even a low table make an adventuresome journey.

"Climbing the Hill"

Crawling needn't be only a flat-surface exercise. Using firm chair-seat cushions, build a series of broad steps and encourage your baby to crawl up and get the prize (a favorite toy) on the highest one. You can reverse the

game by cutting open a large cardboard box and spreading it into a runway (make sure there are no staples or rough edges), and placing it over the pillow steps. This will produce an indoor sliding board. Your baby will probably want to be held for at least the first few descents.

On to Walking

As with crawling, you've been helping baby prepare to walk with your physical stimulation games and exercises. Now give her some more practice. Walk with her whenever you're both in the mood. At first she'll need both hands held; later, one will be sufficient. And give *her* opportunities for practice. The crib and playpen are great supports for pulling up and toddling about. You might try sitting her in front of a low piece of furniture and encouraging her to pull to a standing position. Then let her walk around the table. Or let her push a light kitchen chair.

When she's steadier on her feet, try this: Stand your baby on the floor at one end of the couch and wave a toy or call to her from the other end. Hugs, kisses, and other excited expressions are a wonderful end to a successful trip. Later, encourage her to take a few steps alone. Stand her up, and when she gets her balance, let her go and back away a few steps. "Come here, Ellen, come to Daddy!"

5. Aiding Your Baby's Language Development

Every sound your baby makes is a forerunner of true speech — from the cries of the newborn through the gurgles and babbles of the 6-month-old to the first real words of the 12-month-old. Learning to talk is a developmental process, with a number of steps along the way. You don't "teach" these steps; the age at which a particular one appears is determined by each baby's inner developmental timetable. Nevertheless, parents have a very important role in this process. Your baby needs you to provide 2 necessary conditions for his speech development. First, he needs you to give him good models of speech sounds for him to imitate. Second, he needs opportunities and encouragement to practice his talking skills, just as he practices any developmental skill, such as crawling.

Create a Rich Verbal Environment
Even when the two of you aren't playing together, talk to your baby! Just as you surround him with an interesting physical environment to encourage exploration and play, surround him with words. Listening to your adult language helps your baby learn about important speech sounds. There are other benefits as well. Your voice helps convey your feelings. For most of this year, your tone and expressions are far more communicative than what you actually say. Talking to your baby tells him how special he is to you, since it helps include him in your activities, even from across the room.

Aiding Your Baby's Language Development

What to talk about? The content and nature of your conversations really depend on the situation. Many baby care books offer fairly strict guidelines for your talks: they tell you to keep it simple, concentrate on concrete objects rather than abstract thoughts, and talk about the immediate environment. These are good recommendations, but you needn't feel compelled to follow them all the time. If you did, your language would most likely become boring and unnatural. There are plenty of occasions for using short sentences and for connecting words with objects when you play together. For those other times, whenever your baby is watching you do such things as prepare dinner, fix the leaky faucet, weed the garden, drive the car, or work on your painting or needlework, talk about these activities. Explain why you add salt to a casserole, or how flowers grow from seeds, or name the colors of the threads. And when you just feel like having someone to talk to, your baby will love to hear why you hate spinach, or how much you enjoyed the movie last night, or what the world was like when you were a child. You can be sure she won't spill your secrets.

Encourage her to "talk" by asking questions and conversing as though you expected a reply. "Isn't it hot out today? It sure is—I can't remember such a hot summer, can you?" Pause after each question to give her a chance to answer. "That's right. It wasn't nearly this hot last year." Very often your baby's responses won't be vocal—she may just smile, change her facial expression, or wave her arms. Even if she doesn't make a sound, this type of conversation helps her begin to learn that dialogue is a 2-way street.

Keep your sentences fairly short, and concentrate on the immediate environment. Make naming games a part of your time together. You'll be laying a good foundation for all language development by helping him begin to learn everything has a name. So talk about the things he's interested in at the moment. "Do you see the rattle? Is this a rattle? Yes, it's a rattle. Listen—it makes sounds." Use bathing and changing routines as opportunities to name parts of his body. "Now I'm washing your stomach. Do you know you have a stomach?" "Look, George—this is your foot." During these routines, supply the name of the objects you use as well. "Now this is a washcloth. I use it to wash your *stomach,* and your *arms,* and your *face.* Now your face is clean."

Talking when You Play

Of course, talking to your baby when you're playing together also aids her language development, and makes the interaction much more enjoyable. It's helpful to keep these suggestions in mind:

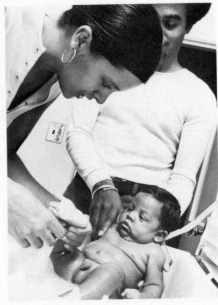

Babytalk

By babytalk we don't mean *gaa gaa doo uzzums* sounds—we mean playing with words, such as elongating vowels and changing the accents on syllables. Many books strongly urge talking to babies only in complete sentences with normal words, and strongly advise against babytalk. They have a point — how can a baby learn to talk if he doesn't hear correct language? But all parents (and nearly all strangers who come up to you in the supermarket) naturally fall into the "Hel-o-o-o-o-o, Bay-b-e-e-e-e" babytalk at times. This sort of wordplay speech has value. For one thing, it's excellent for attracting your baby's attention, and for keeping him in touch when you play together. After all, babytalk is an exaggeration of normal speech, as raising your eyebrows very high or opening your mouth in the shape of an "O" is an exaggeration of normal facial expressions. Babytalk, like

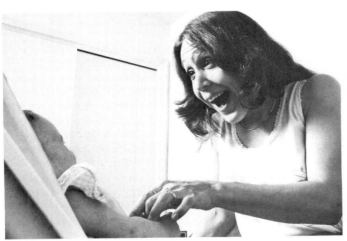

making funny faces, is a way of clowning around — and having *fun*. Babies like it — and so do parents! So if playing with words appeals to you, go ahead and talk this way. It has a place, as long as it's not the main or only language he hears.

Learning through Verbal Games

In addition to these types of conversation, give your baby opportunities and encouragement to practice his speech with Verbal Games.

"Sounds Like Mine"

Even in the early months, whenever she makes any sound (even a gurgle), lean your face over hers and gurgle right back. This usually produces a smile — and maybe even an attempt to imitate your imitation.

Between 3 and 6 months, let your baby try to imitate a sound you make. This is a bit different from the earlier game because now *you* start the ball rolling. Of course, try to limit yourself to the simple sounds he's capable of making: throaty noise, long vowel sounds, and the like.

Try the game "Bob-white." Make a long, low sound — and then add a quick high note on the end. (This is similar to the call of the bob-white bird). Varying the length of the low sounds adds a surprise ending to each game.

During the period 6 to 12 months, your baby begins to make sounds such as *ma, pa, da, di, mi, mu* — so add these to your imitation routines. You might even try springing a few new ones on her, to see what she does. She may be able to make more sounds than you think! Later these sounds will be strung together: *pa-pa-pa-pa-pa-pa*. Now see if she imitates your babble.

**Aiding Your Baby's
Language Development**

If you have a tape recorder, you can record your baby's speech at different times during the year, and play these back so she can try to imitate herself. Don't throw the tapes away. When she gets older, she'll enjoy listening to her own baby sounds, and so will you.

"Which Is What?"
Because your baby is able to understand a number of simple words before he can say them, around 8 months or so he might like to play "Which Is What?" Place a number of

his favorite toys on the floor in front of him, and while you sit facing each other, pick up each toy in turn and talk about it. "See, Benjamin — this is your ball. It's round and blue . . . and it bounces. Watch." "See your dolly? She has arms just like you." During this naming period, let him play with any toy he reaches for. Then, with all the objects back on the floor, ask him to hand you one. "Which one's the block? Can you find the block? That's right — that's the block. Hand it to me. GOOD!"

If he picks up the wrong toy, merely say, "Hey look! That one's the dolly. Here's the block — it's small and hard. Can you hand me the block?" REMEMBER: many babies this age will hold out a toy to you — but will NOT let it go. This is a natural stage of development: showing an object rather than offering it to you. He's not being selfish or a tease. Later he will begin to hand you toys and release them.

"What's the Name?"
Your 9-month-old will like to try imitating words as well as sounds, so encourage her to try repeating the name of an object after you say it. "Here, Susan — this is a ball. Can you say ball?" Remember that before 12 months she'll usually just say part of the name, or make a sound which resembles the name, so don't expect a perfect pronunciation. Instead, you can best encourage your baby's attempts at naming objects by modifying or expanding her pronunciation. For example, when you ask her to say *cup,* and she responds "ca," don't say, "No, that's a *cup.*" Say, "Yes, that's a *cup.* Very good!" The word *no* can be discouraging and even confusing; she may think, "That's *not* a cup?" By responding with a "yes" and then repeating the name correctly, you're giving encouragement — and teaching her the real name.

Singing is also a wonderful way to encourage your baby's language development. Here's where nursery rhymes come in handy, because the words and tunes are so simple. Songs like "Row, Row, Your Boat," "Jack and Jill," and "London Bridge" are standards. Sing each rhyme a few times while he watches and listens. Then repeat a line and pause, so he can try to imitate your sounds.

Books

As a general guideline, use books with large, colorful pictures. Don't worry about the text; for this first year, you don't really *read* books to him, you talk about the pictures.

Books are a wonderful way to help create a rich verbal (and visual) environment. Even before he takes an active interest in turning the pages and playing games with the pictures, your young baby might enjoy looking at books while you make up stories about the pictures. Don't limit yourself to simple baby books. Photograph albums, "women's" magazines, illustrated cookbooks, art books, and even *this* Guide are good sources for pictures.

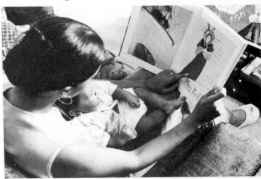

When he becomes more active, at around 5 months, choose books made from heavy paper, plastic, cardboard, or cloth. These will better withstand his rough

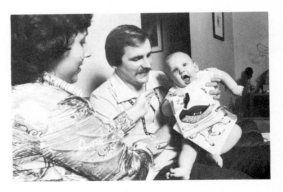

At what age should you introduce your baby to books? Whenever you like, and *he* shows interest. Some babies like "reading" with you as early as a few months; others not until the end of the first year. And some active babies will never sit still long enough to get past the first page. It's important to respect your baby's personality, and his mood. Trying to force him to sit through book time will most likely cause a lot of frustration for everyone involved.

treatment. At this age he'll probably be most interested in exploring the physical properties: opening and closing the covers, turning the pages, maybe trying to put it in his mouth. If he still shows an interest in looking at the pictures and listening to your stories, continue your earlier game.

If not, don't insist on cooperation, because in a few months, when his attention span has increased, he'll be ready to play with you again. And maybe to play some of the following games.

Use books with pictures of:

familiar toys

household objects

familiar things in his world (automobile, tree, flower)

a baby's personal items (clothing, brush, bottle)

and — a real favorite — animals.

As you look at a book together, point to a pictured object while you talk about it, and encourage her to point to it, too. She may use one or both hands instead of her finger. Be sure to repeat the name in a number of sentences: "Look, Claire — this is a pair of shoes. Do you see the shoes? They're just like the shoes you wear."

Or let your baby start the game. Open the book and let her point to an object — and then supply a description or story about it.

With the 9-to 12-month-old, you can play ''Picture Hide and Seek.'' Take a book which has a few objects on each page and ask your baby to ''Find me the dog! Which one's the dog?'' (Just like the "Which Is What?" game you play with toys).

And add some vocal imitation. When you point to a pictured object and say its name, encourage her to repeat it.

With animal books you can play a favorite of most babies: "What does the (cat) say?" Point to an animal and say ''This is a cat. He says 'meow, meow' — can you say that?'' You'll probably have to demonstrate each sound a number of times before she'll answer.

Picture Games

Books aren't the only source of pictures. Fill a small box or bag with:

pictures cut out of magazines, and glued onto cardboard (so they last longer)

family snapshots

old greeting and Christmas cards

and picture postcards, especially museum reproductions of artworks.

Let your baby dump them out and you can make up a story about each one, or play the hide and seek game: ''Show me a picture of Grandma!''

To play ''Match 'Em Up,'' paste pictures of familiar objects (a baby shoe, a spoon, a ball, a toy car, etc.) on the inside of some plastic containers, and give your baby the real things to drop in the corresponding tubs. He might need your help the first few times.

And a game especially for parents: Each night, after putting your baby in his crib, spend a few minutes to tell him the ''story'' of what he did that day. Be sure to include any special accomplishments, such as rolling over for the first time, sitting alone, or taking his first steps. Mention his name throughout your narrative, so he'll know it's a story all about him. If you record some of these tales on tape, you'll have a living diary of your baby's first year, something all of you will enjoy listening to for many years. It's a fine way to share his growth with visiting friends and relatives.

6. Adding Music to Your Baby's World

Even the very young baby usually likes listening to music. Quiet instrumental music will soothe most babies and help them to sleep. Studies show a baby's breathing and pulse rate become very regular when he listens to soft, rhythmic music — possibly because this reminds him of his mother's heartbeats. In fact, recordings of heartbeats have been used successfully in hospital nurseries to help newborns fall asleep. So it's a good idea to make a radio or record player part of your baby's nursery, especially if you have a fussy sleeper.

Music is also good for calming his fussiness, and for keeping him entertained, when he's awake. Your baby may enjoy listening while he is sitting in his infant seat, wind-up swing, stroller, or on your lap.

It's better not to play music constantly; we tend to tune out sounds we hear all the time.

Music and Active Play

Listening to music can be more than a soothing, passive experience. You can make music a part of your active playtime, too.

For musical play, choose records with a strong, bouncy beat: soft rock, pop, folk, jazz, and recordings of Broadway shows. Try setting aside a music appreciation period a few times a week. Turn on the radio or record player and rock your baby to the beat in his cradle, rocking infant seat, or on your lap. It's more fun to introduce a variety of tempos during each period, so that his rocking can be a little different with each song.

When she's old enough to sit alone, move this game to the floor. Your baby may begin to sway in time to the music, especially when watching you do the same. Clapping your hands to the beat might help her "find" the rhythm. Or hold your baby in a standing position and let her dance.

At almost any age, most babies love to dance *with* you — so pick him up and go to town. This is where Broadway music can be great fun; so much of it is written for dancing. And if you feel like singing along, by all means do so.

Music Is Much More Than Records

Singing is a wonderfully personal way to give your baby a musical world. The extent (or lack) of your talent really doesn't matter; babies are a nondiscriminating audience. The melody and rhythm are what attract their attention.

Lullabies are wonderful for bedtime, or to soothe her temporary fussiness when you hold her and sway to the rhythm.

At other times, let her watch your face while you sing, just as she does when you talk to her. In fact, when you feel like exercising all your talents, and if you're theatrically inclined, put on a show, with singing, dancing, maybe even costumes. Everyone likes a good show.

7. Playing Games Together

The following pages suggest additional games for your playtimes together. These have been organized into 3-month age groups, to give you an idea of when each might best be introduced. Most games continue to be of interest for many months.

Keep in mind that your baby has his own schedule of development. He may begin to enjoy games either before or after the recommended age. Also remember that your baby changes a great deal during each 3-month period. A game your 4-month-old might be too young to play could become a favorite a month or 2 later.

When you play together, it's best to respect your baby's own personality and preferences. We offer a fairly large number of games so you and your baby can pick your own favorites. You don't have to play every one; these are just suggestions to get you started. And since babies like variety, you can add variations and make up new games of your own.

In these early months, your baby plays in 2 main ways:
1.) by exploring her immediate surroundings with her
eyes, ears, and hands, and 2.) by taking part in social play
with you and her visitors. Usually young babies are
awake for only short periods of time. Some babies sleep
as much as 20 hours a day! But during her waking
hours, there will be times when she's alert and eager to
play.

Games for Looking

Since your baby spends so much time exploring with her eyes, hold up some interesting things for her to look at: a colorful rattle; a hand mirror (even for babies less than 1 month old); a stuffed animal that has a large, well-detailed face; a simple, brightly colored picture; maybe even a hand or finger puppet.

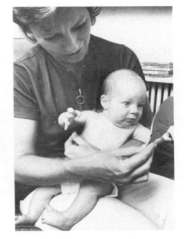

"There It Goes!"

At about 1 month or so, many babies enjoy playing tracking games. All those things she likes to look at become even more interesting when they move. Hold an object about a foot from your baby's eyes, shake it to attract her attention, and then move it very slowly in a small circle, or from one side to the other. Not too far; a young baby follows the movement mainly with her eyes.

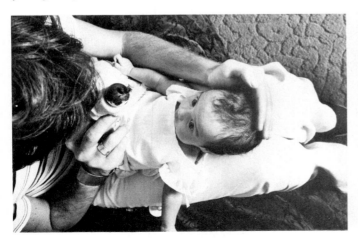

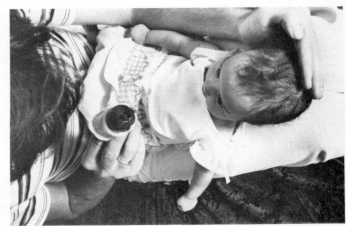

**Playing Games
Together**

Games for Looking

After about 2 months, she begins to move her head more to help keep the toy in view.

Besides toys, you can play these early tracking games with pictures or large photographs, a penlight flashlight, your face, or your hand. Wiggling your fingers, or tying a piece of ribbon on them, makes your hand more attractive.

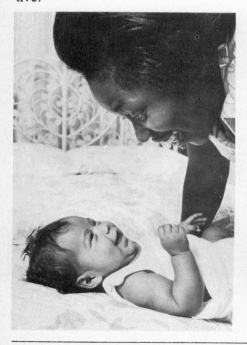 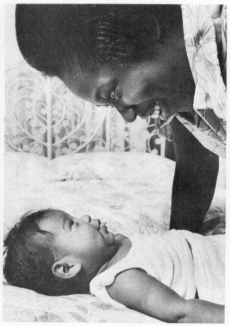 

Listening to the World

To a baby, sound is as interesting as sight. So, just as you give your baby different objects to look at, give him a variety of sounds to listen to. When he's awake in his crib, leave the nursery door open so he can hear the telephone, doorbell, stereo, vacuum cleaner, television, and other household noises. If you play a musical instrument, chances are he'll enjoy listening sometimes.

"So Many Sounds"
You can add sound games to your play together. Introduce your baby to the sounds his toys make. Let him watch you shake a rattle, ring a bell, squeeze a squeak toy, roll a chime ball, wind up a music box. And demonstrate the different sounds *you* can make. Sing, giggle, gurgle, pop your cheeks, click your tongue, snort, whistle, and so forth.

"Hear It Goes"
Play some sound tracking games. Gently shake a rattle or small bell in front of your baby's face and slowly move it from side to side — just like the visual tracking games. But now he also follows the noise.

**Playing Games
Together**

Listening to the World

"Sound and Seek"
Your 2-to 3-month-old baby may actively search for
sounds made out of his sight. When he's lying on his back
and looking to the side, shake a noisemaker overhead,
pause, and say, "Where's the bell? Can you find the
bell?" You might have to ring it again before he'll
respond.

And he may just look at you, but that's part of the fun.
Just start the game over. When he does look in the right
place, ring the bell while he watches. "That's right! Here
it is!" If he finds you too attractive every time, try standing behind his head so he can't turn to see you. And, for
variety, play sound games without a toy. See if he turns
when you snap your fingers, or clap your hands softly.

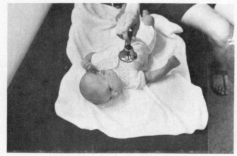

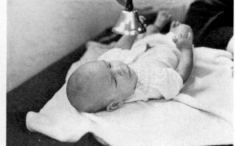

Feeling His Way Around

A young baby will automatically grasp any suitably sized object you place against her palm. This is a *reflex* and usually gives way to voluntary grasping by the age of 2 to 3 months. Still, even the young baby enjoys the experience of holding objects with different properties: wooden clothespins, plastic cooking spoons, an embroidery hoop, and even a cold hot dog. With you guiding her hand, let your baby feel the textures of her crib sheet, of soft toys, and of you! Your nose, hair, skin, tongue, and lips are all interesting to explore. Watch her face light up when you nibble her fingers.

"Hold on Tight"
She'll find *your* fingers fascinating, too. So try some early finger games. With your baby lying on her back, let her grasp your finger and then pull away slightly — in tug-of-war fashion — so she feels the gentle resistance. She'll probably pull back. After a few seconds, draw your hand away and offer it again for a repeat performance.

Or, instead of interrupting this hand holding, slowly pull your baby to a partial sitting position. "Up we go!" Play this game on a soft surface; she just might let go unexpectedly. The very young baby isn't strong enough to support her head very well, so don't lift too high. At about 3 months, you can close your hands over her fingers and pull all the way to a sitting position.

**Playing Games
Together**

Exploring with His Mouth

Although your baby won't begin actively mouthing objects on his own until the 3 to 6 month period, he enjoys exploring things with his mouth at a much earlier age. Not all sucking is for nourishment; many babies will chew on their hands or a pacifier when they're not hungry. So occasionally let him mouth a teething ring or other suitable objects.

''Ya Got Me''
Of course, your finger is a most enjoyable teether. Besides sucking on it, your baby might like this simple game. To begin, let her chew on a finger. Then slowly slip it in and out of her mouth. She wins if she bites you. ''Oh . . . ya got me!''

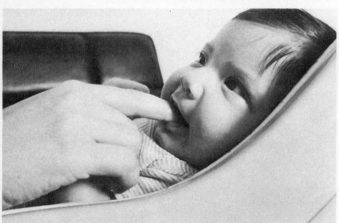 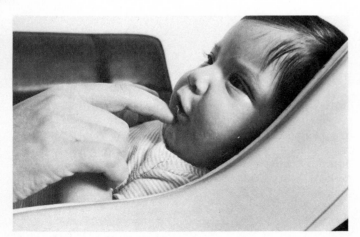

Imitating What You Do

Anything you do that your baby can imitate quickly
becomes a favorite game. After all, you're his favorite
toy. To start with, play the vocal imitation games suggested earlier. At about 2 months, he may like trying to
imitate your facial expressions. First you should establish
eye contact, by looking into his face and talking. This will
earn you his attention. Now, do something simple, like
giving him a big smile, opening and closing your mouth,
blinking your eyes, knitting your brows, and maybe sticking out your tongue. Even if he's not yet interested in imitation, he'll love watching your funny face.

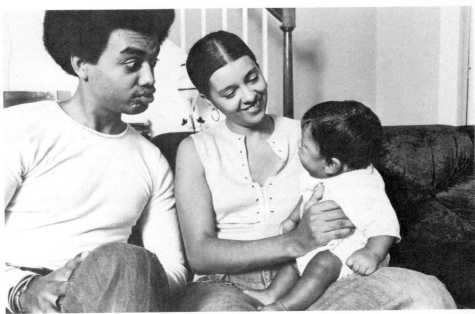

**Playing Games
Together**

During this age period, your baby gains much better control over his head, upper body, legs, and especially arms and hands. Because of these increasing skills, he becomes an active explorer, and opportunities for play and learning are substantially increased. This means you can have more fun playing with him. Also, since he now spends less time sleeping, he has more time for play. So be ready with new games.

A key thing to keep in mind is: Let him know his new abilities have a payoff. When he vocalizes, give him a response. When he waves his arms and legs, hang toys to bat and kick over the crib. And when he begins to reach for and grasp objects, give him a variety of materials to explore.

More Looking Games

''There It Goes Again''
Between 3 and 4 months, your baby may enjoy these new
tracking games: When she lies on her back, slowly move
a toy from one side of her head to the other, or from her
chest to her forehead. At this age she can focus on
objects as close as 4 or 5 inches.

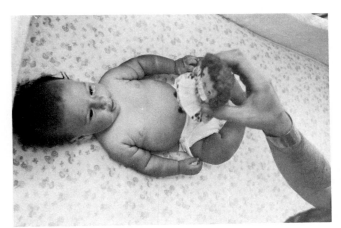
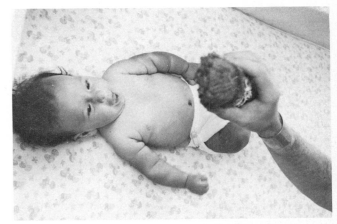

More Looking Games

When you lay her on her stomach, she'll raise her head
and shoulders, supporting the weight on her arms. So try
vertical tracking. Dangle the toy in front of her eyes and
then lift it slowly, encouraging her to keep it in sight by
pushing up with her arms.

She may also like following a toy you move in a wide
circle around her head.

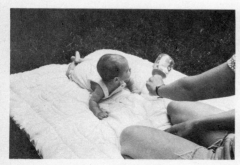  

More Looking Games

"Special Effects"
After about 4 months, your baby's eyesight is very well developed. From this time through the rest of the year, she may enjoy looking at "Special Effects" you can produce:

Blow soap bubbles.

When she's older, she may try to catch them.

Sit under a window on a sunny day and make shadow pictures on the floor.

In the evening, before it gets really dark, make patterns on the nursery walls with a flashlight. Or use the light to illuminate objects in the room.

Play S.O.S. with the venetian blinds. Just open and close them.

Make light dance on the ceiling with a mirror or other shiny object.

Or let your baby join you in watching home movies and slides.

**Playing Games
Together**

Playing with Mirrors

Double your baby's world — produce an instant playmate — with a mirror! Hold one in front of your baby's face so he can stare at the "other baby," reach for his image, pat his friend, or even bestow a kiss, especially with your encouragement. You can join in by pointing to and naming parts of his face. If he reaches for the mirror, let him take it from you. Or put a mirror on the floor and let him play in his own ways. However, never let your baby play with a *glass* mirror without your supervision. He just might accidentally smash it against a crib or chair leg.

One nice thing about mirrors is that they're almost everywhere. Hold your baby in front of wall mirrors, so you can both look at the same time, and make faces at each other. He may also enjoy looking in mirrors while you dance with him. When your baby begins to sit without support, he'll love to play in front of those full-length mirrors that are in your bedroom and in department stores. Three-way mirrors are especially fascinating.

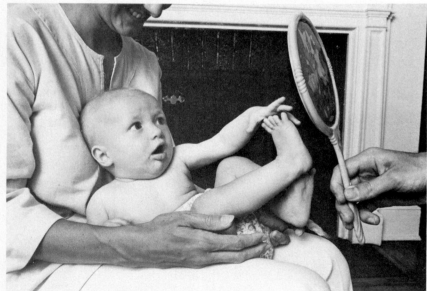

Playing with Mirrors

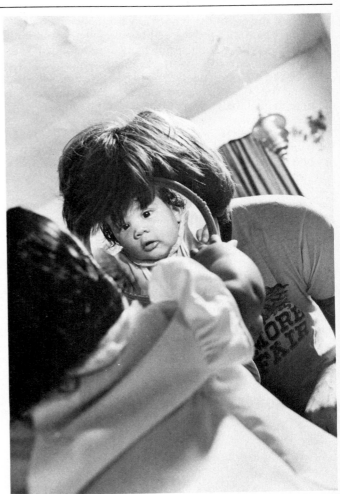

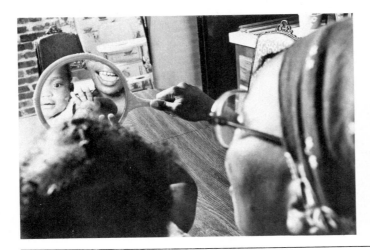

Grabbing Everything in Reach

Between 4 and 6 months, your baby is busily developing
eye-hand coordination. She no longer just bats randomly
at those things you tantalizingly hang over her head; she
reaches with a purpose. At first these attempts are
clumsy, and she often misjudges the distance between her
hand and the object. But practice makes perfect, so this is
the time to introduce ''Reach and Grab It'' games.

''Reach and Grab It''
With your baby lying on her back, or sitting in your lap
or in her infant seat, dangle a set of keys, a small clutch
ball, or other graspable object in front of her eyes. She
may enjoy tracking it for a few moments. When she raises
her arms, slowly bring the toy within reach and encourage
her to grasp it: ''Catherine—get the ball! Ah, you've
got it!'' Then pull the toy away and start over. For
variety, you can pull back slightly, for a tug-of-war game.

Or don't pull away at all. Let her continue to play with it
any way she wants. Instead of dangling a toy, maybe hold
it in your hand.

Now that she's really good at this, make the game a bit
more challenging. Use a small toy, such as a 1-inch
red cube.

Or when she's sitting in your lap, dangle the toy a little
farther away, so she really has to lean forward to grab it.
Not too far; you don't want to frustrate her.

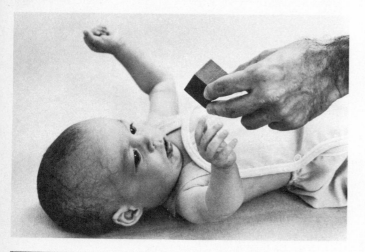

Grabbing Everything in Reach

Of course your baby's reaching and grasping won't be limited to those toys you dangle. He also likes to grab *you:* your nose, mouth, hair, and beard; and the things you wear: clothing, glasses, and jewelry. This is why some mothers find it worthwhile to switch from pierced earrings to clip-ons for the next 6 months. Rather than having him practice on your delicate adornments, you may want to fashion a few "babyproof" bracelets and necklaces. To make one, just string spools, rubber washers, or large wooden beads on a cord.

Even with these precautions, his explorations will sometimes be too vigorous; he'll really pull your hair or hit you too hard. Just tell him he's hurting you, and since he doesn't realize what he is doing, guide his hands with your own. To spare yourself unnecessary pain when you want him to let go of your hair, gently pry his hand open rather than pulling your head away.

Reaching and grasping are only part of hand play. Your baby will also enjoy exploring objects of different sizes and shapes, such as stuffed animals, squeak toys, teethers, cooking utensils, rubber animals, blocks, and plastic pot scrubbers. Just make sure everything is safe for mouthing as well as handling.

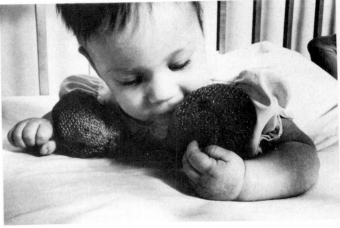

**Playing Games
Together**

Exploring Different Textures

''How Does This Feel?''
Size and shape are only 2 properties which interest
babies. Another is texture. Of course, everything has a
texture — toys, her bottle and clothing, your rug — and
she'll busily explore these on her own.

But she may also enjoy having different textures rubbed
against her skin, so play ''How Does This Feel?'' Raid
your ragbag or a remnant shop for scraps of silk, corduroy, fake fur, velvet, and dotted Swiss, and look
around your house for a terry washcloth, cotton balls,
woolly mittens, rubber toys; whatever you have. As you
play, describe each one; ''Now this one's rough and bum-
py. O-o-o-o-h, this one's really soft.''

Paper Play

One of the best toys is paper. It's everywhere—and it's cheap: cut-up shopping bags, old magazines and telephone books, wrapping paper, typing paper. *But paper is not safe for solitary play,* because it can be torn into small pieces and swallowed. Save it for when you and your baby play together.

Even better than paper are sheets of cellophane and metallized mylar, which are available at hobby and design stores. These materials are particularly tuneful when crunched and squashed, and reflect wonderful dancing lights.

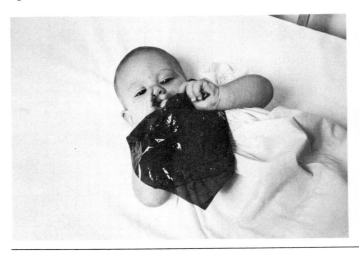

**Playing Games
Together**

Paper Play

In addition to letting your baby play with paper any way she likes, try the following game.

"The Newspaper Shuffle"
The crunch of newspaper is particularly enticing, so try this game, which combines sound with hand play for an added treat. When your baby is lying or sitting on the floor, crumple a piece of newspaper near her ear and toss it at her. Then crumple another and toss it. Crumple and toss again and again, until the Sunday paper is consumed and your baby is surrounded by a sea of paper. Then let her thrash away!

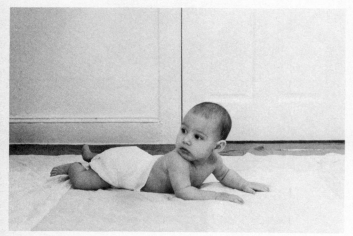

Paper Play

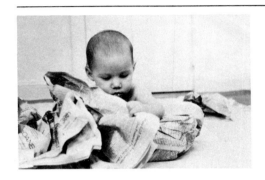

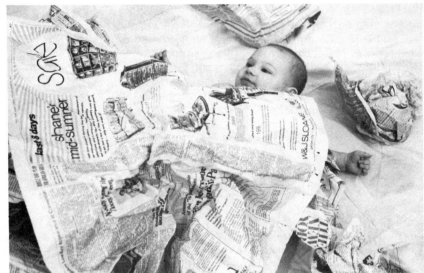

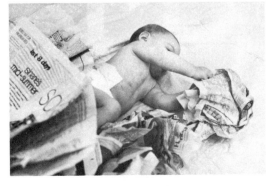

**Playing Games
Together**

More Sounds

"Now Hear This"
Introduce your baby to more sounds with "Now Hear This." Sit her in your lap, infant seat, or on the floor and shake a rattle or bell, crumple dry leaves, squeeze aluminum foil, tap 2 sticks together, or run your fingernail along a comb. The keynote here is variety, so use your imagination. And as with the texture game, talk about each noise as you make it.

"Sound and Seek-2"
At this age your baby might like to play more search-for-the-sound games. Lay him on his stomach and ring a bell or rattle, or squeak a squeeze toy, on the side opposite where he's looking. If he's lying on his back on the changing table or floor, make the noise beside his head. Or hold him in your lap and ring the bell off to one side.

Let him take the toy from you if he reaches for it, because at this age many babies like to make their own noise. Babies like to produce a consequence with their efforts, and sound is a welcome consequence, so occasionally just hand him bells, rattles, and squeak toys, and let him go to town.

Give Your Baby's Nose a Treat

''The First Baby Sniff-It Game''
Introduce your baby to odors. On outings let her smell
different flowers and herbs in the park or garden. Many
leaves give off lovely scents when you crush them in your
hand. At home, sprinkle cotton balls with different odors,
and then one by one, take a sniff, talk about the fragrance,
and let your baby smell. Good sources to tap are:

> the spice cabinet: vanilla, lemon, peppermint, and
> almond extract

> the refrigerator: fruit juices, sweet pickle juice

> the bathroom: perfumes, colognes, and after-shave
> lotions.

Your house is filled with many fragrances you can use
without cotton balls: scented soaps, jars of spices, indoor
plants, scented candles.

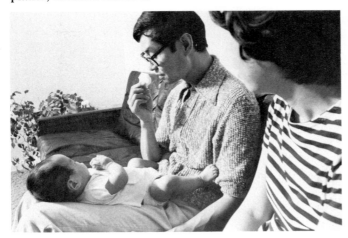

Imitating More of What You Do

When baby is around 6 months old, imitation games take on new importance. Besides the games described earlier, you might like to try getting your baby to imitate you patting your head, putting on and taking off a hat, clapping your hands, playing "drummer," and shaking your head slowly. After he imitates you, stop shaking your head and smile. Does he smile back?

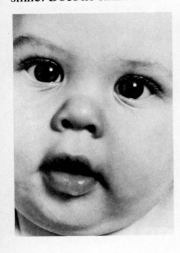

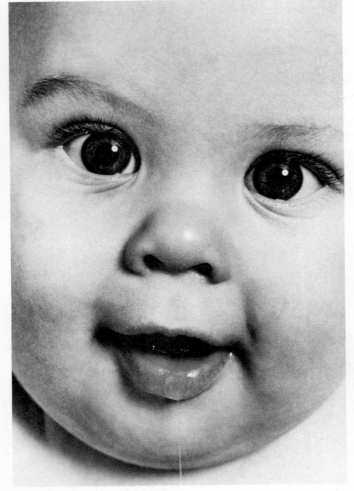

Nursery Rhyme Games

This is the age at which babies begin to enjoy nursery rhymes. Rhyme games are particularly enjoyable because they combine rhythm, singing, and physical stimulation. At first they may seem one-sided, with you providing most of the action. But your baby lets you know how much fun he's having by reaching for you, smiling, laughing, making sounds, and wiggling about.

For early games, you can use some of the following:

1.
A really simple one:

Knock at the door (tap her forehead)
Peep in (lift her eyelid)
Lift the latch (tilt her nose)
Walk in (slip a finger in her mouth)
Go way down the cellar and eat apples (tickle under her chin.)

2.
Make a fist with your hand, and with your baby watching, recite a simple counting rhyme, exposing 1 finger at a time:

Here is a beehive — where are the bees?
Hidden away where nobody sees!
Soon they come creeping out of the hive —
One! Two! Three! Four! Five!

If she grasps your hand, turn this into tug-of-war.

3.
And, of course, the favorite: "This Little Piggy." Recite the rhyme as you pull his fingers or toes in turn:

This little piggy went to market,
This little piggy stayed home.
This little piggy had roast beef,
This little piggy had none.
And this little piggy cried "Wee-wee-wee" all the way
  home.

On the *wee-wee-wee*, squeeze his little finger or toe, run your fingers up and down his arm or leg, and end with a tickle on the stomach or under the chin. The funnier your voice becomes, the more fun he has.

Playing Games Together

Nursery Rhyme Games

Your 4-to 6-month-old may want to move with the rhythm. The following rhymes are especially suited to your baby sitting in his infant seat or on your knees, facing you.

4.
First the standard. Hold her hands in yours and clap while you recite:

Pat-a-cake, pat-a-cake, baker's man,
Bake me a pie as fast as you can,
Prick it and pat it and mark it with a 'B',
And put it in the oven for (baby's name) and me.

When you reach her name, tap her lightly on the stomach. Soon she'll begin to anticipate this ending with great excitement. (Later, when your baby is between 9 and 12 months, try this game without holding her hands.)

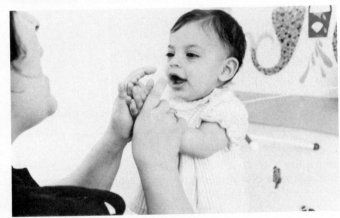

5.
Another favorite is "Row Your Boat." Pull your baby's arms back and forth in a chug-a-chug motion as you sing:

Row, Row, Row, your boat, gently down the stream,
Merrily, merrily, merrily, merrily, life is but a dream.

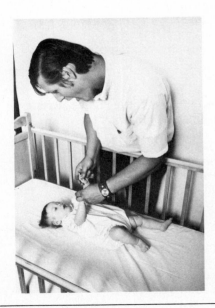

Nursery Rhyme Games

6.
For the 5-to 6-month old, one of the most popular games is "Rock-a-Bye Baby." The standard verse is:

Rock-a-bye baby, on the tree top,
When the wind blows, the cradle will rock.
When the bough breaks, the cradle will fall.
And down will come baby, cradle and all.

Now, while singing the first 3 lines, rock your baby from side to side. But, on the word *fall,* let her fall backward slightly, then pull her to the sitting position again. If you play this game a number of times at 1 sitting, let her fall a little farther each time, to add an element of surprise.

7.
There are 2 ways to add some bouncing games: Sit your baby on your knees and bounce your heels up and down while keeping your toes on the floor; or, cross your legs and sit her on your free foot. Then while you recite a favorite rhyme, give her a ride. If you're stuck for an appropriate rhyme, try:

Ride a cock horse to Banbury Cross
To see a fine lady upon a white horse.
With rings on her fingers and bells on her toes
She shall have music wherever she goes.

But any nursery rhyme or song you might know will work.

8.
For the more adventuresome baby, try "Pop Goes the Weasel." Sit him on the floor, kneel in front while holding his arms up, and recite:

All around the cobbler's bench the monkey chased the
    weasel,
The monkey thought 'twas all in fun — POP goes the
    weasel.

On the POP, raise him off the floor. Most babies love this game because of the dramatic finale.

There are hundreds of nursery rhymes — so don't be limited by our suggestions. We include these just to get you started. Nursery rhymes will probably continue to be your baby's favorite games for the rest of the year.

**Playing Games
Together**

What are some of the big changes at this age? Your baby begins to sit well without support, use his hands and arms in new ways, and crawl. All of these new abilities create more opportunities for play. The ability to sit alone, combined with increased control over his grasping and handling, allow him to explore objects in much more detail. So give him toys with moving parts, and objects with a variety of holes, bumps, and different surface textures. For a special toy of that sort, put together a Feelie Bag, by just filling a small bag with a number of different objects: a rubber sink stopper, fabric swatches, rubber animals, squeak toys, a wooden block, an empty plastic bottle, a yarn ball.

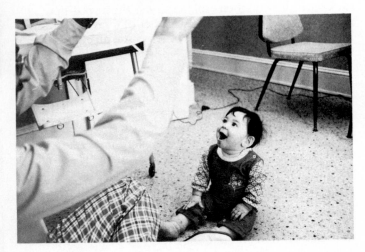

Now that he's beginning to crawl, the whole world is his playground. He'll spend much of his time exploring your house and yard, so be sure your home is baby-proof!

Here are some new games you can add to his growing list of favorites.

Exploration Games

Since your baby will want to explore so many different things, make exploration games a part of your playtime together.

"It's a Family"
In this game, give your baby a variety of objects to explore that have some connection with each other. For instance, his personal care items: comb and brush, an empty powder can, washcloth, feeding spoon, cup, empty shampoo bottle. As he plays with each one, talk about its properties and demonstrate what it's used for. Other families you can introduce include kitchen items: cooking spoons, measuring spoons and cups, mixing bowls, egg beater, pots and pans; and his clothing: diaper, socks, shoes, hat, t-shirt. Of course, you can also use families of toys; such as blocks: foam-filled, wooden, plastic, empty cereal boxes; rattles: clear, dumbbell, etc.; and stuffed animals. Try to describe each one, and explain why it's different from the others.

The family game not only gives your baby the opportunity to explore different sizes, shapes, and textures, but as he gets older, it also helps provide the basis for learning to classify objects into groups.

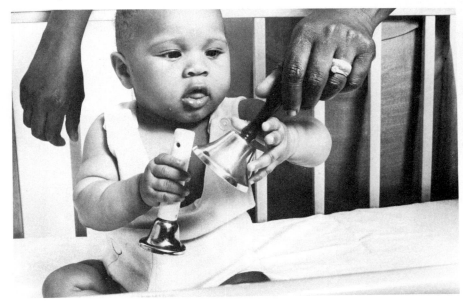

Playing with Nature's "Toys"

Most babies love to play with water and sand. Water play needn't be confined to bathtime; you can half-fill a plastic tub, set it on the floor over a plastic dropcloth, or outdoors on a sunny day, and put in some favorite bath toys. And water play in a wading pool is a wonderful way to spend part of a summer afternoon.

If you don't have access to a sandbox, fill a tub with sand, which you can buy at the hardware or garden store. Good toys for sand play include bowls, cups, strainers, and spoons. Try this game: Encourage her to find a small toy you've buried.

It's wise always to supervise your baby's water and sand play. And it's more fun for everyone when you join in the game.

Let's Play Ball

This is the age when your baby really begins to play with
balls. You may be surprised at the amount of excitement
they arouse. Give your baby a ball and he'll pick it up, try
to bounce it, rub the surface, roll it along the ground,
push it with his head, try to bite it —everything!

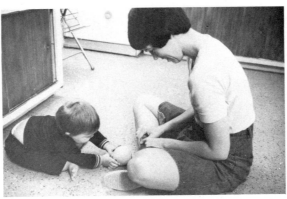

**Playing Games
Together**

Let's Play Ball

In addition to these kinds of explorations, he may
enjoy games like:

"Watch Me Roll It — Now You Try"

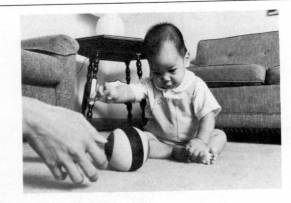

"Chase the Rolling Ball"

"I'm Gonna Bounce a Beach Ball on Your Head"

Let's Play Ball

As he gets older, say around 10 months, you can play:

"Roll It to Me, and I'll Roll It to You"

"Can You Catch It?"

Playing Games Together

String Games

Because your baby has developed fairly good control over his ability to grasp, now's the time to introduce string games. A piece of string changes the way toys can be held and played with, so tie strings to his toys. These should be about 8 inches long. At first he'll want to explore a string with his fingers and mouth. Then, with your help, he begins to discover what strings can do when pulled. String games help a baby to learn about cause and effect.

"A String Makes It Ring"
A good first game: Tie a piece of string on a bell or rattle hanging from the crib rail or cradle gym. Pull it while he watches, then place it in his hand so he can make the noise. If he doesn't respond at first, shake your hand again, so he'll imitate the movement.

"Fishing Fun"
Sit on the floor together, and show him how pulling a string brings a toy to him,

or makes a toy dance and swing.

String Games

At around 8 to 9 months try this: Sit together on the floor, or hold your baby in your lap at table-top height, and place 2 strings within reach, only 1 of which has a toy on the other end: "Which one has the toy? Can you get the toy?" If this is consistently too difficult for her to understand, use a piece of string and a piece of colored yarn instead of 2 strings. For the older baby, try 3 strings.

Tie a small toy to her feeding tray, drop it over the side, and demonstrate how to retrieve it by pulling on the string. When she gets older, and begins throwing toys from the high chair, walker or crib, tying them on strings saves you from having to do a great deal of retrieving.

If he enjoys string games, try this variation:

"Pull the Diaper"
While sitting together on the floor, place a non-rolling toy on one end of an open diaper. Then demonstrate how pulling the other end brings the toy within reach.

**Playing Games
Together**

Playing with a Cardboard Tube

One of the greatest toys is a cardboard tube, like the one inside a roll of paper towels. You can use it to look at each other, whisper in her ear (it really changes your voice), blow on her face and hair, roll a ball through, or lightly tap her on the head. When the tube starts to wear out, discard it. By that time, you'll have used up a few more rolls cleaning up after her meals and you'll have a fresh supply.

Time for Peek-a-Boo

One of the favorite games for this age is "Peek-a-Boo!"
You might have introduced it earlier, but it has many
varieties. The simplest is to carry on a conversation with
your baby watching you from her crib, swing, walker, or
whatever, when all at once you duck out of sight. Then,
just as suddenly pop back into view again with "Peek-a-
boo, I see you!" Sometimes, reappear without saying
anything; she may smile or laugh just to see you again.

Time for Peek-a-Boo

Another version: While you face each other, cover your eyes with your hands, and say something like "Where did Justin go? I can't find Justin." Then off come the hands with "There he is! Peek-a-boo, I see you!" He may want to help you cover your eyes.

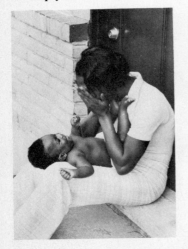
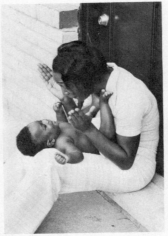

After a few times, cover *his* eyes with your hands. Or, with your help, let him cover his own eyes. Later in the year he may begin to cover his eyes by himself, and wait for you to pull his hands away with the familiar cry.

Time for Peek-a-Boo

For a more dramatic game, cover your head with a diaper, pause a second, and snatch it off with ''Peek-a-boo!'' Sometimes, don't say anything; does she smile at your reappearance alone? Or wait for *her* to pull the diaper away.

Now you're ready to play ''Hide the Baby.'' Make sure she's in a playful mood; many babies won't like the surprise of being covered, at least at first. Drape the cover over her head and snatch it off immediately: ''Peek-a-boo!'' Smile or laugh to reassure her that this is indeed a *game*. She'll soon catch on. Then you can leave the cover on a little longer each time. Surprise her one time by *not* snatching it off; let her do it. Later she will initiate the game, by covering herself up and either waiting for you to pull it off, or snatching it off without your help.

For family fun, two of you hide together, and let the other parent pull the blanket away. Or both parents can hide.

During these 3 months, your baby will practice and perfect many of the skills she's been developing during the previous 9. She sits well for long periods of time, crawls, has good control over arm movements, and can grasp even tiny objects between thumb and finger. Now she's ready to add some new games which take advantage of her high degree of coordination, and she looks to you for guidance and encouragement.

At this age, one of your baby's favorite ways to learn is still by watching you. Imitation games continue to have great appeal. Many of the games described in this section involve more than just having her repeat your demonstration. Earlier, your baby explored the different properties of objects. Now, with your help, she discovers *how* these properties influence the way things work: a toy with wheels can roll, a ring can fit over a stick, a crayon makes marks, nesting bowls and cups fit inside each other, blocks can be stacked into a tower. Of course, she might make these discoveries independently through trial and error, but it's much more fun for her to learn them with you.

The Budding Artist

"Quick On the Draw"
To produce a masterpiece together, take a thick crayon
or felt-tip marker and a large piece of paper (newspaper is
fine.) Then sit down together and show your baby how to
draw a line or scribble. The most important thing is to
demonstrate slowly and explain what you're doing:
"Look, Eric — see the crayon. It's round and fat and red,
and . . . it makes marks. . . like this! Look what I did!
Here — would you like to hold the crayon? Can you
make a line like mine?'' (You may want to guide his hand
at first.) "That's right! Good!"

If the paper tends to move around, tape it to the floor.
Also, since he might occasionally miss the paper, and
since crayons can be chewed, it's best to supervise these
art lessons.

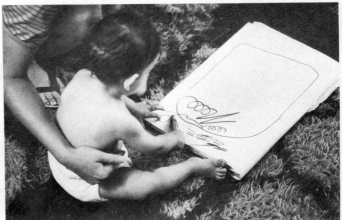

"Paint-by-Hand"
Most babies love to play with soft, squishy things, such as
their food. You can turn this interest to good use. Put a
few dabs of tempera paint on a large piece of paper, show
your baby how to swish it around with his hands, and
then let him create his own room decorations. For
throwaway masterpieces, you can make "paints" by
thickening water with flour or cornstarch, and adding a
few drops of food coloring. Or let him use jello which
you've let soften by leaving it in a warm place. Because it
tends to be messy, do your handpainting on a plastic
dropcloth, or sit your baby in an empty bathtub, or save it
for outdoor play.

Learning How Things Go Together

"Fill and Dump"
The game of "Fill and Dump" really delights most babies. After you've played it together a number of times, your baby will probably spend many hours playing it alone. Take a container, such as a plastic cup or mixing bowl, and collect a number of small objects that fit inside it, such as wooden clothespins, small blocks, spools, rubber animals, or ping pong balls. Now sit together on the floor and spread everything within your baby's reach. He may want to play with each thing in turn. If so, let him. There's no reason to rush. Then, pick up an object and drop it in the container: "See what I can do! Watch the block go in the cup!" After depositing all the toys, dump them out and start all over. Only this time, let him help by taking turns: "See me drop the horse in the can? Now it's your turn . . . can *you* do it?" If he's hesitant, place an object in his hand and help him get started. "You did it, too!" Then let him try without your help.

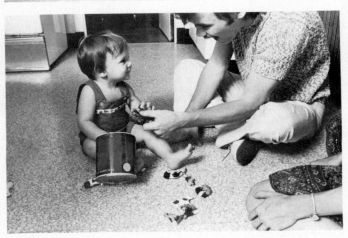

Learning How Things Go Together

For a variation, play "Fill and Dump" with a basket of balls, a container of junk mail, or a box of coasters. Or clip a number of clothespins on the edge of a tub, and show him how to pull them off and drop them inside.

Learning How Things Go Together

In addition to filling and dumping, your 11-to 12-month-
old might like to try nesting and stacking games.

"It Goes in Here"
Demonstrate how to fit one cup or bowl into a larger one,
and then take them apart and let her try. It's easier for her
if at first you hold the larger container. After she catches
on, try nesting a whole series of objects.

Learning How Things Go Together

**Playing Games
Together**

Learning How Things Go Together

"Stack 'Em Up"
Let your baby watch you slip a ring on a spindle. Then
take it off and hand it to him. "Can you do that, too?"
After he understands the connection between the 2 objects, encourage him to stack a number of rings in any
order. Also, at this age he may show more interest in taking
the rings off. In addition, you can demonstrate how to
stack cups, coasters, or blocks.

If your baby becomes frustrated and fussy when playing
filling, nesting, or stacking games, stop and play something else. Babies learn through practice and repetition —
not through frustration and anger.

Beginning to See Differences

"There's a Difference"

Besides learning *why* objects behave the way they do, your baby may like exploring the *differences* between similar things. In this game, let him handle each object or material in turn while you talk about its properties, and about how it differs from the others in the group in texture, shape, size, sound, taste, or weight.

Some groups to explore include:

a paper and a plastic cup

wooden, plastic, and metal cooking spoons

a rubber and a fabric ball

a plastic and a stuffed baby doll

a wooden and a hollow plastic block

a square, circle, and triangle cut out of thick paper

three stuffed animals of different sizes.

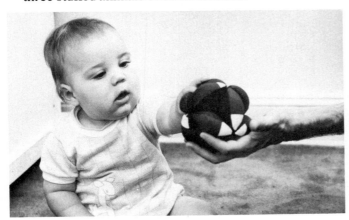

**Playing Games
Together**

Solving Simple Problems

Many babies this age enjoy games that involve solving simple problems. For example, when your baby is holding a toy in each hand, offer him another (one you *know* he wants) or a cookie. How does he handle this problem? By putting one toy down? Both toys down? Transferring both toys to the same hand? Whatever way, he's solving the problem of how to free his hands to take a new object.

"Hide and Seek"
One of the favorite problem solving games is "Hide and Seek," which involves removing a barrier to get at a toy. Like "Peek-a-Boo," this game has many variations. In all of them, be sure your baby watches you hide the toy.

Here is a good introduction to "Hide and Seek". Hold a tantalizing toy in front of your baby: "Oh, Benjamin — look at this — your favorite!" When he reaches for it, put it on the floor in front of him and quickly cover it with a towel or diaper, leaving part of the toy exposed. Now: "Where did it go? Where's the rattle? Can you find the rattle?" For the first few times you may have to remove the cover yourself: "There it is! It was under the towel all the time." Play it again. Pretty soon *he'll* snatch off the cover, and then you can hide the toy completely.

Solving Simple Problems

If she likes this game, try wrapping the toy in paper and handing her the "present", or hiding the toy in a box with an easily opened lid, or slipping a small toy under a larger one.

**Playing Games
Together**

Solving Simple Problems

The following 2 "Hide and Seek" games are for an older baby.

"Screen Test"
Hold your baby in your lap, both of you facing a table top, and place a toy in front of her. To begin, use a piece of cardboard to block the toy from her sight. Now, slowly slide this screen back and forth, revealing and then hiding the object, while you explain what's happening:"Look — there it is. Now it's out of sight." (Sort of "now-you-see-it-now-you-don't.") Then keep the screen in front of the toy and ask her to find it.

For an interesting variation, use a clear screen (such as the top of a plastic shoe box) instead of a cardboard one. If he always runs into a problem when reaching for his toy, show him how to reach behind the barrier.

You can also play these screen games with your baby sitting in his high chair.

"Out of the Frying Pan"
Place a toy in a large, shallow pan, and cover both with a diaper or towel. Now, tilt the pan and slide the toy out onto the floor, keeping it hidden under the towel. Show your baby the empty pan and ask, "Where did your ball go? Can you find it?" If she stares at you with a puzzled look, remove the cover with "Here it is! Right here on the floor!"

Solving Simple Problems

These "Hide and Seek" games involve going *around*
barriers rather than removing them.

"Go and Get It"
While sitting facing each other on the floor, draw her
attention to a toy, and then hide it behind your back.
She has to crawl around you to retrieve it.

Or . . . hide the toy behind a piece of furniture.
Or . . . forget the toy. Hide yourself, and call out.
Or this . . . hide a toy in the room. While he's crawling
toward the hiding place, remove the toy and hide it in a
second place, making sure he sees you do this. The first
few times he may crawl to the first place and stop. So encourage him to keep going.

Or even this . . . move the toy from the second to a third
place. Does he find it?

**Playing Games
Together**

A Game for Parents

One final game — for parents alone. Turn back to the beginning of this section on play and learning and flip through its pages, just looking at the pictures. This quick year-in-a-minute review will give you an idea of the many, many things your baby has done in 12 months — and how much *you* have contributed to your baby's growth, learning, and enjoyment.

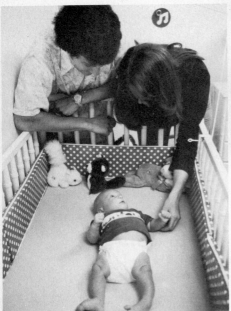

Further Information

We suggest the following books for your further reading because we feel that each one can make a contribution toward better understanding both your baby and your role as parents.

Health and Physical Care

A Sigh of Relief: The First Aid Book for Childhood Emergencies by Martin I. Green. New York: Bantam Books, 1977.

Your Baby and Child: From Birth to Age Five by Penelope Leach, Ph.D. New York: Alfred A. Knopf, 1978.

The Well Baby Book by Mike Samuels, M.D. and Nancy Samuels. New York: Summit Books, 1979.

Baby and Child Care by Benjamin Spock, M.D. New York: Pocket Books, 1974.

Infant Care, U.S. Government pamphlet. Latest revision, 1973. Superintendent of Documents, U.S. Government Printing Office, Washington, D.C. 20402.

Choosing Equipment and Toys

Consumers Union Guide to Buying for Babies by the editors of Consumer Reports. New York: Warner Books, 1975.

Good Things for Babies by Sandy Jones. Boston: Houghton-Mifflin, 1976.

Early Nurturing

The Complete Book of Breastfeeding by Marvin S. Eiger, M.D. and Sally W. Olds. New York: Bantam Books, 1972.

Nursing Your Baby by Karen Pryor. New York: Pocket Books, 1973.

Living with Your New Baby: a Postpartum Guide for Mothers and Fathers by Elly Rakowitz and Gloria S. Rubin. New York: Franklin Watts, 1978.

General Parenting

The Roots of Love: Helping Your Child Learn to Love in the First Three Years of Life by Helene S. Arnstein. New York: Bantam Books, 1977.

New Ways in Discipline by Dorothy Baruch. New York: McGraw-Hill, 1949.

Infants and Mothers by T. Berry Brazelton, M.D. New York: Dell, 1969.

Your Child Is a Person by Stella Chess, M.D.; Alexander Thomas, M.D.; and Herbert G. Birch, M.D., Ph.D. New York: Viking, 1972.

The Magic Years: Understanding and Handling the Problems of Early Childhood by Selma Fraiberg. New York: Charles Scribner's Sons, 1959.

The Mother's Almanac by Marguerite Kelly and Elia Parsons. Garden City, New York: Doubleday, 1975.

The First Three Years of Life by Burton White, Ph.D. Englewood Cliffs, New Jersey, 1975.

Further Information

The organizations listed on these pages are sources of good current information about topics of interest to parents. Each distributes books and pamphlets, and will send parents a list of publications upon written request. In addition, if you should have a specific question dealing with any of these topics, these groups might be able to help you.

In addition to the groups listed here, the federal government has a number of agencies which deal with infancy, and provides many good publications of interest to parents. For more information, you can contact:

Office of Child Development
Public Information Office
Room G-311, Mary E. Switzer Building
330 C Street
Washington, D.C. 20201   (202) 245-1605

Parenting

Parenting Materials Information Center (PMIC)
Early Childhood Division
Southwest Educational Development Laboratory
211 East 7th Street
Austin, Texas 78701

The Parenting Materials Information Center is an information system developed by the Southwest Educational Development Laboratory, a federal project funded by the National Institute of Education. The PMIC provides parents with detailed information about books, journal articles, and movies that deal with aspects of being a parent, such as relating to your child, the family as a social unit, pregnancy and birth, and education. The PMIC publishes a *Users Handbook* which describes these materials and tells you how to obtain them. It is available free of charge.

Infant Education

National Association for the Education
of Young Children (NAEYC)
1834 Connecticut Avenue, N.W.
Washington, D.C. 20009

Association for Childhood Education
International (ACEI)
3615 Wisconsin Avenue, N.W.
Washington, D.C. 20016

Both the NAEYC and the ACEI are professional organizations of teachers and other specialists concerned with the education and well-being of children from birth through adolescence. Each has a strong interest in infant education and publishes a number of excellent materials dealing with stimulation in the first year of life.

Safety

National Safety Council
444 N. Michigan Avenue
Chicago, Illinois 60611

In addition to distributing their own safety publications, this voluntary organization provides a reference service to parents. The National Safety Council will provide, upon request, both the names of organizations which deal with specific areas of safety and information about other safety publications.

U.S. Consumer Product
Safety Commission (CPSC)
Washington, D.C. 20207
(800) 638-2666
Maryland residents only,
call (800) 492-8363

The Consumer Product Safety Commission is a federal agency which provides up-to-date safety information about toys and other infant products.

Health Services

American Academy of Pediatrics
P.O. Box 1034
Evanston, Illinois 60204

The American Academy of Pediatrics, the national organization for pediatricians, publishes and distributes a number of short pamphlets on health care and safety, including a fine first aid chart. The Academy will also help direct parents to health services they may need for their baby.

Further Information

Day Care for Infants

Day Care and Child Development
Council of America (DCCDCA)
805 15th Street, N.W.
Suite 520
Washington, D.C. 20005

This national organization is one of the largest sources of publications dealing with day care. In addition, the DCCDCA has a reference library containing both up-to-date information about day care facts and government regulations, and a listing of licensed day care centers.

For more help with questions about day care in your local area, you can also contact your city's Department of Social Services.

Exceptional Children

Closer Look
Box 1492
Washington, D.C. 20013

Closer Look, a part of the Department of Health, Education, and Welfare, is The National Center for the Handicapped. It distributes pamphlets useful to parents who have a handicapped child, from infancy to young adulthood, and supplies information about the steps parents can take to find additional services. When writing about a specific problem, Closer Look requests that parents supply the child's age and the nature of the handicapping condition.

Infant Research

For parents interested in reading current research of the type we refer to throughout this guide, we recommend the following publications. They can be found in libraries connected with colleges, universities, and medical schools, and many public library systems.

Books

Advances in Child Development and Behavior
Hayne W. Reese, Editor
Published by Academic Press

Annual Progress in Child Psychiatry and Child Development
Stella Chess and Alexander Thomas, Editors
Published by Brunner Mazel

Review of Child Development Research
E. Mavis Hetherington, Editor
Published by the University of Chicago Press

Journals

Child Development
Published by the Society for Research in Child Development

Developmental Psychology
Published by the American Psychological Association

Merrill-Palmer Quarterly
Published by the Merrill-Palmer Institute of Human Development and Family Life

Pediatrics
Published by the American Academy of Pediatrics

In addition, the Society for Research in Child Development publishes *Child Development: Abstracts and Bibliography*. This journal describes many papers on infant research which are published in other professional journals.

Index

Notes

Notes

Notes

Notes

Notes

Notes